I Ching
Natal Chart and oracular interpretation

I Ching
Natal Chart and oracular interpretation

ENOS LONG

SOJOURNER BOOKS

© 2018 by Enos Long

All rights reserved under International and
Pan-American Copyright Conventions.

ISBN: 978-1-9994008-4-2

Other books by the same author:

La raíz del YiJing (I Ching).
Del ZhouYi al Clásico de los Cambios

I Ching: Carta natal e interpretación oracular

Contents

Introduction. 9

How to consult the Oracle. 15

How to get the Natal Hexagram 19

The Yarrow-Stalks Oracle 23

Understanding hexagram readings 27

THE 64 HEXAGRAMAS

1 - The Creative / Activity / Dynamic Force 33

2 - The Receptive 39

3 - Initial Difficulty 45

4 - Youthful Folly 51

5 - Waiting 55

6 - Conflict / Lawsuit 59

7 - The Army 65

8 - Union 69

9 - Little Domestication 75

10 - Treading 79

11 - Harmony / Great 83

12 - Standstill / Stagnation 89

13 - Fellowship 95

Contents

14 - Great Possession.	99
15 - Modesty	103
16 - Enthusiasm	107
17 - Following.	111
18 - Correcting Decay / Corruption.	117
19 - Approach / Leadership	121
20 - Contemplation.	125
21 - Biting Through	131
22 - Elegance / Adornment / Grace	137
23 - Splitting Apart / Decay	141
24 - Return	145
25 - Innocence / No expectations	151
26 - Great Accumulation	157
27 - Nourishment / The Jaws	163
28 - Great Excess	169
29 - Pit doubled / Pit within a pit	175
30 - The Clinging / Fire.	179
31 - Influence / Reciprocity	183
32 - Duration / Constancy.	187
33 - Retreat	191
34 - Great Power.	195
35 - Progress / Advance.	199
36 - Suppressed Light.	205
37 - The Family / The Clan	211
38 - Antagonism / Opposition.	215
39 - Hampered / Obstruction	221
40 - Liberation.	225
41 - Decrease	229

Contents

42 - Increase. 233

43 - Breakthrough / Resoluteness / Parting 239

44 - Close Encounter / Meeting 245

45 - Gathering together.. 251

46 - Ascending 257

47 - Oppression / Besieged / Impasse 261

48 - The Well 267

49 - Revolution / Getting rid of 273

50 - The Cauldron / Sacrificial Vessel......................... 279

51 - Shock 285

52 - Restraint 291

53 - Gradual Development 295

54 - The Marrying Maiden. 301

55 - Fullness /Abundance.. 307

56 - Sojourner / Wanderer. 313

57 - Gentle Influence / Penetration / The Wind 319

58 - Joyousness / The Lake 325

59 - Dispersion / Dissolution / The Flood. 329

60 - Limitation. 333

61 - Inner Truth... 337

62 - Excess of the Small. 341

63 - Already Across. 345

64 - Before Crossing... 351

Get the Natal Hexagram 355

The Eight Trigrams. 369

Chart of Trigrams and Hexagrams 379

Introduction

The *Yijing* or *Book of Changes* (previously spelled as *I Ching*) was intended as a strategic oracle for feudal lords in the Chinese Bronze Age, three thousand years ago, but with the pass of the centuries the book was evolving and become more philosophical, under the influence of Confucianism.

The *Book of Changes* is both an oracular medium and a book of wisdom, but it doesn't try to answer why we are here or where are we going after death; instead it focuses in the business of living. It is also a human attempt to throw light in the natural laws that command change.

Change is the natural state of this world. All things live in continuous flow. All beings are born, grow, evolve and finally decay and die. By observing the natural cycles, the sages of ancient times achieved an intuitive understanding of the laws that regulate change. Change is not chaotic, but it follows a pattern of development. Change is inevitable; situations never are completely static and unchanging

The 64 hexagrams (or sections) of the *Yijing* are a description of the different ways in which situations can evolve, they describe the steps of change and tell us how to act effectively at every moment.

Since change happens through time, each hexagram describes different times. There are times for advancing, times for retreating, times for peace, times for war, and so on. Each hexagram depicts a different time, a different pattern of change. This idea has echoes in the Bible (Ecclesiastes 3:1-8):

> *For everything there is a season, and a time for every purpose under heaven: a time to be born, and a time to die; a time to plant, and a time to pluck up that which is planted; a time to kill, and a time to heal; a time to break down, and a time to build up; a time to weep, and a time to laugh; a time to mourn, and a time to dance; a time to cast away stones, and a time to gather stones together; a time to embrace, and a*

Introduction

time to refrain from embracing; a time to seek, and a time to lose; a time to keep, and a time to cast away; a time to tear, and a time to sew; a time to keep silence, and a time to speak; a time to love, and a time to hate; a time for war, and a time for peace.

Knowing which kind of time we are experiencing allows us to take both preventive measures and to plan the best course of action in advance. In that way we can take the best course between the rough waves of life. Sometimes we may have a smooth sailing, and ride along with the tides with little effort, but in other cases we will have to work hard to manage well the situation.

Content and Structure

The *Yijing* describes change as a permanent cycle between two principles, one active and energetic and the other passive and yielding. Those two principles are the building blocks of the 64 hexagrams of the Book of Changes, they are called *yang* and *yin*. The next table shows how *yang* and *yin* look when drawn as hexagram's lines.

Figure	Description	Attributes
▬ ▬	*Yin* line	Feminine, passive, dark, cold, soft.
▬▬▬	*Yang* line	Masculine, active, light, hot, hard.

Yin and *yang* are relative and changing attributes that interact constantly. Firm and dominant behaviors are *yang*, weak and subordinate are *yin*. *Yang* and *yin* flow constantly, *yang* mutates into *yin* and vice-versa. The flow of *yang* and *yin* is evident in the adaptation to the needs of each moment; some situations require *yang* boldness, and other *yin* tolerance.

All hexagrams are drawings composed by six *yang* and *yin* lines (except the hexagrams 1 and 2, which are pure *yang* and pure *yin*).

The *yang* and *yin* lines form a binary system; by combining both types of lines in six different positions, 64 different hexagrams are created, forming the structure of the *Yijing*. All hexagrams are interconnected between them; when the oracle answers a question it is usual to receive a pair of hexagrams, which describes the flow of the situation.

Each line in an hexagram describes a step in a situation. The lines are counted from bottom to top, being the bottom line the first one. The *Yijing* hexagrams describe how a situation develops in time, starting with the first line and how it evolves until reaching its sixth line.

Introduction

Each one of the 64 hexagrams has some texts attached to its drawing:

The hexagram title, known as "hexagram tag", which is composed of the first one or two Chinese characters that form the Judgment.

The *Judgment* (*guaci*), that describes the characteristics of the situation and its prognosis, either good or bad.

The *Image* (*daxiang*), which analyzes the relation of the trigrams that comprise the hexagram and suggests the best course of action based on the symbolic value of them —you will learn more about the trigrams later–.

Also there are six other texts (*yaoci*), one for each line, which describe the opportunities and dangers of each step.

> Notice that this book always shows the original *Yijing* text as indented lines, our own commentaries to the *Yijing* are show below the indented lines for each text (Judgment, Image and Lines).
>
> Example (from the hexagram 45):
>
> **Fourth Nine**
>   Great good fortune.
>   No defect.
>
> Here comes our commentary...
>
> All the text following the two lines above is our commentary. "Great good fortune. No defect" is the original text.

Reality and discourse

The authors of the *Yijing* had different values from our contemporary society. They lived in a highly hierarchical, patriarchal and feudal society.

Because of this, some ideas or terminology used in this translation may be offensive or strange to a contemporary sensibility. In my comments on the *Yijing* original text, I try to show the original ideas from a modern point of view. I have used gender-neutral words as much as the English language allows me, without damaging the style of the text. Nevertheless, I have been as faithful to the original book text as I can, because my intention is to offer a reliable translation; otherwise my book would be a different book, and could not be called *I Ching* or *Yijing*.

The fundamental principles of life have not changed since the *Book of Changes* was written, we are no better or worse than our remote predecessors. The profound perceptions about human relations that the *Yijing* offers us are still

Introduction

valid and can be applied to our lives in the same way they were in ancient China.

Today as yesterday, fate is determined by both factors outside our reach and by our own capacity. The *Yijing* can help us to understand better the relation between external reality and our will, and because that it is an invaluable tool that will enhance the quality of our lives if we hear its message.

Natal (birth) Hexagram

The *Yijing* is a book about the philosophy of time. Each hexagram has its own time, but in this context, time is not only a number of minutes and hours, but has its own characteristics, its own color and flavor. The 64 hexagrams of the *Yijing* describe the different times that human beings can experience. Hexagrams are intertwined across its changing lines –if you don't know what changing lines are, you will learn that in the following sections–, each hexagram has 64 different combinations of changing lines, so the *Yijing* describes 4096 (64 * 64 = 4096) different times.

The hexagram that describes the time of our birth is our Natal Hexagram. That hexagram –or hexagrams, if you got changing lines– describes the tendencies that will develop throughout our live, our character, which is what will define our destiny.

Our Natal Hexagram reveals our personal characteristics, indicates which lines of development are optimal and which we should avoid and our possibilities in different fields.

The Natal Hexagram can be read as a kind of navigational chart of life, knowing our real possibilities we can take better advantage of our potential and avoid straying into dead ends.

Before getting your Natal Hexagram, it would be good to read the next section, *How to consult the oracle*, to understand the basic principles of a *Yijing* reading.

Of course, in many cases a person may want to ask specific questions to the oracle. Besides getting the Natal Hexagram, the oracle can be consulted with three coins (go to the next page for instructions) or using the **yarrow sticks** method. (p. 23)

The Name of the Book

I used *I Ching* as title, because it's the title most people know. Here, inside this book I prefer to call it *Yijing*, because that is the accepted way of writing the pronunciation of the original Chinese name today, using the *pinyin* system. Note that *I Ching* and *Yijing* are simply two different ways of writing the pronunciation of the Chinese name in Western letters.

The name of the *Book of Changes*, written in traditional Chinese characters is:

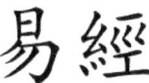

How to consult the Oracle

It has been said that the answer is always hidden inside the question, meaning that you can only get the right answer if you know how to express your question clearly or if you know the right question.

The *Yijing* will not answer your questions unequivocally but instead it will tell you a moral history, sometimes including several protagonists and possible outcomes. It is your task to put yourself inside the history, to understand which part is yours and which is the relation between answer and question.

The oracle will chart for you the possibilities and dangers lurking ahead; if you open your intuition you will understand the message. Perhaps the answer will not be clear at first, but if you keep meditating over it, at some point you will grasp it.

The questions should be clear cut, avoiding asking about several possibilities at once. If you want to know which option is best, you should ask about one option first and then ask again about the other choice in a second consult; never include several alternatives in the same question. Think carefully what you want to ask, take your time; do not ask the oracle in a hurry or in a disturbed emotional state.

Examples:

Should I buy the car that John sells? This question is concise and will simplify understanding of the answer.

Should I go to Paris or London for my next holiday? This sort of question will prevent you from getting a clear answer.

Also you could simply ask the oracle to describe the situation, optionally giving a time frame.

How to consult the Oracle

Example:

What are my chances for getting a new job in the next six months?

Always write down your question before beginning your consult, afterwards you may write the answer in the same paper sheet.

Notice that the oracle may mirror your fears and expectancies in its answer, casting light over your hopes and fears.

In all cases the answer is mainly about you and your interaction with the world around you. The oracle cannot change an objective situation, but can help you to make the most within your circumstances, indicating both your shortcomings and strong points.

Sometimes you will apprehend intuitively the meaning of the answer at once, other times you may have to ponder about it for several days until at least you find what the answer means for you.

Getting your Yijing reading

The consultation process will generate six numbers, and you will draw a hexagram according to them.

Most people use the coin-tossing method to get the numbers, but we also describe the ancient yarrow-stalk method in **The Yarrow-Stalks Oracle**.

Some people like to follow a predefined ritual before divination; if you are inclined to do so, the ritual may help you to put your mind at ease.

Indeed focusing your mind is what matters most, if you concentration wanders during the consultation it may affect the final outcome. In an ideal world you should not consult the *Yijing* if you are not relaxed and without distractions, an altered state of mind doesn't improve the practice of divination.

Using the coins to get an oracular reading

It is said that this method has been in use since the fourth century BC, the yarrow-stalks method is older, but because the coin-tossing method is faster and easier it is more widely used at the present time.

Traditionally three Chinese coins are used, but you can use any kind of coins, provided that all them are equal.

The coins should be tossed six times on a flat surface to get the six lines of a hexagram. You will draw the hexagram from bottom to top, according to how the coins fall, as the following table shows:

How to consult the Oracle

Coins	Numbers	Results	
Three tails	2+2+2=6	A changing *yin*	━╳━
Three heads	3+3+3=9	A changing *yang*	━○━
2 tails and 1 head	2+2+3=7	A static *yang*	━━━
2 heads and 1 tail	3+3+2=8	A static *yin*	━ ━

As you can see tails are worth 2 and heads 3; when you add the numbers for the three coins you will get 6, 7, 8 or 9 for each coin toss.

Broken lines are *yin* and whole lines are *yang*. If there are one or more changing lines, they will generate a second hexagram, with all changing lines inverted: *yin* will become *yang* and vice versa.

After you toss the coins six times you will have a six lines drawing which depicts the oracle answer.

Example (the first column shows the line number and coin toss value for that line):

	Hex. 55	Hex. 21
L6: 6	━╳━	━━━
L5: 8	━ ━	━ ━
L4: 7	━━━	━━━
L3: 9	━○━	━ ━
L2: 8	━ ━	━ ━
L1: 7	━━━	━━━

As you can see, the changing lines are drawn differently from the non-changing lines, adding an X or a circle in the middle.

In the previous example, the hexagram on the left (55) is the first one that you will draw. In this example, it has two changing lines: a *yang* line in the third position and a *yin* line in the sixth position.

The second hexagram (21) is similar to the first, but the two changing lines are replaced with their opposite ones. If the changing line is *yang*, replace it with a *yin* line and vice versa.

If there are no changing lines, you will get a single hexagram.

How to consult the Oracle

After drawing the hexagram/s see the **Chart of the Trigrams and Hexagrams** (p. 379), to get the number/s of the hexagram/s.

Returning to the previous example, where we got the hexagram 55 that mutates to the 21; we must read the Judgment, the Image and the third and sixth lines of the hexagram 55, but only the Judgment and the Image of the hexagram 21.

The hexagram 55 is the starting point of a situation that will lead to hexagram 21, which describes the final situation. Note that both hexagrams can be linked in other ways, see **Understanding hexagram readings** (p. 27) to learn how to interpret hexagram reading.

What are changing lines

We get a changing line when a coin toss has three tails or three heads –6 or 9 value–. The changing lines generate a second hexagram; if there are no changing lines, we get a single hexagram, which depicts a slowly evolving situation.

Changing lines are the steps of change that are activated in the hexagram reading; because that we will experience only the situations described by the changing lines we got.

Changing lines are also the lines more charged with energy. *Yang* and *yin* always change, *yang* mutates into *yin* and vice-versa. When the *yang* or *yin* lines are strongly charged with energy, they flip, mutating into its opposite, that is the reason changing lines generate a second hexagram.

How to get the Natal Hexagram

The hexagram that corresponds to the date and time of birth is the Natal Hexagram and it is the equivalent to what the astrologers call Natal Chart or Birth Chart. That hexagram describes the trends that will develop throughout life and the development of character, which is what defines destiny.

The Natal Hexagram reveals the main characteristics of the person, indicates the opportunities and dangers that may arise; it also shows the possibilities in different fields of life, like work, social relationships, travel, etc.

The Natal Hexagram can be read as a kind of navigational chart of life, useful to take better advantage of our potentialities and avoid deviating from the right path by taking dead ends.

Steps to get the natal hexagram

The Natal Hexagram is obtained from the date and local time of birth. The exact time is not mandatory, but by knowing the time, it is possible to get a much clearer description of a person's life chances.

As we explained previously, each hexagram is formed by two trigrams, one corresponds to the three upper lines and the other to the three lower lines.

The steps to get the Natal Hexagram are:

1. Get the upper trigram, corresponding to the year of birth.
2. Get the lower trigram, corresponding to the month and day of birth.
3. Get the changing lines, which depend on the local time of birth.
4. Taking the two trigrams and the changing lines, we can see which hexagram we have.

How to get the Natal Hexagram

> Detailed instructions are provided in **Get the Natal Hexagram**, in page 355.

A practical example

For a person born on September 4, 1992, at 18:20 hs.

First we will get the upper trigram, as the century of the birth is even (XX), we will go to the table of the upper trigrams for the even centuries. That table indicates that the upper trigram for the year 1992 is:

Now we will seek the lower trigram, going to the table of lower trigrams for each period of the year, we will find that the lower trigram for the period 08/17 - 09/30 (August 17 to September 30) is .

Finally, since we know the time of birth, we can see which changing lines the natal hexagram has. Going to the table of changing lines for even days we will see that for someone born between 18:00 and 18:44, the lines that mutate are 4 and 5.

Knowing the two trigrams for the Natal Hexagram, we should see which hexagram they form, at the Chart of Trigrams and Hexagrams.

Now we can now draw the Natal Hexagram with its changing lines. The following table shows the result of your example.

The first column shows the line number. Remember that the changing lines are marked with an X or with a circle, for that reason we marked the upper trigram with two circles on the yang lines in positions 4 and 5; because those two lines changed.

The second hexagram (22) is similar to the first, but the two changing lines are replaced with its opposite ones. If the changing line is yang, replace it with a yin line and vice versa.

As you can see in the table in next page, we got the hexagram 13, **Fellowship**; when it mutates, originates a second hexagram, the 22, **Elegance**.

Fellowship indicates that you are very linked to the community that surrounds you.

Elegance means that it is very important for you to behave with delicacy and cordiality, with discretion and elegance.

Now we should look at the two lines that mutate in *Fellowship*, which are:

How to get the Natal Hexagram

#	Hex. 13	Hex. 22
6	▬▬▬▬▬	▬▬▬▬▬
5	▬▬●▬▬	▬▬ ▬▬
4	▬▬●▬▬	▬▬ ▬▬
3	▬▬▬▬▬	▬▬▬▬▬
2	▬▬ ▬▬	▬▬ ▬▬
1	▬▬▬▬▬	▬▬▬▬▬

Fourth line: Tendency to isolate oneself from others due to distrust. It can be a recurring theme, you will always have to overcome your initial mistrust before you can trust your neighbor. The good thing about this provision is that you will not take undue risks, the bad thing is that you can lose some opportunities due to your prejudices.

Fifth line: Conflict and mistrust keeps people apart and causes unnecessary suffering. If you take the first step and show your sincere commitment, the union will be restored and everyone will be happy again.

This is only a basic idea of the meanings of all parts of this Natal Hexagram (the Judgment and Image of both hexagrams, and the changing lines of the first hexagram):

You are very careful with your image (22) and position in the social group to which you belong (13). Despite your natural elegance and cordiality, you are very cautious and suspicious (4th line). You will be someone very difficult to cheat, although your prejudices can hinder your relationships (5th line). Your membership in the social group is very important and you will always keep in mind the proper conduct for each situation (the Image, Hex 13).

There seems to be a repetitive situation of approaching and distancing from others; you approach others because you need them and because you miss the fellowship after having left, but also you have a hard time withstanding the foolishness and imperfections of others.

You are well suited for working with other people because you know how to behave in public, and how to communicate with groups, but you also know how to draw the line when others misbehave. You also know how to project the proper image and will be an example for others.

How to get the Natal Hexagram

Learn how to relax, sometimes you get too stressed out.

Possible fields or work: Diplomacy, public relations, sales, manager, artist.

The Natal Hexagram also allows us to analyze both the internal and external sides of a person, by studying the characteristics of the the two constituents trigrams of the first hexagram obtained. We should user the upper and lower trigrams that we got from the tables related with the years and periods of the year.

The upper trigram shows the person's performance in the world, his/her social personality and how is seen by others.

The lower trigram describes the inner, hidden and subjective part of the person, his/her feelings, aspirations, dreams and fears.

We can see the descriptions of each trigram at **The Eight Trigrams** (p. 369). There we can see all the characteristics associated with each trigram, its strengths, defects, sympathies, etc.

The Yarrow-Stalks Oracle

The yarrow stalks oracle method has been in use for the last three thousand years as the traditional way to consult the *Yijing*.

The stalks used by the ancient Chinese were dried stalks of the Asian Yarrow, *Achilea mongolica*, in Europe the closest species is the European Yarrow, *Achilea millefolium*. Notice that some people use thin wooden or bamboo sticks instead Achilea stalks.

The number of sticks is fifty. We do not know the size of the sticks in ancient times, but any thickness, length and material will suffice, if you can handle them easily in your hands.

If the number of sticks is not fifty, they will not produce the correct results; hence they should be stored safely to avoid losing any stick. It is advisable to keep the sticks wrapped in a clean linen cloth or at least store them in a container that keeps them clean.

Notice that the probabilities of get changing *yang* and *yin* lines are not the same using the sticks than when using coins to get an oracle.

With coins, there is the same chance of obtaining changing *yang* or yin lines, but with the sticks, there are more chances of obtaining changing *yang* lines than changing *yin* lines. When tossing coins there is a one in eight chance of obtaining a changing line –either *yang* or *yin*–, when using sticks there is one in sixteen chance of getting a changing *yin* line, but three in sixteen chances of getting a changing *yang* line. The probabilities of getting non changing *yang* and *yin* lines are evened with coins, but with sticks there is slightly more chance of getting non changing *yin* than non changing *yang* lines.

In practice, both oracular methods work equally well. The main difference is that coin tossing is easier and faster but using the sticks is more complicated

The Yarrow-Stalks Oracle

–at least until you are used to it– and takes more time. You can see how to get the oracle with coins at **How to consult the Oracle** (p. 15).

Usage

After you have written your question, unwrap the 50 sticks and put one of them back in the linen cloth wrap, since only 49 will be used. Follow the steps below six times to obtain the six lines that will draw the hexagram –there may be two hexagrams if there are changing lines in your answer– that will be the oracle's answer. Lines will be drawn from bottom to top.

1. Divide the 49 sticks at random in two heaps and put them on the table, on your right and left sides.

2. Take one stick from the right-hand heap and place it between the little and the ring fingers of your left hand.

3. Take the left-hand heap with your left hand and start taking groups of four sticks from it, placing them away (in a heap that we will call Group A), until you have 4 or less sticks remaining in your left hand. Place this remainder between the ring and the middle fingers of your left hand.

4. Take the right-hand heap with your left hand and start taking groups of four sticks from it, placing them away (in Group A), until you have 4 or less sticks remaining in your left hand. Place this remainder between the forefinger and the middle finger of your left hand.

5. Now you will have either 9 or 5 sticks in your left hand: the first one that you put there before counting groups of four, and the two remainders of the counting. If there are 9, count 2; if there are 5, count 3; write down that number. Notice that you will have to write down three numbers for each line of the hexagram.

6. Put away the sticks in your left hand (in a heap that we will call Group B), leaving only the single stick between your little and ring fingers. Divide the sticks in Group A in two heaps at random and put them on your right and left sides. Go back to step 3 and repeat the previous steps until you have written down three numbers (3+3+3, 2+2+2 or different combinations of 2 and 3). Notice that the second and third time you repeat the process, you will have either 8 or 4 sticks. If there are 8, count 2; if there are 4, count 3.

7. Once you have written down three numbers you already have defined one line of the hexagram. Join all the 49 sticks on the table (Groups A and B) and go back to step 1. After you have the numbers for the six lines, the divination will be concluded. Write the three numbers for each

line in a separate line, starting from bottom –for the first line–, to top –for the last line–.

After you consultation is done you will have written down some numbers (always from bottom to top) as the following example shows:

6th line	2+3+3=8	A static *yin* line ▬ ▬
5th line	2+3+2=7	A static *yang* line ▬▬▬
4th line	3+2+2=7	A static *yang* line ▬▬▬
3rd line	3+3+3=9	A changing *yang* line ▬O▬
2nd line	3+2+3=8	A static *yin* line ▬ ▬
1st line	2+2+2=6	A changing *yin* line ▬X▬

As you can notice each number corresponds to some kind of line.

Broken lines are *yin* and whole lines are *yang*. If you have any changing lines in your hexagram, a second hexagram will be generated by replacing every changing line by a non-changing line. If the changing line was *yang* it will be replaced by a *yin* line and vice versa.

The first hexagram shown in the above image (31), will change or mutate to the second one (17), as you can see in the following table:

31	17

The first hexagram (31) has two changing lines. To get the second hexagram, copy the first one, but replacing changing *yang* lines by *yin* lines and changing *yin* lines by *yang* lines. In this example only the first and third lines change.

Of course, if there are no changing lines you will not have a second hexagram.

The Yarrow-Stalks Oracle

For information about the interpretation of the answer see **Understanding hexagram readings** (p. 27). To know the hexagram numbers for your own Yijing readings, please see **Chart of the Trigrams and Hexagrams** (p. 379).

What are changing lines

We get changing lines when a line has a 6 or 9 value. The changing lines generate a second hexagram; if there are no changing lines, we get a single hexagram, which depicts a slowly evolving situation.

Changing lines are the steps of change that are activated in the hexagram reading; because that we will experience only the situations described by the changing lines we got.

Changing lines are also the lines more charged with energy. *Yang* and *yin* always change, *yang* mutates into *yin* and vice-versa. When the *yang* or *yin* lines are strongly charged with energy, they flip, mutating into its opposite, that is the reason changing lines generate a second hexagram.

Understanding hexagram readings

The interpretation of oracular responses is more of an art than a science, use the guidelines outlined below as useful tools to structure and analyze the answer got from the oracle, rather than absolute rules.

General guidelines

Although basically you would only need to read the changing lines, Judgment and Image, if you are not familiar with the Book of Changes, it would be good to read the entire hexagram, because that way you will get a clearer idea of the time you will have to live through.

After reading the full text of the hexagrams (it can be one or two, if there are changing lines), concentrate on the specific parts referring to the reading you got; first read the Judgment and the Image of the first hexagram, if there are changing lines, read them –only in the first hexagram– and then read the Judgment and the Image of the second hexagram.

If you got only one hexagram, the situation will not change very quickly and you should only read the Judgment and the Image to know how the circumstances will develop and what kind of behaviour is most appropriate.

If you got two hexagrams, the first hexagram describes the immediate situation and the second its future development, although both may be linked in other ways, see *How to interpret the second hexagram*, further down in this same section.

Sometimes the oracle will be easily understood as you read it, you will be able to see clearly how the answer you get applies to your life.

Other times, the answer may seem like a coded message, which has little to do with the reality that surrounds you; in that case, keep the oracular response in your mind, as a pending matter; meditate on it, don't dismiss it. Let some time go by, maybe you could reread the answer the next day. If you persist, at the some moment, you will be able to see clearly how the hexagram reading applies to your life.

How to interpret the changing lines

It is useful to apply some rules to avoid contradictions in the interpretations of answers with several changing lines and thus better understand the readings.

Always remember that the lines are numbered from bottom to top.

If the number of changing lines is between one and five, you must read all the changing lines in the first hexagram.

Note that if only the first or sixth line changes or if more than 4 lines are change, the emphasis will be on the second hexagram.

When several lines change, the top line is the most important, because it defines the conclusion of the situation. If there is a contradiction between the top line and other changing lines or the Judgment or Image, take the text from the top line as the most valid oracle.

Note that, within each hexagram the lines are identified with titles such as: First Six, Third Nine, Top Six, etc. This is because only changing lines are read, which are those with a value of 6 (*yin* lines) or 9 (*yang* lines). So "First Six" means the changing *yin* line in the first place, "Third Nine" means the changing *yang* line in the third place and "Top Six", means the changing *yin* line in the sixth place.

Alternative procedures for interpreting changing lines

Each changing line links the first hexagram with a second hexagram. If several lines change, a second hexagram would be produced, but each of these changing lines can also be changed individually –without modifying the other lines– generating a different hexagram for each line, read only the text of the changed line in that hexagram, it will serve as an additional explanation for the text of the original changing line.

Use this method with caution and only when several lines mutate and the meaning of a line needs to be clarified.

No line changes

There's only one hexagram. Read the Judgment and the Image. The situation is stable or may evolve slowly.

Only one line changes

Read the text of the changing line in the first hexagram, as well as the Judgment and Image of both hexagrams. The line takes precedence over the Judgment. In case of contradiction between the line and the Judgment, take the line as the valid oracle.

If the changing line is the top line, in the sixth position, the time of the first hexagram is passing; in that case read only the text of the changing line and the Judgment and Image of the second hexagram.

Two, three or four lines change

Read the changing lines in the first hexagram, in addition to reading the Judgment and the Image in both hexagrams.

Five lines change

Read the changing lines in the first hexagram, in addition to reading the Judgment and the Image in both hexagrams.

The situation described by the first hexagram will soon be over.

All lines change

The situation described by the first hexagram will conclude soon, so the second hexagram is the most important. Do not read the changing lines, only read the Judgment and Image of each hexagram.

Note: The hexagrams 1 and 2 have an special text to read when all lines mutate.

Only the first line changes

The first line has not yet entered fully into the situation, so you may pass to the second hexagram, without fully experiencing the time described by the first one.

Only the last line changes

The last line is saying goodbye to the situation, which is why you may pass to the second hexagram, without fully experiencing the time described by the first one.

Relationships between changing lines

The lines describe the evolution of the situation, from the bottom to the top, each line illustrates a different moment of the situation –which may be good or bad– but they also describe relationships between different people .

The lines have a natural hierarchy, which is why they often describe relationships between people of different social positions.

Understanding hexagram readings

The first line represents someone in a low social position, with little experience, a beginner or someone who has no power. It can also indicate an influence or a person that is just entering the situation now.

The second line symbolizes a wife, an assistant, an employee with some responsibility, an official who is located far from the center of power, someone who has an internal task within an organization or a family.

The third line is placed in a transition point and can represent an intermediary.

The fourth line represents a minister, an executive officer who works in a position close to an authority figure, such as a leader, a manager or a ruler.

The fifth line represents a manager, a governor, a king, a leader or the head of a group or family.

The sixth line represents a sage, a spiritual leader, a counselor, or someone who has distanced himself from the situation. Sometimes it can represent someone who went too far and who becomes a transgressor.

Adjacent lines can be linked through a bond of solidarity, especially between *yang* and *yin* lines.

The lines in the positions 1st, 2nd, and 3rd are related to the lines in the 4th, 5th and 6th positions by a correspondence relationship. *Yang* lines correspond to *yin* lines and vice versa.

For all these reasons, the changing lines can describe the dynamics of a situation, showing its protagonists in action and how they relate to each other.

How to interpret the second hexagram

If there are one or more changing lines, you will have to interpret two hexagrams.

If you get two hexagrams, the first hexagram describes the immediate situation and the second its future development, although both can be linked in other ways.

In some situations the first hexagram describes the situation in the outside world (objective reality), and the second indicates the feelings and tendencies in the mind of the consultant (subjective reality).

Note that, as we indicated earlier, in the event that more than 4 lines mutate, the emphasis will be on the second hexagram.

The Trigrams

Each hexagram is composed of two trigrams, one corresponds to the three lower lines and the other to the three upper lines.

The interaction of both trigrams determines the character of the hexagram. In the Image, this interaction is used as an example to follow appropriate behavior for each hexagram.

The trigrams are associated with many symbolic meanings, which can greatly enrich the interpretation of the hexagrams.

The lower trigram is related to the inner world: feelings, judgments and hopes and the superior to the external world: the objective situation.

You can see ample information about the trigrams in **The Eight Trigrams** (p. 3 69).

A practical example

The following oracular answer is an answer to the question: *Job Possibilities*. We got the hexagram 55, **Fullness**; which has two changing lines and thus originates a second hexagram, the 21, **Biting Through**. The first column shows the line number and value obtained for each line.

	Hex. 55	Hex. 21
L6: 6	━╳━	━━━━━
L5: 8	━━ ━━	━━ ━━
L4: 7	━━━━━	━━━━━
L3: 9	━━◯━	━━ ━━
L2: 8	━━ ━━	━━ ━━
L1: 7	━━━━━	━━━━━

Fullness describes a time with many opportunities, but it is also full of inconveniences, and it will not last long, so it is important to take advantage of it well before it ends.

Biting Through indicates that firm measures must be used to remove an obstacle.

The two lines that change in *Fullness* are:

Understanding hexagram readings

Third line: Unfavorable conditions will block any attempt on your part to overcome them. The broken arm means that your influence and power will be diminished if you try to make a failed attempt to move forward.

Sixth line: This line describes someone who, instead of facing the problems of daily life, takes refuge in the memories of the past, withdrawing from the outside world.

This is a possible synthesis of the meanings of all the parts of this response:

You will have good opportunities to progress in your work (Judgment and Image of hex. 55), but you will have to overcome some obstacles to achieve it (indicated by the hexagram 21 and the image of 55). Do not delay, but do not act without preparation; If you are not careful, the impediments will stop you and may even harm you (3rd line).

Keep a positive attitude, focused on the means at your disposal to advance, do not escape reality by taking refuge in false illusions of superiority (6th line).

The third and sixth lines are linked by a correspondence relationship; the third line symbolizes an employee in a transition position (the consultant), who does not have much power; the sixth line is a weak and inoperative boss who does not fulfill his duty and who can block the employee advance by refusing to accept reality.

If you waste the moment for advancement, you will lose the opportunity. If you can take advantage of the opportunities, you will obtain important, although transitory, advantages. You can benefit in the long term, because you will get a significant improvement in your reputation and, over time, this will open your way to a wider circle of action.

1

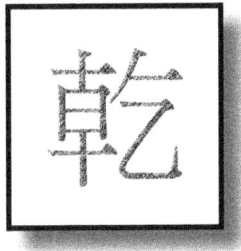

qián
The Creative / Activity /
Dynamic Force

This is one of the eight hexagrams that are comprised by the same trigram repeated twice, in this case *qián*, The Creative. Please see **The Eight Trigrams** (p. 369) for more information.

Associated meanings

Spirit power, creative, force, dynamic, strong action, vigor, constant, heaven, heavenly generative principle (male), father, sovereign, power above the human, yang power, active, vigorous appearance.

Judgment

> The Creative.
> Outstanding success.
> The determination is favorable.

This hexagram is comprised of six solid, *yang* lines, representing light, action and strength. It describes a great accumulation of energy and consequently the need for steadfast action to channel such power in the proper direction.

The figure of the dragon appears as protagonist in five of the seven line statements (only the first and second hexagrams have seven line statements).

The Chinese dragon, different from the western dragon, is not evil, but beneficial. It is a legendary animal, a powerful force that surges from the waters, and is associated with rain, floods, heaven and the hexagram 1. It also has supernatural godly power. It is at home either under the waters or flying in heaven and has supernatural energy. Also it is related with the supreme authority (the emperor).

1 - The Creative / Activity / Dynamic Force

In this hexagram the dragon symbolizes somebody with its same qualities, and the lines show its ascension from a low position (under the water) up to the sky.

This is one of the few hexagrams that mention the "four cardinal virtues": *yuan*: outstanding (fundamentality, primal, originating, spring season, head, sublime, great, grand); *heng*: success (prevalence, growing, penetrating, treat, offering, sacrifice); *li*: determination (perseverance, constancy, correct and firm) and *heng*: favorable (advantageous, suitable, beneficial, lucky). One or more of the cardinal virtues appear in 50 different hexagrams, but only the hexagrams 1, 2 (with some modification), 3, 17, 19, 25 and 49 have the four virtues in its Judgment. Since the *Han* Dynasty onwards they have become keywords of Confucian thought, four qualities or virtues applicable both to Heaven and to the noble-minded person.

In the Confucian tradition the dragon is associated with the four cardinal virtues. Any oracle encompassing the four cardinal virtues indicates that success is granted, but only if you don't stray from the good; for this reason determination in the right way is the key to success.

The Image

> Heaven action is strong and dynamic.
> Thus the noble never ceases to strengthen himself.

In the same way that heaven revolves daily, the creative person should be ready for incessant action, a movement that keeps going along through time, renovating itself each day.

Strong action should be matched to the needs of each moment. The creative person should keep touch with reality and with other people as well.

First Nine

> Submerged dragon.
> Do not act.

The dragon is at home either under the waters or flying in heaven.

It was believed that dragons caused rain when they ascended into the sky, hence they were beneficial since the rain watered the crops.

In this line the dragon is hibernating; still not ready to make its mark in the world. It means that the time is not yet ripe for action and that you should wait and keep a low profile until you are ready.

Career: There will be no changes. Premature action would be dangerous because you are not yet prepared for it.

Private life: Quiet life. Do not start anything new.

Health, Feelings and Social life: Good health. Rest is advised. Be discreet.

Second Nine

> Dragon in the field.
> It is favorable to see the great man.

You are entering your field of action in life, where you will find your peers.

The word translated as "field" also means "hunt". The hunt symbolizes the search for your destiny and your vocation.

To see the great man means that having a mentor would be very useful at this stage; but it also indicates that you should rise spiritually and in understanding.

Career: You will have good opportunities to advance, provided that you get support from your superiors.

Private life: Your good conduct and reputation will gain you the respect of other people and will help you to advance successfully.

Health, Feelings and Social life: Good health. Excellent moment for establishing relations with other people.

Third Nine

> The noble is active throughout the day.
> At night he is cautious, as if in danger.
> No defect.

You will be creatively active all day long. Enduring strength and alertness will keep you out of trouble.

A wide scope of opportunities will spread before you along with your reputation.

Do not procrastinate nor allow others to influence you improperly. You will have to marshal wisely your resources to keep pace with your responsibilities.

Career: You will have many duties and concerns, but if you are cautious enough you will not make any mistakes.

Private life: You will need all your strength to handle your obligations. Be very careful to avoid complications with other people.

Health, Feelings and Social life: Excellent health, but sometimes you will feel stressed out.

Fourth Nine

> Hesitates before jumping over the chasm.
> No defect.

You will test your capability for success, deciding your future.

The choice is yours; you can ascend and play an important role in the world, gaining fame and power or stay low and dedicate yourself to personal matters.

Career: A decision must be made between different opportunities. You may have to wait for a time and make some trial runs before deciding what you will do.

Private life: This is a period of transition. You will vacillate until you find which path you will take.

Health, Feelings and Social life: Be open to new experiences. If you are sincere, confusion will fade away and you will know which is your true path in life.

Fifth Nine

> Dragon flying in the sky.
> It is favorable to see the great man.

To fly in the sky means to have reached a high position in the place where you belong, because the sky is the natural world of the dragon.

The sky is the highest sphere where only dragons, that is to say, the most capable and creative persons can abide.

The flying dragon symbolizes an outstanding person at work, having great influence and being an example for other people. The flying dragon also indicates that you can advance freely and achieve lofty goals with ease.

To see the great man means that still after having reached such a high place, having a guide would be very useful.

Career: Great success and fast progress. You will be widely recognized and respected.

Private life: Your desires will be fulfilled and you will be very successful.

Health, Feelings and Social life: Excellent health. Your mind will be clear and insightful and you will have great influence over other people.

Top Nine

> Arrogant dragon.
> There will be occasion for repentance.

If you go too far in your ambition you will lose contact with the real world and will get lost.

Arrogance will sever your links with other people and when you most need them you will not get any help.

If you recognize your limits and do not forget your fellow men you may still prevent trouble.

Career: It may be a good time to retire or fall back. If you push too far you will have heavy losses.

Private life: Your obstinacy will isolate you and will get you into a lot of trouble.

Health, Feelings and Social life: Your health will suffer if you ask too much of your body. Egocentric views will let you without friends.

All lines are Nine

A group of dragons without heads.
Auspicious.

Only the first two hexagrams, The Creative and The Receptive have an additional line statement, to be read when all lines change.

Each dragon is strong; a group of dragons is a powerful force that hardly can be stopped.

To be without heads means that the dragons act by common accord, without having a chief among them.

When all lines mutate *The Creative* changes into the hexagram 2: *The Receptive*. By combining the strength of *The Creative* with the devotion of the *The Receptive* you will achieve a perfect balance and will be able to handle any situation easily, hence the prospects will be entirely good.

Career: You are part of team of distinguished individuals, working in good harmony.

Private life: It is a good time for cooperating with your family and friends. Shared creative participation will be very favorable.

Health, Feelings and Social life: Excellent health and very good social interaction.

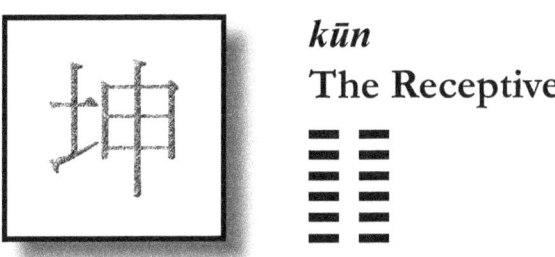

kūn
The Receptive

This is one of the eight hexagrams that are comprised by the same trigram repeated twice, in this case *kūn*, The Receptive. Please see **The Eight Trigrams** (p. 369) for more information.

Associated meanings

Earth, nature; receptiveness, responsiveness, compliance, acquiescence, docility, devotion, subordinate; matter, field, spatial extension; feminine, nurturing, mother, yin force.

Judgment

> The Receptive.
> Outstanding success favorable for the determination of a mare.
> If the noble takes the lead he goes astray,
> but if he follows, he finds a master.
> It is favorable to find friends in the west and south;
> avoid friends in the east and north.
> A quiet determination is auspicious.

A mare is strong but docile. Hence, do not try to impose your will but follow someone's example or guide.

You are part of a group or team and you should work for the good of the whole, not just for your own personal gain or benefit.

If you have employment, it would be best for you to progress inside the place where you are working instead of trying to go ahead on your own. If you are part of a family, be loyal with them and do you share of the work for the sake of your family.

South-west means going towards other people and to work with them, north-east indicates advancing in solitude.

Going with friends signifies to surrender to a community-sense work, where solidarity and cooperation are involved.

Quiet determination means that you should do what is required from you and persevere with steadfast and calm resolve.

This is one of the few hexagrams that mention the "four cardinal virtues": *yuan*: outstanding (fundamentality, primal, originating, spring season, head, sublime, great, grand); *heng*: success (prevalence, growing, penetrating, treat, offering, sacrifice); *li*: determination (perseverance, constancy, correct and firm) and *heng*: favorable (advantageous, suitable, beneficial, lucky). One or more of the cardinal virtues appear in 50 different hexagrams, but only the hexagrams 1, 2 (with some modification), 3, 17, 19, 25 and 49 have the four virtues in its Judgment. Since the *Han* Dynasty onwards they have become keywords of Confucian thought, four qualities or virtues applicable both to Heaven and to the noble-minded person.

Any oracle encompassing the four cardinal virtues indicates that success is granted, but only if you don't stray from the good; for this reason determination in the right way is the key to success.

The Image

> The earth condition is receptive obedience.
> Thus the noble, who has a munificent character, sustains all living creatures.

Like the earth nurtures all beings, the virtuous person will be generous and tolerating, helping and guiding all living beings.

Be open-minded and compassionate to the needs of other persons.

Do you duty for the sake of others more than for your own advancement.

First Six

> Walking on hoarfrost one reaches hard ice.

Walking on hoarfrost (*lu shuāng*) has several connotations:

The coming winter; signs of decay.

An approaching marriage. Two *ShiJing* (The Classic of Poetry) odes use the same characters with that meaning.

The Receptive - 2

Ceremonial walking on hoarfrost for the autumnal sacrifices.

The first meaning is the more common interpretation, here walking on hoarfrost indicates that danger is coming and good conditions are coming to an end, because the hard and cold winter is approaching. Be alert for signs of trouble and do not let matters slip out of hand.

Also the reference to hard ice may indicate that your advance will be stopped cold soon.

Career: The period of easy advancing is coming to an end. Be alert to plots against you. An alliance may help you.

Private life: Trouble is brewing. The path that you follow may be more slippery that you expect. Do not be ingenuous or care free, but take precautions.

Health, Feelings and Social life: You may have trouble with your feet or mobility issues.

Second Six

Right, square and large, inexperienced.
But nothing will be not favorable.

The square is a symbol of earth. An alternative translation would be: "honorable, straightforward and extensive, without practice". In any case the line means that by being correct and strong you can make all things flourish easily.

Be sincere and follow your instincts, you will do the right thing.

Career: Your natural qualities will help you to prosper in your trade.

Private life: Be open to life and accept what happens with ease. Your good nature will assure success.

Health, Feelings and Social life: Good health and an open heart will make you happy.

Third Six

Hidden brilliance.
The determination is suitable.
If you are in the service of a king you will not have achievements,
but will carry to conclusion.

Concentrate your efforts in your duty and do not seek distinctions for yourself.

Your talents will be rewarded when the time is ripe, for now it would be best for you to focus in servicing others.

If you are not independent but work for somebody, you will do a good job, but you will not get any credit for it at the present time.

Career: You will not have immediate success but will achieve your ends in the long run, provided that you handle matters with modesty and perseverance.

Private life: Stay in the background, you will prosper in an unassuming way, possibly working from home.

Health, Feelings and Social life: Be modest and discreet. People will appreciate you more if you do not outshine them.

Fourth Six

A tied up bag.
No defect, no praise.

Keep your opinions and plans private. Do not draw attention to yourself.

Caution is advised, do not commit, keep your neutrality and distance until the situation clears.

Career: You have reached an impasse. Because there is trouble ahead, stay in your place, be prudent and do not take sides.

Private life: The situations is stationary, you will neither gain nor lose. Discretion and prudence will keep you safe.

Health, Feelings and Social life: You are something of a recluse, but your reserve will save you from trouble. Time for resting.

Fifth Six

Yellow lower garment.
There will be outstanding happiness.

Yellow is the color of the earth and indicates moderation and following the middle path between the extremes.

Also, the yellow lower garment symbolizes humility and virtue in somebody that occupies a place of honor (the fifth line is the ruler's place).

If you are sincere but polite, people will respond well to you sensible approach.

Career: Your ability to handle matters smoothly and with modesty will help you to progress greatly.

Private life: Moderation and tact will make your life flourish.

Health, Feelings and Social life: Excellent health and very good social life.

Top Six

>Dragons fight in the open country.
>Their blood is black and yellow.

The *yin* principle is the complement of the *yang* force, but it should be subservient and do not take the lead.

Here a mad fight between the two forces, the true *yang* dragon and the rebel *yin* false dragon will cause calamity. Black is the color of heaven and yellow is the color of the earth, they identify the true and false dragons.

An unpleasant and violent competition for power will only cause misery for both sides. Be cooperative, not competitive.

Career: Power struggles should be avoided, because they will damage everybody involved and may make you to lose your position.

Private life: Conflict and fights will cause many troubles and loses.

Health, Feelings and Social life: Envy and intransigence may destroy your happiness.

All lines are Six

>Long term determination is favorable.

Only the first two hexagrams, The Creative and The Receptive have an additional line statement, to be read when all lines change.

Final success will be achieved through the practice of constant determination.

You are doing things just fine, keep in the same line and you will have lasting success.

Career: Be loyal to your commitments and plans.

Private life: Firmness of purpose and allegiance to your principles will be advantageous.

Health, Feelings and Social life: Good health and dedication to a cause will keep you well engaged socially.

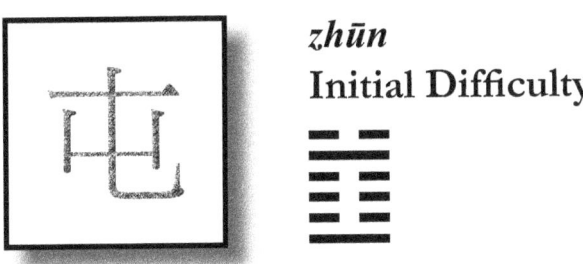

zhūn
Initial Difficulty

Associated meanings

Difficult; to sprout, begin to grow; leadership; assemble, accumulate, hoard; to garrison soldiers, massed, bunched.

Judgment

> The Initial Difficulty.
> Outstanding success.
> The determination is favorable.
> It should not be pursued any goal.
> It is favorable to appoint officials.

In the first stages of growth, immature beings and new ventures need nurturing, care and firm determination.

This is the right moment to set the basis of future developments, to affirm the innate potential, as the root must be steady into the soil before sprouting. The situation is unstable and the task couldn't be done without the help of collaborators. Goals cannot be attained until some order and development is achieved. That means that long term planning is required.

This is one of the few hexagrams that mention the "four cardinal virtues": *yuan*: outstanding (fundamentality, primal, originating, spring season, head, sublime, great, grand); *heng*: success (prevalence, growing, penetrating, treat, offering, sacrifice); *li*: determination (perseverance, constancy, correct and firm) and *heng*: favorable (advantageous, suitable, beneficial, lucky). One or more of the cardinal virtues appear in 50 different hexagrams, but only the hexagrams 1, 2 (with some modification), 3, 17, 19, 25 and 49 have the four

3 - Initial Difficulty

virtues in its Judgment. Since the *Han* Dynasty onwards they have become keywords of Confucian thought, four qualities or virtues applicable both to Heaven and to the noble-minded person.

Any oracle encompassing the four cardinal virtues indicates that success is granted, but only if you don't stray from the good; for this reason determination in the right way is the key to success.

The Image

> Clouds and thunder: The image of the Initial Difficulty.
> Thus the noble sorts the threads of warp and woof.

The competent person should order and classify things in order to convert potential capabilities into a real force.

Clouds and thunder is a reference to the two constituent's trigrams which depict a situation with plenty of possibilities but also in a chaotic state. To sort the threads of warp and woof is a metaphor for the act of government.

Resolute leadership is a required to order the situation and achieve final success.

First Nine

> Looking to overcome an obstacle.
> It is favorable to maintain the determination.
> It is favorable to appoint assistants.

It may be necessary to try different approaches before being able to surpass an obstacle; hence some hesitation will be unavoidable, but the final goals should not be forgotten.

By recognizing the merits of your subordinates and making them feel useful, you can get help from them and establish a good foundation for further expansion.

Career: Good moment to assemble a team, to push forward and to set the rules of the game.

Private life: Time to take the reins of the situation and to offer guidance to friends or family. Do not let others make you doubt yourself and do not deviate from your own rules.

Health, Feelings and Social life: Some mobility problems may affect you feet. Irresolution.

Initial Difficulty - 3

Second Six

    Difficulties impeding progress.
    Horse and cart separate.
    It's not a villain, but a pretender.
    The girl has determination and does not plight her troth.
    After ten years she will pledge herself.

The horse separated from the cart symbolizes the difficulty in making cooperative efforts work.

An obstacle still impedes the advance and some misunderstandings are complicating the teamwork.

Somebody will provide help from an unexpected quarter. The newcomer will not be appreciated at a first glance, you may hesitate, waiting for the right moment before taking on any obligations or to compromise your will.

The Chinese character translated as "plight" also means "conceive", "breed", indicating that you will achieve a fruitful alliance at the end.

Ten years indicates a long period, like in the hexagrams 24.5 and 27.3.

Career: Establishing an alliance or forming a good team will take some time, but its advantages will make worthwhile the delay and effort spent in building it. Good long term prospects.

Private life: After experiencing some hardships, conflicts and doubts a marriage or a firm friendship will be achieved. Possible birth in the family.

Health, Feelings and Social life: Mobility troubles. Distrust, irresolution.

Third Six

    Chasing the deer without forester, entering in the depths of the forest.
    The noble sees the signs and desists.
    If he went forward, he would regret it.

Blinded by your desire, you may advance in dangerous and unknown ground without taking the proper precautions or lacking a good guide. The deer represents the desire; the forest symbolizes the unknown and the dangers ahead where you may be taken by your ambition. The signs are subtle indications that –if disregarded– will lead you amiss.

Career: Lack of planning and foresight will lead you to failure and humiliation. Restrain and prudence is advised.

Private life: The heart forges ahead chasing its own unattainable dreams. The awakening will be painful.

3 - Initial Difficulty

Health, Feelings and Social life: Feelings of being lost or disconnected from others. Obsession.

Fourth Six

> Horse and cart separate.
> Look for the union.
> Advance brings happiness.
> Everything will be auspicious and without blemish.

The forces at your disposal are scattered and discordant. The cart symbolizes a project that cannot advance forward for lack of union.

You are not qualified to solve the problems by yourself, getting an ally is the only way to resume your advance and carry out things to a successful end.

Career: Associating with other people or becoming part of a group is the best way to achieve good results. Good prospects for teamwork.

Private life: Recognizing that you cannot do everything by yourself and looking for help in friends or family will make your life more agreeable and prosperous.

Health, Feelings and Social life: Indecision, hesitation.

Fifth Nine

> Difficulties dispensing favors.
> Determination in small matters is auspicious.
> Determination in major ways brings misfortune.

Preserve your energy, wait for a more propitious time. For now only small things can be done successfully. Big achievements will fail.

You will not be able to help others in any significant way.

Career: It is advantageous to focus in the small matters at hand with care. Ambitious projects will fail. Inversions will be unsuccessful.

Private life: It is a difficult time for helping others. You will not be able to solve the problems of your friends or family, and will only bring misfortune on yourself if you get entangled in trouble. Only small things can be achieved.

Health, Feelings and Social life: Feelings of inadequacy towards others. Insecurity.

Top Nine

> Horse and cart separate.
> Tears of blood are spilled.

Initial Difficulty - 3

Blood tears represent an exaggerated attitude; more stressful in the lament than what really corresponds. You have gone too far and now you are mired in difficulties.

There are no helpers and you will find no suitable place for moving, but neither remaining in your current position will do you any good.

If you yield to reality and give up your obstinacy you will be able to start anew.

Career: You cannot neither advance nor hold to your current position. Accept your losses and start again from the beginning.

Private life: You may lose your property or be separated from a beloved one.

Health, Feelings and Social life: Chronic depression. Obsession and despair.

4

méng
Youthful Folly

Associated Meanings

Ignorance, immaturity, inexperience; cover, hidden, in darkness; go with covered eyes against; deception, conceal, cheat.

Judgment

> The Youthful Folly is successful.
> It is not I who seek the young fool, the young fool seeks me.
> At the first oracle I inform, but a second or third time is troublesome; and I do not instruct the annoying.
> The determination is favorable.

Immaturity is a learning stage. A young fool can be successful; because the close contact with experience will help him to acquire some wisdom. Also, the learning process should be taken care showing respect to the master; otherwise the teacher's effort will be wasted Unruly students will bring humiliation over themselves.

The Oracle speaks here, telling the people who seek its advice to take seriously its instruction and to avoid asking the same question again and again. In such case they would just waste their time.

The Image

> Under the mountain flows a spring: The image of the Youthful Folly.
> Thus the noble makes his actions resolute and cultivates his virtue.

4 - Youthful Folly

The mountain is strong, consolidated, but the spring flowing out of it runs in search of the formation of its own course. The spring runs the risk of stagnation, as when the youthful inexperience takes the wrong road, delaying the maturation process.

To cultivate one's virtue means to develop the own strong points or natural gifts. That is the way to success.

First Six

> To develop the foolish man it will be favorable to discipline him.
> The fetters must be removed,
> otherwise there will be regret.

Discipline is good for strengthening the will, but it shouldn't be carried too far. If the restrains (symbolized by the fetters) are excessive they will sap the student creativity and good will. After all, discipline is an excellent tool but not a goal in itself.

Career: Clear rules should be enforced, but not to the point of hindering efficiency or dampening creativity.

Private life: Some quarrels. Family rules should be applied wisely, not blindly.

Health, Feelings and Social life: Weak or impeded feet. Exercises will strengthen mobility.

Second Nine

> Supporting the Youthful Folly is auspicious.
> To take a wife is auspicious.
> A son can take care of the family.

The student weakness should be tolerated. Expecting too much and too soon from people that are starting to learn is not a realistic expectancy.

The wife is here a symbol of weakness, to be able to take one indicates a kindly and considerate attitude, how a stronger being can manage a relation with a weaker person.

The pupil that is educated with kindness, in turn will be able to take care of his own family in the same way.

Career: This is a good moment for assuming more responsibilities and accepting subordinate partners.

Private life: You may take responsibility over other people or perhaps even marry.

Health, Feelings and Social life: You will feel a new drive and have high levels of energy.

Third Six

Do not marry a girl who, on seeing a man of metal,
loses her self-possession.
No place is favorable.

This line describes how a weaker person can lose his will and blindly imitate or follow a stronger person as a role model. It is not right to allow other person to follow you in such a slavish way. That kind of situation doesn't lead to success or to a sustainable relation.

Also, sometimes a weaker person can relate to a stronger or richer one only with the idea of getting selfish advantages. In such case nothing good will come of that relationship.

Career: Do not trust people that follow you blindly, keep your independence of action at all costs. Do not fawn over your superiors.

Private life: Do not be servile; maintain your self-respect. Do not encourage others to be dependent from you.

Health, Feelings and Social life: Emotional disturbances may affect stomach and bowels.

Fourth Six

Trapped by his folly he will suffer shame.

A fool who is not ready to give up his foolish ways and is too proud to change, will arrive to a dead end, losing touch with reality and becoming trapped in his own fantasies. No other outcome than shame is possible.

Career: Impasse and humiliation due to lack of imagination and stubborn adherence to impractical ways.

Private life: Do not close yourself to reality; be open to new ways for doing things. Be ready to adapt and learn.

Health, Feelings and Social life: Back problems. Trouble with the upper limbs. Feelings of inadequacy.

Fifth Six

Children's folly is auspicious.

Being flexible, willing to learn and accepting guidance will be favorable.

4 - Youthful Folly

An open-minded person knows his limitations and where to look for help. This describes the exact inverse situation of the previous line.

Career: Delegating responsibilities in trustworthy and knowledgeable people will complement well your weak points. Do not hesitate in asking advice.

Private life: Being open to friends and family and willing to follow good counsel will be favorable. Recognizing your own limitations and asking for help will be positive.

Health, Feelings and Social life: Good emotional balance. Happiness.

Top Nine

> Punishing Youthful Folly.
> It is not favorable to commit harassment,
> but it is favorable to defend yourself against transgressors.

When a fool is stubborn he may require punishment, but only to the point that is required to curb his bad behavior. The amount of punishment depends on the person; in some cases a light punishment may be enough in other cases stronger punishments may be more appropriate.

Punishment is the last resort and should not be applied as revenge or in anger.

The same Chinese word is translated as "harassment" and "transgressors", literally means "bandit, invader, enemy, robber, violent people, outcasts, plunderers". The basic meaning would be: do not become a bandit, defend against bandits.

Career: Leaders should know when and how to apply punishment, not only to protect themselves but to make people follow the proper rules. You may have to go to court or press charges again somebody.

Private life: Some people will not stop taking advantage of you until they are stopped forcefully, strong words or acts may be required. Conflicts should be temporary, not a perpetual feud. Be alert against robbers. Do not oppress other unduly.

Health, Feelings and Social life: Depression, self-reproach.

5

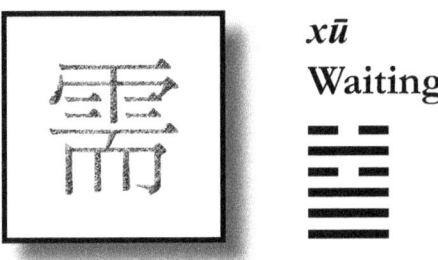

xū
Waiting

Associated Meanings

Wait, tarry, stop; get wet; serve.

Judgment

> Waiting.
> With brilliance and sincerity you will succeed.
> The determination is favorable.
> It is favorable to cross the great river.

Waiting is not the same than giving up. Having clarity of purpose one can wait patiently, looking carefully at the situation to see when the right moment for advance comes.

In ancient China, crossing rivers, either at a ford or when the river was frozen, was not an easy task. It implicated dangers and hardships; hence crossing the great river means to carry out a difficult undertaking.

The Image

> Clouds ascend to heaven: The image of Waiting.
> Thus the noble drinks, eats and parties.

Clouds gathering in the sky symbolize a process or situation that is evolving slowly. The conclusion of that process will be rain, which also indicates the liberation of the stress.

5 - Waiting

To drink eat and party means to be at ease and to have a good and optimist state of mind. The waiting time can be enjoyed, and normal live must go on without being put on hold until your goals are attained.

Nourish yourself and keep in touch with other people while you wait.

First Nine

> Waiting in the suburbs.
> It is favorable to have perseverance.
> No defect.

Your life is still undisturbed and nothing unusual happens yet.

If you stay away from danger and remain committed to your daily chores you will have no trouble.

Career: Continue with your business as usual. Neither news nor challenges will disturb your work.

Private life: Peaceful time. Quiet country life.

Health, Feelings and Social life: Good health and contentment, although you may feel a bit isolated.

Second Nine

> Waiting in the sand.
> They say little things.
> Finally there will be good fortune.

Waiting in the sandbank, near the river means that you are about to cross the river. Crossing a river symbolizes undertaking a dangerous enterprise. Some people may not understand your goals or distrust your capability to perform them, but their gossip will have no importance. In time you will carry out successfully your objective.

Career: You are waiting on a threshold, about to start some important project. Since you are now in the open, people can see what you are looking for. Keep you focus in your final goal and don't mind the critics.

Private life: This is a transitional time. Your life is about to change and some friends or family, who cannot understand you, will criticize your moves.

Health, Feelings and Social life: You will feel some anxiety because you have big expectations.

Third Nine

> Waiting in the mud attracts bandits.

You advanced too far and too soon and now you are in a vulnerable position. You are in danger of being attacked or slandered.

The way out of the bad actual situations is not clear; you are obstructed for the time being. Utter prudence and circumspection are advised.

Career: Your career is obstructed temporarily and there is danger of demotion. Some bad people may try to take unfair advantage of you.

Private life: Rushing things led you to trouble. Be careful, you are isolated, and in danger of being robbed. Do not take things at face value.

Health, Feelings and Social life: Insecurity, alienation. Digestive and sexual problems.

Fourth Six

Waiting in blood.
Outside the pit!

To be in a bloody pit means that you have fallen in a trap or are in a critical situation. Rushing things only will worsen your problems. Keep your head cool, let things take its course and wait until you can see a clear way out.

Career: Your position or career is in danger. Maintain your composure; do not let yourself to be dragged into further troubles. Stay calm and quiet until the situation resolves by itself.

Private life: Try to shun any confrontation with other people and avoid violence at all costs. Any movement may increase the danger.

Health, Feelings and Social life: Danger of injury. Possible hospitalization and surgery.

Fifth Nine

Waiting with wine and food.
The determination is favorable.

Waiting in the middle of abundance, you can replenish your strength and enjoy the current moment. You are at the proper place, enjoy it while you can.

Career: Time of peace and relaxation with good prospects for advancement.

Private life: A quiet, relaxed and fruitful moment.

Health, Feelings and Social life: Happiness and contentment.

5 - Waiting

Top Six

> One falls into the pit.
> Three uninvited guests arrive.
> Treat them with respect and in the end there will be good fortune.

The character translated as "pit" here (and also in the fourth line) in addition means "cave, hole, underground dwellings". It indicates that you are trapped in darkness, you cannot see the way out and there is no hope left.

The three uninvited guest indicate new persons, ideas or influences that will change entirely and unexpectedly the situation for good.

If you treat the unexpected guests in the proper way, you will gain insight and will be able to come out of the pit.

Career: New opportunities and may be a new post or responsibilities will renovate your career.

Private life: It is a good time to accept new people and ideas in your life. Only in that way you will overcome your troubles.

Health, Feelings and Social life: You will have an unexpected chance to recover your health and happiness, provided that you are receptive to new ideas or new people.

6

sòng
Conflict / Lawsuit

Associated Meanings

Conflict, litigation, dispute, quarrel, to demand justice, accusation, arguing, grievance.

Judgment

> Conflict.
> You are sincere but you are hold back.
> Cautiously stopped halfway brings good fortune.
> Going to the end is ominous.
> It is advantageous to see the great man.
> It is not favorable to cross the great river.

Righteousness it not enough to win the conflict and no matter if you win, the costs may be higher than the advantages.

The Judgment suggests stopping halfway; that means to find a middle ground where both litigants can agree.

The great man is a mediator that can help both sides to find a peaceful solution.

The fact that it is not favorable to cross the great river indicates that to take the conflict ahead is not convenient. Going to the end –not reaching a compromise– would be disastrous; there is danger of a never ending conflict that will drag you down for a long time.

6 - Conflict / Lawsuit

This hexagram is related with civil lawsuits, the other hexagram with a similar meaning is the number 21: **Biting through**, which indicates a criminal lawsuit.

The Image

> Sky and water move in opposite directions: The image of the Conflict. Thus the noble, in all his tasks, plans well before starting.

The sky is located far above the waters, and water always goes down; this symbolizes two parties –litigants– with opposite goals and perspectives.

In order to prevent conflicts it is necessary to plan ahead and to delimitate clearly the responsibilities and duties of every involved person. Stating your position clearly at the beginning, also will minimize the danger of any future confrontations.

First Six

> If one does not perpetuate the affair, there will be some gossip,
> but eventually it will be auspicious.

This is the initial stage of the conflict where it is still feasible to stop it without negative effects. At this point it would be easy to find mutual understanding with minimal discussions and without losing face.

Career: When divergences arose, do not delay in reaching an accord, before the matter goes out of hand. The more people get involved the more difficult will be to fix the situation.

Private life: Making some minor concessions now will save you a lot of trouble in the long run.

Health, Feelings and Social life: Bad habits should be napped in the bud, before they can cause harm. Be tolerant and yielding with aggressive people.

Second Nine

> One cannot succeed in the suit and escapes back to his home.
> The inhabitants of his city, three hundred families,
> will not suffer misfortune.

Confronted with a superior power the only reasonable action is to go back to a safe position. A conflict can expand towards the surroundings and it may harm people that are not directly related to it, hence a prompt retreat will secure the safety of your friends and associates.

Returning home also indicates to take a low profile approach.

In ancient China, the man who lost the litigation should have to pay a fine or commute a harsh penalty by payment. His vassals –the inhabitants of his city– would be forced to pay the fine for his feudal lord, hence if the lord retreats before losing his case they would suffer no harm.

Career: Stepping back to a secure position is the best possible decision. There is danger of losing it all if the conflict is left unchecked.

Private life: Renouncing to a fight that you cannot win is the only way to secure the future of your family.

Health, Feelings and Social life: Without moderation and restraint your health will be compromised. Avoid getting involved in conflicts with other people.

Third Six

Subsisting on old virtue.
Determination in front of danger.
There will be good fortune in the end.
If you are in the service of a king
you will not be able to complete your work.

The traditional ways are the safest option, especially when confronting powerful contenders.

This is not the right time to improve or change anything; the situation cannot be improved yet but it can be sustained. Steady but traditional work will achieve the best results in the end.

Behave with restraint and modesty to avoid attracting unwanted attention.

Career: Complying to the letter with your obligations without trying to improve your orders is the best way to keep your position. Some projects may be stopped or postponed.

Private life: For now it would be best to keep to true and tested customs without changing your lifestyle.

Health, Feelings and Social life: This is not the proper time to try new medications or to change anything in your health-care treatments.

Fourth Nine

One cannot win the fight.
Turns back and accepts fate.
Changes his attitude and finds peace.
The determination is auspicious.

When the right is not on your side, the correct thing to do is to resign and go back.

Accepting fate and resigning your ambitions will bring peace to you. It is auspicious to act that way.

Career: Faced with a weaker opponent you will find that the best way is to accept things as they are and to avoid seeking further advantages by the exercise of raw power.

Private life: Listen to your conscience and accept reality, do not try to force other people to do things your way.

Health, Feelings and Social life: Reducing the stress and ambitions in your life will improve your health. Be cooperative and adaptable instead trying to impose your will.

Fifth Nine

> Litigating.
> Outstanding fortune.

The fifth line is the ruler of the hexagram and it symbolizes a just arbiter situated in an elevated position.

To resolve the conflict in a fair way you should recourse to a just person in position of authority.

It is important not only to search for a proper mediator but to take the right course towards the desired goal.

Justice will be done. If you are in the right you will be highly successful.

Career: A successful solution of the conflict will lead to a promotion or to good business opportunities.

Private life: Seek help from a third party to solve any conflicts or grievances you may have.

Health, Feelings and Social life: Moderation in your desires and behavior will make your happier and healthier.

Top Nine

> If you get rewarded with a leather belt,
> by late morning it will have been snatched away three times.

The leather belt is a symbol of rank and authority.

To lose it several times means that the victory will not be sustainable, that the conflict will never end.

Career: Your triumph will be short lived and it will have to be kept through continual strife.

Private life: The price of victory will be constant disputes and your position will never be secure.

Health, Feelings and Social life: Recurring health issues caused by a stressful situation.

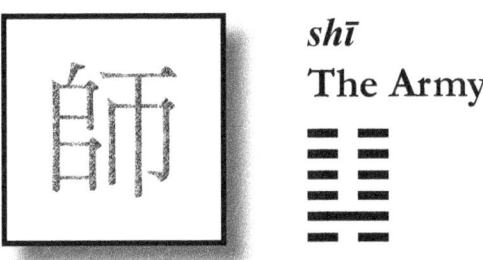

shī

The Army

Associated meanings

Army, troops, legion, militias, a disciplined group, multitude; master, leader; take as a master, imitate, follow a role model or norm; military virtues.

Judgment

> The Army.
> The determination brings good fortune for a strong man.
> No defect.

An army requires strong leadership and clarity of purpose, expressed with firm determination.

Good organization and strict discipline are needed to avoid the army becoming a mob.

Caution is required to avoid falling in danger.

The Image

> The earth contains water inside it: The image of The Army.
> Thus the noble takes care of and increases the crowd.

The trigram *Kan* appears in the lower part of this hexagram. *Kan* the symbol of moving water, but also indicates danger; the trigram *Kun* is the upper trigram and it symbolizes the Earth (please see **The Eight Trigrams** for more information). The Army is like water put in movement, powerful and dangerous, but in this case, it remains hidden in the depths of the Earth until it is

7 - The Army

mobilized. A strong leader can drive the masses and gives them direction, like water channeled in a precise direction.

The noble indicates a person of high ideals and capacity that supports and contains the people like the Earth contains the water. He knows how to attract followers to his cause and how to motivate and direct them.

First Six

> The Army should set forward in orderly rows.
> If discipline is bad there will be misfortune.

The Army requires organization and discipline, in other way it will never work properly. From the start, clear rules and goals must be established; rushing ahead without planning or lacking discipline should be disastrous.

Career: The first steps of any new project should be planned carefully and responsibilities should be delimited clearly, to prevent further troubles. The more people are involved the more need for strict rules.

Private life: Do not start new projects lightly or with ill-considered haste. Take your time to plan things carefully and be sure that the people that are going to help you know well what you expect from them.

Health, Feelings and Social life: Putting some order in your lifestyle will improve your health. Lack of self-control may damage your health and make your life less good that it could be.

Second Nine

> In the midst of The Army.
> Good fortune.
> No defect.
> The king gives rewards and promotions thrice.

This is the position of the leader, the only *yang* line in this hexagram. The king giving rewards and promotions symbolizes a ruler who supports and promotes an able person as leader of the army (the second line); it also means to receive blessings from heaven.

Career: Good moment for receiving promotions and getting recognition from your superiors.

Private life: Good connection with other people. You are appreciated and your actions are in tune with time.

Health, Feelings and Social life: Excellent health and happiness.

Third Six

> Perhaps The Army carries a corpse in the carriage.
> Ominous.

Note that in ancient China sometimes a child impersonated the dead during sacrifices. From this viewpoint carrying a corpse may mean that the army leader is no present but is substituted for another one during battle, who is not up to the task. Hence, this line may indicate deficient leadership, lack of capacity and misunderstandings in the handling of the resources at your disposal.

Such lack of leadership will be disastrous.

Career: Leadership failure. Either the leader is incompetent or he is replaced by an incompetent at a critical moment and that fact causes big losses. Somebody may be out of a job.

Private life: Not a good moment for starting anything new. Be careful and do not dare to delegate responsibility, instead manage with care each one of your obligations.

Health, Feelings and Social life: Health issues, grief, sadness. Somebody in your family may die.

Fourth Six

> The Army camps on the left.
> No defect.

To camp on the left means to withdraw to the barracks. By avoiding battle you can keep clear from trouble.

Career: Time to hunker down and wait until it is safe to continue ahead.

Private life: An introspective moment, not good for social relations, or changes in lifestyle. There is no shame in taking some time for yourself.

Health, Feelings and Social life: Be happy with what you have and exercise restraint. Do not overtax yourself, try to rest.

Fifth Six

> There is game in the field.
> It is favorable to capture them for questioning.
> No defect.
> The eldest son should lead The Army,
> if the younger brother leads, the carriages will be used to carry corpses.
> The determination is ominous.

7 - The Army

The "game in the field" means that there is no way to postpone facing an important problem and that your adversary is in the open.

To "capture for questioning" means that you should analyze the situation carefully before taking action.

It is important to wait until the new facts are understood clearly before taking action, to solve the present crisis and start the fight.

The eldest son is a symbol of good leadership; without it defeat will be the final result.

"The determination is ominous" means that you must exercise restraint in battle and stop advancing as soon as your goals are accomplished. It also indicates the need for self-discipline and moderation to avoid dangerous excesses.

Career: An exciting opportunity will open up when something new changes the balance of power.

Private life: The appearance of a new factor or information will change the situation. Act with firmness and moderation.

Health, Feelings and Social life: A critical surgical procedure may be ahead. Choosing the right surgeon and waiting until the proper diagnosis and all possible ways of treatment are explored is of imperative importance.

Top Six

The great king has the mandate to found a state and inherit the house. Small men should not be used.

After achieving your goals you should consolidate your situation. Distribute your resources wisely to avoid further problems.

Both inferior people and low desires should be kept in check.

Career: After the objectives had been achieved it is necessary to delegate responsibilities and to establish a proper administrative structure. To avoid undermining your achievements you should select carefully the right person for the job.

Private life: You will need helpers to manage your gains. Take care of choosing people that are not small minded.

Health, Feelings and Social life: It is important to keep the balance in your life and to not compromise your newly gained health with unhealthy habits or bad friends.

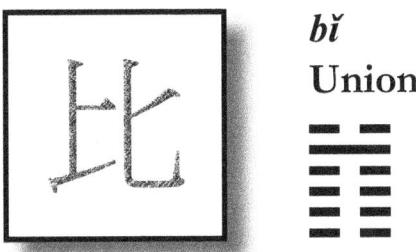

bĭ
Union

Associated meanings

Union, go together with, joining with others, put together, holding together, assemble, associate with, alliance, combine, ally with, pair, match.

Judgment

> Union brings happiness.
> Look deep and divine to see if you have great long-term determination;
> if so there will be no defect.
> They will come from the lands without peace.
> Those who arrive late will have misfortune.

In order to achieve union you should feel confident that it is good for you; because only with no doubts you will be able to have enough determination to accomplish a worthy union.

The phrase "lands without peace" refers either to people with doubts or to unruly people; if they muster enough confidence, they will join the group, but if they hesitate for too long or refuse to comply with the ruler, they will miss the opportunity.

The text describes the summons from a ruler to his tribal chieftains. Those who arrive late will not be well received and may be even punished. There is a proper time for joining a group, those who enter too late will not be able to become full members.

8 - Union

The Image

> On earth there is water: The image of Union.
> So the kings of old established ten thousand different states
> and kept close relations with all the feudal lords.

The earth supports the water, which in turn humidifies earth, fertilizes it; this shows how a proper union can benefit all participants.

Then thousand indicates a large number. There are masses of water on the earth just as there are many countries on the world. In the same way than flowing water, friendly cultural and commercial relationships between different nations fertilize the world.

In the same way a leader maintains mutually beneficial relations with his associates, keeping the communication channels well opened like flowing waterways. It is important to cooperate between people and assign each one the proper task.

First Six

> If there is sincerity, the Union will be without defect.
> Full of sincerity as an overflowing earthenware vessel.
> Finally, through others, happiness will come.

Sincerity is essential to keep good relations with friends and associates. The earthenware vessel symbolizes a sincere and true approach, full of substance and not a mere appearance. It shows that something of real value is offered and that there is no disguise. Having such a good attitude and offering a real value you will gain the trust from everybody and the reunion will bring happiness to all parties.

The overflowing earthenware vessel also indicates that your capacity for sincerity will attract people. The mention to "others" means that valuable people outside of your usual sphere of acquaintances will be attracted.

Career: Your proposal will be appreciated and your sincerity recognized. Good business and/or a promotion are coming.

Private life: Excellent moment to interact and collaborate with friends and family. You are a valued member of your household or group of friends.

Health, Feelings and Social life: Shared feelings and good communication with other people will make you happy.

Second Six

> Union from the inside.
> The determination is fortunate.

Affinity with a certain person (the fifth *yang* line, the one with a superior position) will be firstly manifested inwardly as a shared feeling. Such sincere relationship will bring good fortune.

"Union from the inside" also indicates that you should remain loyal to your comrades and close friends.

Career: Be ready to share your ideas with your colleagues and associates, you will find a sympathetic ear. It is a good moment to work as part of a team.

Private life: You belong to a close knit group or family. If you keep up your loyalty to your friends you will be happy and prosperous.

Health, Feelings and Social life: Stable and peaceful moment.

Third Six

> Union with worthless people.

The two Chinese characters translated as "worthless people" also mean: "bandit, disreputable or despicable people". It may indicate that you give trust to the wrong people and that you are being deceived.

No prognostication is appended, but mixing with bad company will prevent you from establishing relations with better people and surely will not lead you to a positive outcome.

Career: You should reconsider your alliances and loyalties, you are not going anywhere with your current associates.

Private life: Relations with people or low morality will keep you down.

Health, Feelings and Social life: Substance abuse and unworthy habits will damage both your physical and spiritual health.

Fourth Six

> Solidarity with people outside.
> Determination brings good fortune.

Manifesting openly your affinity with other persons will bring good fortune. Also it may mean that you are establishing a positive connection with somebody who is outside of your normal sphere of acquaintances.

This line also depicts the moment when the decision of joining somebody or to pursue some goal is openly taken.

Career: Very good moment for striking new alliances and expanding your horizons.

Private life: Going out and expressing your feelings openly will be fortunate.

Health, Feelings and Social life: Expansive moment. Do not be shy, get in touch with new people.

Fifth Nine

> Manifest Union.
> The king uses beaters for hunting prey on three sides,
> but lets the animals in front of him go.
> The villagers are not wary.
> Good fortune.

"The ancient rule for hunting expeditions was that after the beating was completed and the king was ready to commence taking game, one side of the enclosure into which it had been driven was left open and unguarded. This was proof of the royal benevolence which didn't want to make an end of all the creatures inside". (*Legge*)

As the leader, he motivates people and puts them in motion, but without forcing the final decision on anybody.

The people related to him ("the villagers": people in the same organization or family) know and trust him.

This union between high (the leader, the fifth line) and low (the people) brings good fortune.

Here the union is completely voluntary; people decide by themselves if they want to join the leader, and they do so because they believe in him.

Career: This is good moment for a public relations campaigns, starting promotions and incorporating new people to your organization.

Private life: You are a natural leader, your friends know and trust you and because that they will support you.

Health, Feelings and Social life: Good conditions.

Top Six

> Union without a leader.
> Misfortune.

Union - 8

The union was not achieved because lack of a focusing point and bad leadership. The consequences are isolation and regret.

The lack of a leader may be caused for disagreement among members or groups within an organization, such conflicts will conduce to a complete breakdown.

Career: This describes a project or business that is faltering because of disagreements, feuds or lack of will.

Private life: You missed the moment for the union, and as a result you are left alone.

Health, Feelings and Social life: Depression and isolation.

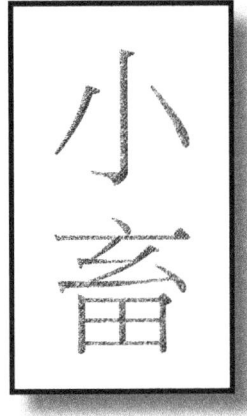

xiǎo chù
Little Domestication

Associated meanings

Accumulate, nurture, support, cultivate, farming, domesticate take care of little things. All done in small scale.

Judgment

> Little Domestication is successful.
> Dense clouds, no rain from our western borders.

The clouds in the sky indicate partial results, a work in progress that still cannot bring out the desired outcome. Rain symbolizes the positive consequence of your efforts.

Only small steps can be taken at this time, this is not the proper time for great expenditures or a full scale advance.

Exercise restraint and moderation. Long term planning is required. For now you can only set the groundwork to consolidate the requirements for a future expansion.

It is important to give attention to details and to keep the final goal in mind. Gather information, polish your plans and be sure that nothing will be left to chance when you can at last make a bold advance.

The Image

> The wind crosses the sky: The image of Little Domestication.
> Thus the noble refines the outward manifestation of his virtue.

9 - Little Domestication

Although you don't have yet the means to produce big effects, you can use your knowledge to improve your image and promote your goals.

The outward manifestation of virtue implies things like kindness, politeness, good social graces and tolerance.

First Nine

> Returns to the own road.
> How could it be wrong?
> Good fortune.

It is preferable to go back instead of being exposed to danger. This means you should exercise self-restraint.

The term translated as "own" also means "source, origin", meaning that you should go back to your own vocation or to the original point from where you have strayed.

It also indicates returning to normal life after being stranded.

Career: Time to fall back, cut expenditures and concentrate in the basis of your business.

Private life: You may renew old ways or acquaintances.

Health, Feelings and Social life: Happiness coming from the past.

Second Nine

> Led to return.
> Good fortune.

After looking at how other people in similar position than you behave, you will decide to go back.

Also your own experience may teach you that the conditions are not right at this time and that by going back you will avoid trouble and be successful.

This moment marks the end of a cycle. The next time you may have better results, but for now it is time to reshuffle and deal again.

Career: Your position is not sustainable. Follow the lead of others and start afresh.

Private life: It is time to reevaluate your goals. Avoid conflict and follow the advice of your friends.

Health, Feelings and Social life: Do not isolate yourself, you cannot follow ahead alone.

Third Nine

> Rays are removed from the carriage wheels.
> Man and wife avert their eyes from each other.

The carriage with the spokes of its wheels removed points to a project that has been stopped completely. No matter how much power is applied to move forward a carriage, if the wheels are broken it will not advance at all.

The man and his wife that do not look at each other symbolize lack of cooperation, indifference, people with different objectives or having severe dissensions. Also the man-wife conflict may symbolize lack of understanding and good will between a boss and an employee.

Career: Lack of cooperation and poor team leadership has mired the advance.

Private life: Conflict in the family or with close friends. Until some real dialog is restored there will be no chance of fixing the current problems.

Health, Feelings and Social life: Solitude and disappointment. Sexual or digestive problems.

Fourth Six

> If you are sincere, the blood disappears and concerns are cast aside.
> No defect.

Sincerity can act as a soothing factor. After trust is restored the risk of spilling blood will be avoided and all involved people will feel at ease.

Only by being truthful and inspiring confidence in others, you will be able to defuse this conflict and avoid further mistakes.

Career: Do not hide facts from your collaborators or from your boss, full disclosure is the only way to avoid misunderstanding and distrust and to prevent dangerous mistakes.

Private life: Dissent and contention thrive because misunderstandings and suspicions. If you inform all concerned people about the real facts and let them know your true feelings, they will be more cooperative and understanding.

Health, Feelings and Social life: Face reality, both external and internal. Do not hide your own feelings and recognize what you really are. This is the only way to get some balance and relaxation in your life.

Fifth Nine

> If you are sincere with your neighbors
> the alliance will bring prosperity for all.

9 - Little Domestication

You sincerity will draw other people to collaborate with you.

By sharing your prosperity you will increase it.

Career: A climate of trust between superiors and inferiors will help to increase your business. Teamwork will drive new projects ahead with benefits for everyone. Promotion or advancement in your career.

Private life: Shared feelings and common goals with friends and family will improve the life of everybody involved.

Health, Feelings and Social life: Feelings of communion with other people. Good health and happiness.

Top Nine

> The rain fell and he could rest.
> His spiritual power brings him recognition.
> The determination is dangerous for a wife.
> The moon is almost full.
> Enterprises are unfortunate.

By the sum of small steps a project or plan has been driven to completion. The rain symbolizes relaxation after a storm and shows that it is time to stop and rest.

The Chinese character translated as "spiritual power", also means "moral integrity, ability, character, virtue". It indicates that your value is recognized and people trust you.

The mention to a wife indicates that all achievements were produced not for the use of force, but on the contrary, by careful, measured steps, not with *yang* bravado but with *yin* cunning and perseverance. The *yin* power is at its strongest when the moon is almost full, so now it is the proper time to cease advancing; continuing ahead would be counter-productive and would put in danger all your present achievements.

The moon almost full indicates that a cycle is ending and changes are coming.

Career: Time to stop and consolidate your gains. You are trusted by your superiors, but if your ambition drives you ahead you will lose not only your actual gains but possibly your position as well.

Private life: Your friends and family trust you. Be content with what you have and with your current position, because your ambitions may ruin your life if left unchecked. Do not try to control everything around you.

Health, Feelings and Social life: Time for relaxation. Do not push your luck overextending your forces, or your health will be compromised.

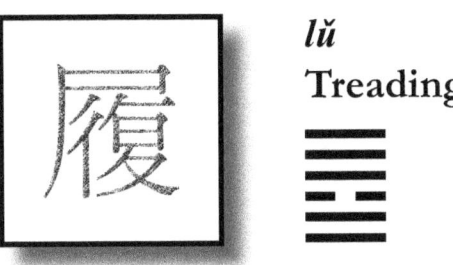

lǚ
Treading

Associated meanings

Step on, track, walk or follow a trail or way, stepping on the tiger's tail; footwear, shoes; conduct, behavior, ceremonies.

Judgment

> Treading the tiger's tail.
> The man is not bitten.
> Success.

Stepping on the tiger's tail means that you will cope with a perilous endeavor or circumstance. It also indicates to conduct yourself correctly, to behave properly in the face of danger.

This is not a good time to be adversarial, but to remain constant in your beliefs or convictions and to advance with politeness and care.

The tiger symbolizes a powerful and wild force; when facing individuals that are equally dangerous, you should proceed in a way that doesn't antagonize them, advancing softly and with utmost care, but with firmness. In that way, although the tiger will notice that somebody is treading over its tail, it will tolerate it.

The Image

> Above the sky, down the lake: The image of Treading.
> Thus the noble distinguishes between high and low
> and makes certain the will of the people.

10 - Treading

The distance between heaven and the lake symbolizes the range of different behaviors in human society. The noble takes in account such differences and understands that each person acts according to his will. Indeed the Chinese word translated as "will", also means "purpose, goal, determination". Hence the noble tries to understand the different purposes and goals that motivate people and to take in account the feelings and the expectations of them, acting tactfully and with care, especially when facing dangerous persons.

First Nine

> Simple Treading.
> Advance without defect.

You are taking the first steps and since you still don't have any heavy responsibilities on your shoulders, you are free to follow your own feelings and to take life easily. Such easy going attitude is correct at this point.

Career: Not being bound by any obligations you are free to choose any course of action that suits your own inclinations. You can freely take a new job or leave your current position.

Private life: As long as you don't complicate your life, you will be able to move freely.

Health, Feelings and Social life: Good health. Natural happiness.

Second Nine

> Treading a smooth and easy way.
> The determination of a lonely man brings good fortune.

The word translated as "lonely" also means "dark, solitary, secluded". The "lonely man" indicates a wise man that follows his own path without asking for fame, fortune or worldly recognition. Because he is unassuming and doesn't ask too much, his way is easy. His way is also smooth because he follows what he really feels and has no doubts.

Career: By focusing in the work at hand without thinking in recompenses, you will attain excellent results with minimal stress.

Private life: You are comfortable with your solitude.

Health, Feelings and Social life: Stable health and good emotional balance.

Third Six

> A one-eyed man can see, a lame can tread.
> The tiger bites such a one who treads on his tail.
> Misfortune. A warrior acts as if he were a great lord.

Trying to live beyond your capabilities or forces will lead to disaster. Ignoring your limitations, like a man blind in an eye who thinks that his sight is excellent or a lame that believes he can run, will be unfortunate. To act as a lord means to act boldly.

The tiger biting such overconfident fellow indicates an important setback or loss.

This line can be translated in different ways: "a warrior acting like a great lord" would indicate overconfidence and recklessness, but it also may be translated as: "a warrior that acts in behalf of his prince"; this second translation supplies an alternative interpretations; it indicates a man who sacrifices himself doing something that he is not able to handle, but not motivated by foolishness but because he is following his duty.

Career: Do not be overconfident, or you will experience trouble.

Private life: Reckless attitudes are dangerous. Do not go beyond your capabilities. You may have an accident.

Health, Feelings and Social life: Physical/emotional crisis triggered for excessive stress and daring.

Fourth Nine

> Steps on the tiger's tail with great caution.
> At the end there will be good fortune.

The situation is difficult and you are under pressure, but with extreme caution and circumspection you still can succeed.

Career: Your position is correct but stressful and only with utmost care you will be able to carry on successfully your plan or assignment.

Private life: You know well your goals and what is at stake. With extreme caution you will get good results from the difficult present situation.

Health, Feelings and Social life: You have plenty of fears and preoccupations, but taking adequate precautions your health will improve.

Fifth Nine

> Resolute Treading.
> The determination is dangerous.

You are firmly resolved to carry on with the task at hand, but such strict determination may be dangerous because it will not allow you enough flexibility to make adjustments along the way.

A breakthrough point is close. Be ready to notice any changes in the circumstances; reevaluate your situation on a daily basis and be flexible in dealing with it.

Career: Keep your goals in mind but be ready to make compromises if needed. If you are too rigid you will fall into danger.

Private life: The situation is dangerous. Firm resolution is a good thing, but you also need flexibility to face any new threats that may appear.

Health, Feelings and Social life: Try to keep things in balance, if you are too stressed-out you will reach a breaking point.

Top Nine

> Watch the trodden path and examine the omens.
> The cycle starts back.
> Great good fortune.

When you are at the end of the road it is time to stop and review the path taken. If the consequences of your actions are good that would be a good omen. New paths will open up with plenty of possibilities ahead.

Career: You have reached the end of a cycle or carried on a business to conclusion. Try to learn from your past actions. If you apply to your future projects the lessons learned from your previous venture, you will enjoy lasting success.

Private life: At the end of a cycle it is time to learn from the trodden path and to use that knowledge to grow as a person.

Health, Feelings and Social life: Time to reevaluate your progress and your feelings. A new cycle starts.

tài
Harmony / Great

Associated meanings

Great, extensive, exalted, superior, prosperous, successful; harmony, peace, quiet; liberal; extreme, influential, spread out and reach everywhere, permeate, pervade.

Judgment

> Harmony.
> The petty depart and the great are coming.
> Good fortune and success.

People from all walks of life can cooperate with solidarity. There is no place for meanness or petty selfish interests.

The great that are coming means that the result of such harmony will be very good and will bring prosperity for everybody.

This is a period of material and spiritual balance where everything is in its proper position.

It is an excellent time for teamwork and reaching accords. A culture of sharing and cooperation will drive your business ahead.

Harmony and tolerance makes social interaction easy. Grievances go away and people trust each other.

The Image

> Heaven and earth are closely related: The image of Harmony.
> Thus the sovereign regulates and completes the course of Heaven and

11 - Harmony / Great

Earth, and assists Heaven and Earth in the right way;
thereby helping the people.

Heaven and earth represent the forces of *yang* and *yin*, male and female, activity and passivity. They are complementary forces and when they relate to each other harmoniously all people prosper.

For the ancient Chinese, the interaction of heaven and earth produced the seasons. The sovereign regulated the activity in his domains to match the course of the seasons and the pass of the time.

Applied to actual circumstances this teaches us to follow the course of nature, to not strive against it but to flow along with nature and make good use of the favorable circumstances.

First Nine

> When reeds are pulled,
> they pull up others of the same kind together with them.
> Enterprises bring good fortune.

The roots of reeds are intertwined, so when one strand is pulled out it will take other grasses alongside. When somebody starts some endeavor in flourishing times, such action has a summoning effect and others will follow the good example and cooperate freely.

Career: This is an excellent time for starting up a business or to make your business grow. You will find plenty of valuable help because the prospects are very good. Good time for getting a promotion.

Private life: You will receive help from family and friends and will achieve your goals.

Health, Feelings and Social life: Good health and excellent communication with your loved ones.

Second Nine

> Bear with the uneducated, wade the river, do not neglect the distant.
> Thus factions disappear.
> One get honors if stays in the middle path.

To wade the river means to go beyond your area of expertise, to enter a new field of action, to learn something new.

To "wade the river" can be also translated as "put to use those who wade the river". In such case that would be another reference to the uneducated, since people who wade the river, do so because they don't have boats or a carriage; they are uncultured people.

This is a good moment to make long-term plans and to take precautions against contingencies. You will need to include people of different backgrounds in your plans to make them work; do not use only your friends or the people that you already know. Sometimes valuable helpers and friends can be found behind a rough façade. Do not be prejudiced when you meet new people. Be ready to accept people from all walks of life. Think outside the box.

Career: Try to find new talents, no matter if they lack formal education, they will be valuable helpers. If you keep vigilant, planning ahead and avoiding excesses you will get recognition from your superiors and you will be able to carry on difficult endeavors.

Private life: Show tolerance and be open-minded, avoid associating exclusively with members of your own group. You may receive help from unexpected quarters. Good moment for making new friends.

Health, Feelings and Social life: Act with care and be ready to accept new ideas that may help you. Try to avoid any excesses and keep a balanced lifestyle.

Third Nine

There are no plains without slopes.
There is no going forth without a return.
Fortitude under trying conditions.
No defect.
Do not regret this truth.
Enjoy the happiness you still possess.

All things in life are subjected to change and finally pass away. By fully accepting the transient nature of life you will be able to fully enjoy the good moments and to be strong when bad times come.

Career: The situation is not stable. You may have losses and gains. Make good use of what you have but be ready to accept some losses. Do not take any risks.

Private life: You will have ups and downs. Be careful with your money, friends and family, you may be deceived by someone. Mind your own affairs. Take each day as it comes.

Health, Feelings and Social life: Your health may get diminished, but your troubles will pass in time. Enjoy what you still have and be strong until conditions improve.

Fourth Six

> Flapping, fluttering.
> Not using his own rich resources to deal with his neighbors.
> Without having to ask gets confidence.

Flapping and fluttering indicates fluctuations and hesitation.

Seek a way to establish a good relation with others without pushing your weight around. In that way you will get the trust of others who will see that you are sincere and humble.

Career: You will get genuine cooperation from people only if you show empathy and establish a personal relation with them. Take all the time you need until you find a way to get ahead.

Private life: You are not sure about how to deal with you neighbors or friends, but such indecision will make you cautious and in time you will gain the cooperation of them after they see that you are sincere.

Health, Feelings and Social life: You have plenty of doubts and concerns, but finally your situation will stabilize.

Fifth Six

> The sovereign *Yi* gives his daughter in marriage.
> This brings happiness and great fortune.

An alliance between low and high will bring prosperity to all people involved.

Career: You may get promoted. Cooperation is the key to success.

Private life: Possible marriage. Happy union, the family will grow. Prosperity.

Health, Feelings and Social life: Excellent health and spiritual stability. You will receive a gift from above.

Top Six

> The wall falls back into the pit.
> Do not use the army now.
> Proclaim your commands only in your own town.
> The determination brings humiliation.

The "walls" refers to the city walls, battlements or ramparts. The typical fortification for a city was a high wall surrounded by a pit.

A natural cycle is at its end. The falling city walls symbolize some plan or structure that is crumbling down and cannot be sustained by force anymore. It indicates as well that you are now in a vulnerable position.

You should concern yourself with your immediate surroundings and put order there. If you are overextended you will be shamed.

Do not try to fix your troubles by the use of force.

Career: Downsizing is the best way to diminish your losses. Trying to fight back would be counter-productive because you are not strong enough. Put in order your own sector or department, do not involve yourself with matters outside of your immediate area or responsibility.

Private life: Care and mind for your own nuclear family. Concerning yourself with bigger matters will give you sorrow.

Health, Feelings and Social life: Illness. Mobility issues.

12

pǐ
Standstill / Stagnation

Associated meanings

Standstill, stagnation, obstruction, hindrance, stoppage, blocked, dead end; bad, wrong.

Judgment

> Standstill.
> Worthless people are unfavorable to the determination of the noble.
> The great is going away, the petty is coming.

This is a period of stoppage, when able persons are hindered by evil and small-minded people.

There is lack of cooperation and the tide of events favors petty people. Those with a self-serving agenda will obstruct the efforts of the best minded persons.

Growth is not possible anymore; the prevalence of selfish people makes this a time of decay, because their intolerance and greed will block any intent of progress.

Personal difficulties will hinder your plans. From a psychological viewpoint, you may be lured by other people or by your own low desires to take the wrong path. Do not try to force the advance, be patient and wait until the situation improves.

12 - Standstill / Stagnation

Image

> Heaven and earth are not related: The image of Standstill.
> Thus the noble, restrains his virtue, and avoids calamities.
> He does not accept receiving rank or salary.

Heaven and earth represent high and low. When high and low do not cooperate, when people from different walks of life plot against and mistrust each other, things don't prosper and nothing good can be achieved.

Weakness (the three lower *yin* lines) is within and strength (the three upper *yang* lines) is outside, indicating morally weak people in a situation of power.

The Chinese character translated as "virtue" in: "the noble restrains his virtue", also may be translated as "capabilities, qualities". It means that when advancing is not possible without compromising your moral standing, you should withdraw and do not lend you own capabilities to evil associates or worthless friends. It is better to take a low profile approach and avoid displaying your talents.

You may be sorely tempted, but by keeping apart from the bad people that are in power, you will avoid falling in trouble.

The temporal progression of the situation described by the *Yijing* hexagrams is always from bottom to top, lines enter the hexagram at the base and leave it at the top; because that the three first lines are considered to be "inside" and the three upper lines are "outside".

First Six

> When reeds are pulled,
> they pull up others of the same kind together with them.
> The determination brings good fortune and success.

This is the beginning of a stagnation period. The pulled reeds dragging other herbs indicate a capable person withdrawing from the bad company, avoiding getting involved in weakness, dragging out of the public life other good people with him. Success, under these circumstances, means to be free of wrongdoings and avoiding shame.

Career: A strategic retreat, alongside some close associates will save you face in the long run. Keep up your standards and do not let others drag you into any dubious behavior.

Private life: It is better to remain aloof than to involve yourself with bad people. Stay close to those of your friends that share your own goals, and keep clear from low life people who may involve you in trouble

Health, Feelings and Social life: Do not let others fool you or drive you away from your real calling. Magic cures usually don't work.

Second Six

They support and tolerate.
Good fortune for the petty.
By accepting the Standstill the great man will have success.

Small people will adapt to and follow any leader, without thinking twice in the final consequences. But the *Yijing* is written for high minded people, who in this time should avoid getting involved in the generalized misconduct.

Accepting the Standstill means to fully realize that this is not the proper time for action, that you should stand aside until the Standstill ends. Keep your hands clean and do not involve yourself in any wrongdoings.

Career: Although common people will adapt to and support any misguided leadership, you know that their aims are not right and you will remain on the side until the situation changes. In this way you will not be tarnished by any bad deed and will have success in the end.

Private life: It is better to be alone that in bad company.

Health, Feelings and Social life: Time of impasse. Wait and see. It is better to be conservative.

Third Six

They bear the shame.

Those who are in posts above his capabilities will be humiliated. People who raised using flattery and obsequiousness will not be able to handle well their responsibilities and will disgrace themselves.

Career: Do not try to do what is above your capacity, or you will be embarrassed and possibly demoted.

Private life: If you try to start something that you cannot actually handle you will embarrass yourself.

Health, Feelings and Social life: Risk of overexertion and shame.

Fourth Nine

Who follows the commands of Heaven will have no defect.
His comrades will share the blessings.

The phrase "commands of Heaven", may be translated as well as "fate" or "orders from above". It means that if you follow truthfully your real vocation

12 - Standstill / Stagnation

or your duty you will be blameless and you will benefit your companions as well.

Career: A strong leader will do the right thing and by doing so also will benefit all his associates. You may be promoted.

Private life: Your friends and family look at you for leadership and will give you their support. Good luck.

Health, Feelings and Social life: Following your real calling will lead you to happiness.

Fifth Nine

> The Standstill is stopping.
> Good fortune for the great man.
> It can fail! It can fail!
> Tie it to a luxuriant mulberry tree.

Finally there is a way to put an end to the Standstill. But it is up to the great person (the fifth line usually symbolizes a person in a commanding position, like a king or a ruler) to put things to right. The phrase "tie it to a luxuriant mulberry tree" means that all possible precautions should be taken to prevent failure, since stopping the standstill is not an easy task.

Also to tie something to a tree indicates that you should focus and concentrate all your resources in a single objective in order to succeed, avoiding dispersing them.

Tying a talisman to a tree is some kind of protective magic that still is used in some places, and the fifth line may reflect that ancient belief.

Career: You can improve the situation and make things move ahead again, but you will need collaborators to perform that difficult task. Your position is not secure; you should build a solid basis before moving and manage all details with extreme care.

Private life: The situation will improve, but only if you put substantial effort to correct it.

Health, Feelings and Social life: After taking care of some issues your health will improve.

Top Nine

> The Standstill is overthrown.
> First standstill, afterwards joy.

Standstill / Stagnation - 12

This is the end of the stagnation period, when the roads are unlocked and it is possible to move ahead again.

Career: Your career or business will prosper, you may get promoted or start a new business.

Private life: New options will appear in your life and they will bring joy.

Health, Feelings and Social life: A time of isolation and chronic health problems will end. Improvement of health and happiness.

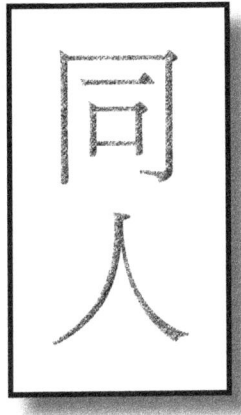

tóng rén
Fellowship

Associated meanings

Gather people, assemble, join, partake in; identical, together, fellowship; in agreement, identified.

Judgment

> Fellowship in the fields.
> Success.
> It is advantageous to cross the great river.
> The determination brings good fortune for the noble.

People assemble naturally when a common purpose joins them, when they share a common vision and commitment. The fact that the union is in the fields indicates that it is a union of people of similar standing.

A group of like-minded people can achieve big success if all them work for the sake of the group and avoid in-fighting and hidden agendas.

In ancient China, crossing rivers, either at a ford or when the river was frozen, was not an easy task. It implicated dangers and hardships; hence crossing the great river means to carry out a difficult undertaking.

Determination is required to keep things going smoothly and to stay in the right path.

13 - Fellowship

The Image

> Heaven and fire: The image of the Fellowship.
> Thus the noble organizes the clans and discriminates among things.

The fire under heaven symbolizes a gathering point, a point of interest that attracts and unites people.

A gathering of people should be organized and every person should be given the task more appropriate for their abilities.

By following specific goals and rules of behavior the group gathered together will become a fellowship instead of a mob.

First Nine

> Fellowship in the front door.
> No defect.

The union is forming in the open, not behind closed doors. There are no hidden agendas. To pass over the door indicates entering in the fellowship, to cross a threshold, taking on a new relationship and making a commitment.

Career: A good chance to start a new job or to be promoted. Openness and sincerity are required.

Private life: New possibilities and new relations will enrich your life. Be ready to cooperate and interact with others.

Health, Feelings and Social life: Good moment for sharing your feelings with others.

Second Six

> Fellowship in the clan.
> Shame.

Selfish purposes will weak the community and will make way to factions that in the end may break the group. Those with egoist and mean ends will be sorry.

Career: Weak and egotistical individuals will cause some trouble.

Private life: Be careful of prejudice and malice.

Health, Feelings and Social life: Discord and suspicion.

Third Nine

> He hides weapons in the bush and climbs the high hill,
> but for three years he will not rise.

This line describes somebody that retreats from social life and seeks a secure position, afraid of others.

Mistrust and conflicts are inspiring paranoid attitudes in some persons. Instead cooperating, people are wary and try to get the upper hand on others. There is no communication, everybody is isolated.

The three years indicate a full period that will pass before the impasse is left behind.

Career: There will be no advancement. Business will be paralyzed for a while.

Private life: Lack of confidence will prevent you from receiving or giving help. Some people may plot or file a lawsuit against you.

Health, Feelings and Social life: Your health will not improve nor turn worse. Emotionally there is no connection with other people but distrust.

Fourth Nine

He climbs to his wall he but cannot attack.
Good fortune.

You feel alienated from others and distrust them. But before attacking them you will realize that such thing is not possible, and finally you will reach an agreement. Good fortune is the result of stopping the conflict and resuming cooperation.

Career: The sooner you realize that a deal with your adversary is possible, the sooner all involved parties will benefit.

Private life: Try to leave behind suspicions and conflicts with people. There is no need to be in the defensive or take the offensive.

Health, Feelings and Social life: Relax and you will be happy.

Fifth Nine

The men in Fellowship first weep and mourn, but then laugh.
Great armies come across.

You are separated from the group where you belong. Conflicts keep divided the people and cause unnecessary suffering. If you take the first step, making clear your commitment, that will bring joy to all the people involved; laugh symbolizes the relaxation and happiness after the fellowship is restored, when an agreement is achieved; like powerful armies that stop being belligerent and join in peace.

Career: Finally an agreement to solve the present conflicts is possible. Doubts will linger until all involved people make clear their commitment, but the final result will be harmony and new opportunities.

Private life: Reconciliation is at hand. Take the first step to show your commitment and real feelings, in that way you will improve the relation with your fellows.

Health, Feelings and Social life: Expressing your feelings will do you real good.

Top Nine

Fellowship in the field.
No repentance.

The fellowship in the field means reaching a proper and convenient union, but without intimacy. The time for a close fellowship has passed, but in spite of that you can cooperate with others in a good way.

Career: You can participate successfully in common projects. You are in the periphery, not taking part in the decision process, but you are happy with that situation, and your position is secure.

Private life: Your relation with other people is good and useful but you are not too close with them.

Health, Feelings and Social life: Your life is stable. You are neither happy nor sad.

14

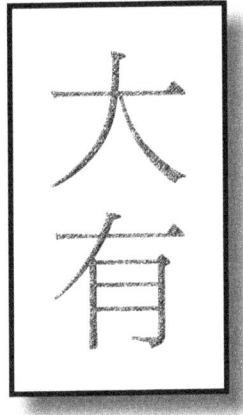

dà yŏu
Great Possession

Associated meanings

Great possession, great wealth, abundance; sovereignty,

Judgment

> Great Possession.
> Outstanding success.

Clarity and creative strength combined will give you plenty of possibilities to achieve your objectives.

You have many resources and the know-how to use them well, that will bring about outstanding success.

The Image

> Fire at the top of heaven: The image of Great Possession.
> Thus the noble punishes evil and promotes good,
> following the good will of Heaven.

Fire at the top of heaven indicates that you have clarity of mind, which makes you able to have an acute perception of what happens around you. It also means that you are in the spotlight, in the sight of every one.

Such keen awareness and visibility also increases your responsibility to make good use of your wealth and insight, curbing evil and promoting what is good.

14 - Great Possession

First Nine

> No relationship with harmful things.
> No defect.
> There will be hardship but no defect.

You are a beginner, endowed with great resources. Until now you have not faced great trouble and your record is clean

If you are alert and don't misuse your resources you will make no mistakes in spite of the hard times coming.

Career: Be careful and do not hurry ahead blindly. Do not let others lure you in more than you can chew.

Private life: Care and prudence will keep you secure. You may have some problems but you will remain without blame.

Health, Feelings and Social life: You may have some health issues. Be careful with what you put in your body.

Second Nine

> A great carriage for carrying things.
> One has a goal.
> No defect.

The words "a great carriage", suggest that you have not only plenty of resources but that you are able to put them to good use effectively; because they can mobilized swiftly and applied where you need them.

Having a goal, without any defects, means that you can apply you energies positively in one single direction, with clear purpose, and without making mistakes.

Career: Good time to move your projects ahead with clear intent and focus. You will have plenty of work and perhaps a promotion.

Private life: You know what you want and how to achieve it. Your plans will go on flawlessly.

Health, Feelings and Social life: Strong health and stamina. You are dedicated to your work.

Third Nine

> A prince presents his offerings to the Son of Heaven.
> A petty man is not able to do so.

Wealthy people should put his wealth to the service of higher purposes, like a prince presenting offerings to the emperor.

Offering to the Son of Heaven indicates to use your wealth not only for yourself but to benefit others as well, to act with greatness.

Monopolizing all resources for egoist purposes is the mark of a small-minded person.

Career: You should follow your duty impartially, be ready to cooperate with others and work for the benefit of your organization without asking what is for you.

Private life: You are in position to help others and participate in community goals. Do not hamper yourself with petty self-interest.

Health, Feelings and Social life: Do not trap yourself in your ivory tower; be ready to share your feelings.

Fourth Nine

He is not arrogant.
No defect.

The Chinese character translated as "arrogant" also means "fullness, plenitude". Besides the basic meaning of not being boastful, proud or overbearing, it also indicates that you know how to control yourself, and will not exceed the proper measure.

Career: Your situation is stable. Be modest and keep a balanced approach to avoid trouble.

Private life: You may be tempted to impose your views; do not do it and you will avoid blame. Be humble and avoid ostentation. Don't expect important news.

Health, Feelings and Social life: You prefer to keep a low profile. Possible lack of stamina.

Fifth Six

His sincerity will earn the trust and respect of others.
Good fortune.

Your sincerity will make people trust you. Dignified, but accessible and humble, you will gain the admiration of the people around you.

Career: You will progress helped by your clarity of mind and the support from your followers.

Private life: Your friends and family look to you for guidance.

Health, Feelings and Social life: You will be well liked by the people around you. Good health.

Top Nine

> He has the protection of Heaven.
> Good fortune.
> Nothing that is not favorable.

To have the protection of Heaven means that you will receive recognition and support from high spheres. It also indicates divine help or blessings.

Because you have plenty and resources and a keen mind, everything will be favorable.

Career: Promotion and success.

Private life: You will receive help and support from important people.

Health, Feelings and Social life: Inspirational state of consciousness.

15

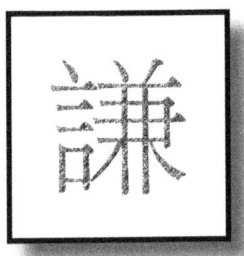

qiān
Modesty

Associated meanings

Modest, humble, yielding, moderate, temperate, unassuming, reverent.

Judgment

>Modesty.
>Success.
>The noble carries things to completion.

Modesty allows carrying things through without putting the ego in the way. By concentrating in the work at hand and avoiding conflicts with others, modest people can enjoy a very balanced lifestyle.

Modesty doesn't meant that you are insecure of weak, only that you know how to relate with other people and how to project a non-threatening image that draws the better in other people and has a soothing effect around.

The Image

>A Mountain in the middle of the earth: The image of Modesty.
>Thus the noble reduces what is excessive and increases what is insufficient.
>Weighs and distributes things evenly.

A mountain hidden under the earth is the image of a self-effacing attitude, it means no ostentation, also it symbolizes hidden treasures, resources at your disposal that you held in reserve. You don't boast about your virtues –what is excessive– but instead work on your weak points, increasing what is insufficient. In this way you will keep improving yourself and will avoid arousing jealousy.

15 - Modesty

First Six

> An extremely modest noble can cross the great river.
> Good fortune.

In ancient China, crossing rivers, either at a ford or when the river was frozen, was not an easy task. It implicated dangers and hardships; hence crossing the great river means to carry out a difficult undertaking.

Modesty opens the way to achieve great enterprises.

Career: You are able to start difficult projects and coordinate the efforts of your subordinates successfully. Extreme dedication is required though. Good time for advancement and promotions.

Private life: Propitious time to start some new project or to travel or relocate. Your sincere dedication will guarantee success.

Health, Feelings and Social life: Good health. This is the right time for a change.

Second Six

> Modesty expresses itself.
> The determination is fortunate.

The Chinese character translated as "expresses" literally means the "cry of a bird", indicating that modesty is calling out publicly. It indicates that your achievements will speak for themselves and make evident to everybody your worth. If you keep up your commitment and your work you will be fortunate.

Career: Your abilities will be recognized. Possible promotion and advancement. Keep up the good work.

Private life: Your family and friends appreciate your efforts and support you. You are in the right path.

Health, Feelings and Social life: Your actions will speak by themselves; you do not need to speak too much. No need to innovate.

Third Nine

> A noble meritorious for his modesty carries things to completion.
> Good fortune.

You occupy a place of honor. Persevere in your efforts until you achieve your goals.

An alternative translation would be "working modesty", instead "meritorious modesty". In both cases the meaning is diligent work.

You will be supported by the people because they respect your accomplishments and devotion to your work.

After you accomplish your objectives do not forget your loyalty and commitments.

Career: You can complete your enterprises by diligent effort, helped by plenty of support. Your work will be very successful.

Private life: This is a very good moment. You will be held in high esteem and your dedication will assure your good fortune in carrying on whatever plans you have.

Health, Feelings and Social life: People will turn to you for guidance because they trust and like you. Good health.

Fourth Six

Nothing that is not favorable for manifested modesty.

Your sincere commitment and dedication will make you very successful. The Chinese character translated as "manifested" also means "display, fly a banner", that means that you should make yourself known publicly and display your work.

Career: You are entirely dedicated to your duties without putting your ego in the middle. That makes you respected and well liked and it makes possible to you to carry on important enterprises.

Private life: You are on a roll. Your dedication and trustworthiness is well known; you will have plenty of support.

Health, Feelings and Social life: By being unassuming and temperate you will have success and happiness.

Fifth Six

Without wealth can employ his neighbors.
It is advantageous to take the offensive.
Nothing that is not favorable.

Do not be reactive but proactive. Do not limit yourself to fix the troubles as they appear, but act with strength and determination to avoid things getting out of hand.

Modesty doesn't mean weakness or submission. Use whatever means you need to restore justice but without using excessive or uncontrolled force.

15 - Modesty

Career: Your position is strong, but you have to take care to avoid things going downhill. Your example and guidance will be needed to keep the proper order.

Private life: Money cannot fix problems between people. Use your influence to correct any wrongs and stop wrongdoers.

Health, Feelings and Social life: Do not be reluctant to accept help from other people; you may need them to solve some problems. Do not disregard your health issues, take care of them without delay.

Top Six

Manifest Modesty.
It is favorable to launch armies to punish the capital city.

To punish the capital city indicates self-discipline, since the capital is at the heart of the country. It means that when something is wrong you shouldn't blame others but look inside yourself or inside your own intimate circle for the cause of the trouble.

Career: It is imperative to put in order your own sphere of influence. Reforms to correct any errors must be carried on without any delay.

Private life: The current problems only can be fixed by putting order in your own household.

Health, Feelings and Social life: Discipline and restraint are required to maintain your good help, both physically and emotionally.

16

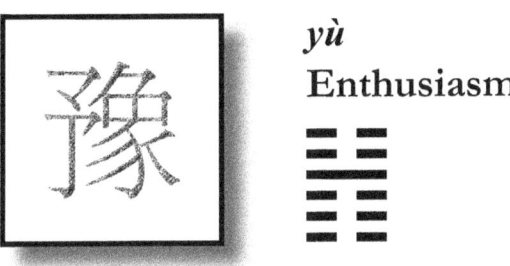

yù
Enthusiasm

Associated meanings

Joy, happy, amusement, recreation, enthusiasm, contentment, at ease; think beforehand, take precautions, anticipate, planning ahead.

Judgment

> Enthusiasm.
> It is favorable to appoint officers and to set the army in motion.

A strong leader stirs with happiness and passion the people who follow him. To appoint officers means to choose capable persons who share the same ideal as helpers.

Setting the army indicates not only to enlist troops, and to organize them in a capable force but to go ahead with some project.

Proper timing is very important, acting before the right moment comes or being late will make you fail.

The Image

> Thunder comes out from the earth: The image of Enthusiasm.
> So the kings of old made music to honor merit, and lavishly offered it to the Supreme Lord to be worthy of their dead ancestors.

Music, like thunder, indicates something that attracts the attention of people. Music awakes feelings within and influences and puts people in a receptive mood. Music symbolizes an attractive and harmonic message that makes all

16 - Enthusiasm

listeners vibrate in the same tune. In that way people can collaborate more effectively, and share a higher purpose than selfish interest.

First Six

> Manifest Enthusiasm is ominous.

Showing off your achievements or bragging about your connections will put you at odds with the people around you. Such conduct would be a source of trouble.

Career: You can have temporary gains, because your boss favors you at the present, but in the long run you may become isolated. Keep a low profile to prevent future trouble.

Private life: Do not boast about your riches or your highly placed friends. You will have problems ahead if you are not discreet now.

Health, Feelings and Social life: Living above your means will cause you a lot of trouble, both physically and socially.

Second Six

> Solid as a rock.
> His chance will come before the end of the day.
> The determination brings good fortune.

"Solid as a rock" means that you should trust your own judgment and do not deviate from your chosen path. Do not let other people or passing fads deviate you from your objectives. You should be ready to advance or retreat as the situation evolves, without hesitation and without heeding what other persons say, acting always with determination.

Career: Keep you focus on your plans but also be ready to make adjustments as you go. Trust your own insight more than the chatter of other people. If you keep alert you will not miss any good opportunity coming your way.

Private life: Do no let others deviate you from your aspirations, but be ready to take any corrective actions that may be needed to prevent trouble.

Health, Feelings and Social life: You are alert and resolute. Excellent health and stamina.

Third Six

> Enthusiasm that looks upward brings repentance.
> Hesitation brings remorse.

Lack of autonomy and indecision will make you to lose a good opportunity.

Procrastinators will not be rewarded.

Career: Do not keep waiting for others to show you the way or help you; such attitude will only shame you.

Private life: Looking at others with envy and hesitation will not solve anything but in the end you will regret your lack of decision.

Health, Feelings and Social life: Lack of energy and focus. If you never take the initiative you will achieve nothing.

Fourth Nine

Enthusiasm causes great things.
Do not hesitate.
Friends are quick to join your side.

The right time for action has come, take your chance before the opportunity fades.

A true leader will be sure of his way and will attract like-minded people around him with excellent final results.

Career: Optimum chances for carrying on your projects, you will receive plenty of support and you may be promoted.

Private life: You are blessed in your friends, they trust and support you. Your goals are shared by your family. You will be fully successful.

Health, Feelings and Social life: Great abundance of energy and determination.

Fifth Six

Determination.
Persistently ill but not dying.

To be ill without dying indicates a period of stoppage, your will experience pressure and trouble but your determination will keep you going.

Career: Any advancement in your business or career will be blocked and you will suffer plenty of problems. Keep up the struggle without losing faith in yourself.

Private life: People around you will not support and will hamper you. Keep going on.

Health, Feelings and Social life: You will suffer a long or chronic illness.

16 - Enthusiasm

Top Six

> Confused Enthusiasm.
> But if one changes course after it is over, there will be no defect.

The time of the Enthusiasm is ending. If you don't adapt to the new circumstances but instead press ahead blindly it would be a mistake. You will have a final chance to make amendments, do not waste it.

Career: Your endeavors will not prosper and you may be demoted. The situation is not stable, be ready to adapt and change your plans when needed.

Private life: Do not get carried away with unrealizable projects. Be ready to reconsider matters and to make adjustments.

Health, Feelings and Social life: If you realize that you are being deluded you will be able to overcome your mistake.

suí
Following

Associated meanings

Follow, pursue, conform to, accord with, respond, follow a way or religion, accepting guidance, acquiring followers.

Judgment

> Following has outstanding success.
> The determination is favorable.
> No defect.

Continuity, persistence and flexible adaptation to the demands of the changing times are the keys to success in this time.

Following has a dual aspect, to be followed and to follow; hence knowing when to follow and when to lead others is very important. Following also is related with helping and serving other people.

Before getting your own followers you should know how to follow the right track, being open-minded and flexible enough as to hear what other persons have to say and to change course when it is needed.

This is one of the few hexagrams that mention the "four cardinal virtues": *yuan*: outstanding (fundamentality, primal, originating, spring season, head, sublime, great, grand); *heng*: success (prevalence, growing, penetrating, treat, offering, sacrifice); *li*: determination (perseverance, constancy, correct and firm) and *heng*: favorable (advantageous, suitable, beneficial, lucky). One or more of the cardinal virtues appear in 50 different hexagrams, but only the hexagrams 1, 2 (with some modification), 3, 17, 19, 25 and 49 have the four virtues in its Judgment. Since the *Han* Dynasty onwards they have become keywords of Confucian thought, four qualities or virtues applicable both to Heaven and to the noble-minded person.

Any oracle encompassing the four cardinal virtues indicates that success is granted, but only if you don't stray from the good; for this reason determination in the right way is the key to success.

The Image

> In the middle of the lake is the thunder: The image of Following.
> Thus the noble, at dusk, enters and rests in peace.

Chinese people believed that in winter the thunder (*yang*, creative energy), rested in the depths of the lake.

Notice that the characters translated as "at dusk" also may be translated as "when it is time to be reticent" or "when you are in darkness". Therefore, the meaning of the image is that you should rest and restore energies when it is not propitious to go ahead.

There is a time for action and a time for resting, the wise person should grasp intuitively the right moment, since the meaning of Following is to be in touch with the time. The important thing is to be adaptable enough as to pursue the right course of action at every moment.

First Nine

> The situation is changing.
> The determination is favorable.
> Going outside to find associates is worthwhile.

This is a good moment to broaden your horizons, meet new people and accept new influences. To be ready for the coming opportunities you should be open to new alternatives, reconsider your priorities and goals, do not stick blindly to outmoded ideas.

Use your self-determination to select what is good for you and choose your goals wisely.

Career: New opportunities and a possible promotion will appear. To progress you should be ready to innovate. Do not isolate yourself, you will need some partners to make the most of this time.

Private life: Be flexible, do not stick mindlessly to the same old routine. Do not be afraid to face new challenges and meet people.

Health, Feelings and Social life: Communicating with others and going outside your home will bring good things into your life.

Second Six

> He clings to the boy and lets go the strong man.

The boy symbolizes a trivial, immature, superficial choice and the strong man a sound and wise alternative or decision.

Relating with nice and care-free people only for the sake of having a good moment is not bad, at least if done occasionally; but if you choose such persons as your day-to-day relationships you will miss far more valuable people.

The essential point is that to get better things you have to discontinue your relations with low quality elements.

Career: Choosing the easy thing over far-sighted choices will not conduce you to anything good. Try to work with experienced people and avoid those that do not have the knowledge, qualities or commitment required to do a god job.

Private life: Choose wisely your friends; relating with immature people will make you to lose far better persons.

Health, Feelings and Social life: If you follow you base instincts you will lose the spiritual thing, the deep thing.

Third Six

> He is involved with the strong man and lets go the boy.
> By following one gets what one seeks for.
> The determination is favorable.

This situation is the inverse of the previous line. It indicates a good and wise choice, a mature decision.

This is a good time to outgrow relationships and habits that are no longer suitable for a mature person.

By following a good model with perseverance you will achieve your goals advantageously.

Career: You will acquire new knowledge. Your contacts will benefit you in your career and perhaps you will get promoted. To progress you will have to leave some things behind.

Private life: You are in the right path, relating with good people. Your persistence will be rewarded. Do not let anyone to hold you back.

Health, Feelings and Social life: You are in the doorstep of a new spiritual level, follow your insights with determination.

Fourth Nine

> By following there will be a catch.
> The determination is ominous.
> He is truthful and bright on the way.
> How could there be defect in this?

The Chinese word translated as "catch" also means "hit the mark, find, succeed". You may find or achieve some tangible thing, succeed in your pursuit or catch a perception or an idea.

Things will go well for a while, but if you are complacent, in the end you will have trouble.

Keep up your standards and do not trust blindly the people around you, some of your supporters may have hidden agendas.

Career: Be careful and stick to the truth. Flattery is dangerous, do not fawn on your superiors; be wary of insincere people around you as well.

Private life: Sincerity is the best conduct. Be on guard against false friends.

Health, Feelings and Social life: You are sincere and your mind is clear. Be careful or excesses.

Fifth Nine

> Sincerity leads to excellence.
> Good fortune.

Pursuing a higher goal with sincerity will help you to get the trust of others and achieve good fortune.

Notice that this line may be translated alternatively as "Faithfulness is rewarded". Hence, commitment and dedication to your duty will bring you success.

Career: Do not aim low. This is an excellent moment to develop in earnest your business or career.

Private life: People recognize that you are truthful and fully dedicated to the common good. Nothing but good things will happen to you.

Health, Feelings and Social life: Excellent health, both physically and spiritually.

Top Six

> Strong ties between those who follow the same path.
> The king makes an offering in the Western Mountain.

The top line frequently describes a sage of somebody who is outside the situation, since the time of the hexagram is ending at this point.

Following - 17

You may be called from your retirement to help others.

The figure of the king making an offering in the Western Mountain indicates that your work or your ideas will be recognized by the authorities and set as an example to be imitated for others.

Career: You efforts will be recognized. You will have new opportunities and a new stage for your work.

Private life: You are bond to somebody powerful who will introduce you to a new circle. A new road opens up.

Health, Feelings and Social life: You will experience a spiritual awakening.

18

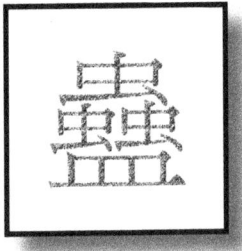

gǔ
Correcting Decay / Corruption

Associated meanings

Decay, corruption, poisonous worms in the food or the stomach, poison, evil influence, seduction, madness, insanity, curse, spell. The central meaning of the hexagram is to correct the corruption inherited from the past.

Judgment

> Correcting Decay has outstanding success.
> It is favorable to cross the great river.
> Before the first day three days.
> After the first day three days.

Decay may have been caused by carelessness, mistakes or lack of flexibility when facing changing situations.

Before correcting a spoiled situation it is important to understand the causes of it, which is the reason the Judgment says: "before the first day three days". Also, when correcting decay, people will need some time to adjust to the new rules, things cannot be fixed in no time; hence the text says "after the first day three days".

Correcting a spoiled situation implies to keep the foundation, but to eliminate all rotten parts; to keep the essence of the thing, but to get rid of the corruption that crept inside along the time. Renovating a situation that was neglected for too long takes time and requires a great effort, but the results will be good if you are willing to do a thorough job, such kind of job is indicated by the phrase "It is favorable to cross the great river".

18 - Correcting Decay / Corruption

In ancient China, crossing rivers, either at a ford or when the river was frozen, was not an easy task. It implicated dangers and hardships; hence crossing the great river means to carry out a difficult undertaking.

The Image

> The wind blows under the mountain: The image of Corruption.
> Thus the noble puts in motion the people and cultivates their moral values.

The wind blowing in the base of mountain gives the idea of stagnation, of air trapped in a valley. In the same way people may get trapped in outmoded ideas and bad habits, unable to change and improve. They should be awakened and learn new and better ways of doing things; that is the meaning of the text in the Image. New values and positive action should replace the lassitude and negative attitudes of the past.

First Six

> Correcting the decay left by his father.
> Since there is a son the father will have no defect.
> Danger.
> Good fortune in the end.

The mention to the father indicates mistakes caused for ways that are no longer valid; trouble that comes from the past. What is needed is a renovation and since the time of decay if just beginning, fixing the wrong things shouldn't be too difficult; in that way the father will have no defect.

On the other hand, if things are left to themselves, without any correction, there will be danger of stagnation. The more time passes the more difficult will be fixing the problems inherited from the past.

Career: You need to change your way of doing business of fix something bad in your new assignment.

Private life: Time to outgrowth your quaint ways. Look ahead instead of looking back at the past. If you don't adapt to the new times you will not fulfill your possibilities.

Health, Feelings and Social life: There is a chance for improving your spiritual and physical health, but only if you are open to new possibilities.

Second Nine

> Correcting the decay left by his mother.
> One shouldn't be too hard.

Correcting Decay / Corruption - 18

The mention to the mother and the warning about avoiding being too hard, indicates that the mistakes to be corrected should be handled with softness and gentleness, without making the people involved to lose face.

A tempered approach, taking in consideration the limitations of the people who caused the trouble, is the best option.

Career: Sensitive issues should be corrected in a discrete way. Something should be done, but without going to extremes.

Private life: Something is not well in your family; try to correct it with utmost care. Do not be hard on the feelings of others.

Health, Feelings and Social life: Learn to control your emotional states, but with balance and gentleness. Do not repress harshly your feelings, moderate and balance them instead.

Third Nine

Correcting the decay left by his father.
There will be some regrets, but no great defect.

You may need to step in some toes to fix problems that have been neglected for a long time.

You will have no help from others and some people may even complain, saying that you are too harsh, but the important thing is to fix the issues, so in the end all will go well because you have enough will and strength to straighten up the situation.

Career: You have a hard job to do and you will not be able to avoid antagonizing some people, but you should do your work disregarding any complaints.

Private life: Your efforts for renovating the situation will stir some resistance, but you are on the right path; do not let others make you doubt about your goals.

Health, Feelings and Social life: This is not a time for taking half-measures. The important thing is to correct your defects, that is the only way to improve your life.

Fourth Six

Tolerating the decay left by his father.
He will regret going this way.

Inactivity will get you to nowhere. Weakness and rigid adhesion to the past only will cause your current troubles to grow worse.

Career: If you do not take care of correcting the situation you will be shamed.

18 - Correcting Decay / Corruption

Private life: Do not keep ignoring the need to mend what is wrong, or you will be sorry.

Health, Feelings and Social life: Indulging in bad habits may cause a bad illness.

Fifth Six

> Correcting the decay left by his father.
> You get praises.

Long standing problems should be corrected with the help of others. To get praises means that you efforts will be recognized and supported by others.

Career: You may be promoted if you handle well the problems that you face now; your efforts will be recognized and your reputation will increase.

Private life: Your friends and family will support you in your quest for renovation.

Health, Feelings and Social life: Time to fix your problems with help from others. Spiritual rebirth.

Top Nine

> Does not serve kings or lords.
> He seeks much higher goals.

The last line many times indicates somebody who is outside the situation. Here it symbolizes a wise person detached from worldly affairs, focused in spiritual goals and self-improvement.

Career: This may be the time to retire from your work and pursue your own private goals, because you do not care about money any longer.

Private life: Detached but no unfriendly, you are no longer interested much in the affairs of other people.

Health, Feelings and Social life: You are a truly free spirit who only seeks spiritual growth.

19

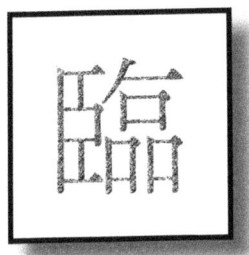

lín
Approach / Leadership

Associated meanings

Approach, becoming great, oversee, supervise, inspect, leadership.

Judgment

> Approach.
> Outstanding Success.
> The determination is favorable.
> On the eighth month there will be misfortune.

You should be ready to make the most of the new opportunities that area approaching, because they will not last a long time. Eight months represents an ephemeral period, after it ends, the growth and prosperity will stop.

The three lower lines symbolize people that are prospering. The three upper lines indicate persons of higher rank who work with the three lower lines, helping and overseeing them.

This is one of the few hexagrams that mention the "four cardinal virtues": yuan: outstanding (fundamentality, primal, originating, spring season, head, sublime, great, grand); heng: success (prevalence, growing, penetrating, treat, offering, sacrifice); li: determination (perseverance, constancy, correct and firm) and heng: favorable (advantageous, suitable, beneficial, lucky). One or more of the cardinal virtues appear in 50 different hexagrams, but only the hexagrams 1, 2 (with some modification), 3, 17, 19, 25 and 49 have the four virtues in its Judgment. Since the *Han* Dynasty onwards they have become keywords of Confucian thought, four qualities or virtues applicable both to Heaven and to the noble-minded person.

19 - Approach / Leadership

Any oracle encompassing the four cardinal virtues indicates that success is granted, but only if you don't stray from the good; for this reason determination in the right path is the key to success.

The Image

> Above the lake is the earth: The image of Approach.
> Thus the noble is tireless in his efforts to educate the people
> and doesn't know boundaries in protecting and supporting them.

The image of this hexagram shows a hidden body or water, located under the earth. It symbolizes a type of leadership based on nurturing and educating the people, as a gardener waters the garden to make plants grow.

Like a garden, this time will flourish only for a while, until fall comes, hence no time should be wasted.

This is a good moment for supporting and teaching people, delegating authority in them. In that way they will grow as fully responsible persons.

First Nine

> Joint approach.
> The determination is favorable.

Your influence will attract like-minded people; joining forces with them will benefit everybody. Be ready to cooperate with others, but keep your own goals in mind.

Career: Working with people who share your same aims is the proper thing to do, but do not let others choose the path for you. Good time for teamwork; you may get promoted or assigned to a new job.

Private life: Excellent opportunities for making new relationships and starting new projects with your friends or family.

Health, Feelings and Social life: Communing with others, sharing a common purpose, will fulfill your life. Do not forget who you are.

Second Nine

> Joint approach.
> Good fortune.
> Everything is favorable.

You will get recognition from your superiors. Since you have the strength and knowledge to push forward your projects, nothing will stop your advance.

Career: You will get support from influential people and will be able to overcome any obstacles in your path. Be ready to cooperate with others.

Private life: New opportunities are coming. People like and support you. With help from your friends and family you will prosper greatly.

Health, Feelings and Social life: Blessings from above will give you strength and insight to grow as a person.

Third Six

Sweet approach.
No goal is favorable.
If he becomes anxious about it, there will be no defect.

Becoming too cozy and over-confident would be an error, but if you are really sorry for your carelessness you can still avoid making big mistakes.

Be wary of flattery and do not be lazy or rash.

Career: If you are not cautions you will regret it. Be careful of your actions and keep an eye on the people around you. Do not take any risks.

Private life: Do not take things for granted. The situation looks good but if you let your guard down you will have trouble.

Health, Feelings and Social life: Over-indulgence in food will make you ill. Time for self-restraint.

Fourth Six

Approach reaches its climax.
No defect.

The fact that the approach is at its climax and that there is no defect indicates that you can handle the situation with ease, being able to lead your subordinates well. All is running smoothly, if you keep focused in your duty you will have no trouble.

Career: The fourth line is the place of the minister, a senior executive in a subordinate position. Your mature and levelheaded leadership will assure success.

Private life: You will be able to support and guide your family very well without making any mistakes.

Health, Feelings and Social life: Good physical and spiritual balance.

Fifth Six

> Wise approach.
> It is fitting for a lord.
> Good fortune.

A wise leader can employ others in order to serve him, trusting and promoting the capable persons (the second *yang* line) and because that he will be successful.

Career: You are an efficient manager who knows how to find able subordinates and delegate tasks to them.

Private life: You will prosper and enjoy a happy family life.

Health, Feelings and Social life: By keeping mind and body relaxed, you are ready to handle everything in the proper way. Your mind is clear.

Top Six

> Sincere and generous approach.
> Good fortune.
> No defect.

A generous and humble sage is a blessing for the people whom he teaches (the first and second lines). He is ready to share his experience with others in order to help worthy people with his wisdom.

Career: You may be a consultant, or somebody who provides guidance to other people. Your valuable advice is widely sought.

Private life: You are generous with your experience and knowledge, helping people around you with your wisdom.

Health, Feelings and Social life: A magnanimous and benevolent approach towards other people helps you to have good relations with everybody.

20

guān
Contemplation

Associated meanings

Contemplate, look at, observe, watch, regard, examine, evaluate; scenery, sight, aspect.

Judgment

> Contemplation.
> The ablution was done but not yet the offering.
> His dignified appearance inspires confidence.

The sacrificial rituals in ancient China started with a purification ceremony. Here is described the moment between such ceremony and the offering, the sacrifice preparations were started but it still has not been performed.

Besides knowledge, the act of quiet contemplation can provide spiritual balance and insight. After acquiring such spiritual insight, one becomes a living example for other people, like the worshiper in the Judgment, who symbolizes a highly developed person performing an important task. Such person will be publicly looked on and will inspire trust in the spectators.

Contemplation means to acquire knowledge about something by carefully observing it, but it is not possible to look at something without changing it, because the observer will also be seen by others.

The Image

> The wind moves upon the earth: The image of Contemplation.
> Thus the ancient kings inspected all regions looking at the people and giving instruction.

The wind moving upon the earth means to look far away, trying to understand the customs of other people with an open mind. The ancient kings symbolize wise persons that know how to adapt ancient wisdom to the reality of the people, to instruct and guide them.

From a personal viewpoint, the image is telling us to widen our horizons, to take a fresh look at the situation, and also to adapt and apply old beliefs to the current situation.

First Six

> Childish contemplations.
> No defect for the small man.
> For the noble is humiliating.

Lack of understanding is not a fault for an ignorant or young person. Some persons may have limited understanding of the situation, lacking analytical capacity. Indeed ignorance would be excusable in young people, but in a mature individual it would be shaming, since such person should know better.

In any case, the one described here doesn't understand the situation, and because that he will not be able to act correctly.

Career: You have in your hands more that you can manage, mainly because you lack enough knowledge and experience to understand and handle the situation well. It would be better to wait or retreat; if you go ahead you will be shamed.

Private life: Immaturity and lack of knowledge may put you in an awkward position. If you recognize your limitations you will avoid facing humiliation.

Health, Feelings and Social life: Confusion and ignorance.

Second Six

> Furtive contemplation.
> The determination is favorable for a woman.

The Chinese word translated as "furtive", also indicates to "peep through a door crack". In ancient China women neither could leave her homes nor have a superior education, hence it would not be expected from them to have wide knowledge of the world; for that reason furtive contemplation is related to a woman.

Indeed somebody looking through a door crack cannot have a good knowledge of what is looked upon, since such person cannot see the whole scene.

Hence, this line indicates somebody —either a man or a woman— who has a narrow field of view and cannot understand the whole situation.

You may lack knowledge or be limited by dogmatism, looking on reality from a distorted viewpoint. This kind of limited contemplation would be excusable in somebody with limited possibilities, like a woman in ancient China, but not in a capable person.

Also this line may point to some kind of spying in favor of a weak faction.

Career: You don't have the full picture of the situation. If you are a subordinate who is only following orders, you may not need a full understanding about what is happening, but if you are leading others, your lack of knowledge will prevent you from achieving good results.

Private life: It would be advisable for your to widen your perspective and to look beyond your narrow sphere of experience. Women will have better chances than men.

Health, Feelings and Social life: You have some constrains, they may be physical or mental.

Third Six

Looking at the progress and setbacks in my life.

Some maturity has been reached at this point. It is time to try to make sense of your past life, to understand and eventually change the way you behave.

Making a realistic balance of your possibilities will make clear to you what you can do from now on.

Career: Time of impasse and uncertainty. Try to understand better the situation before doing anything.

Private life: You may have gains and losses. Understanding the reasons of what is happening will help you to know yourself better.

Health, Feelings and Social life: Look at the result of your actions to understand better who you are. You may experience a setback in your health.

Fourth Six

Contemplation of the glory of the kingdom.
It is favorable to act as a guest of a king.

Contemplation of the glory of the kingdom means to broaden your horizons and discover new possibilities. You can use your talents to support a worthy cause or business.

The phrase rendered as "favorable to act as a guest of a king", also may be translated as "favorable for having audience with the king"; it means that you can progress by contacting the right person who is in a position of authority.

Career: Your advice is valuable. First see where it can be employed better, and then apply your capabilities to the job. You may be offered a new job or a position as advisor. The scope of your responsibilities and reach will be greatly enhanced.

Private life: Do not limit yourself to the old track. Be an active member in society, you can play an important part and influence positively other people. You have the ear of important people and your advice is valuable.

Health, Feelings and Social life: A more active life is possible. Share your wisdom with others.

Fifth Nine

Contemplation of my life.
The noble has no defect.

You occupy an elevated position. Your decisions affect not only your own life but also other people.

The text says "no defect" because you will keep clean or errors by watching with attention the result of your actions. Only by contemplating the effect of your actions you will know if you did the right thing.

Career: Your position is secure and stable. This is an introspective moment, when you realize that you did well, but also understand that you have to be careful with your actions because you have plenty of responsibilities.

Private life: The fifth line is the place of the regent; likewise you have a respected position in your family. You are aware of your responsibilities; by examining carefully your actions you will stay free from errors.

Health, Feelings and Social life: Good health and spiritual insight.

Top Nine

Contemplation of his life.
The noble has no faults.

The sixth line many times depicts a wise person who is not concerned by worldly matters.

You can see with detachment and a good perspective not only what happens around you but also your own actions, because you no longer care for success and money. As a result you can see things as they really are. Your clarity will prevent you from making any mistakes.

"Knowing others is intelligence; knowing yourself is true wisdom. Mastering others is strength; mastering yourself is true power." (*Laozi*)

Career: You are able to do what is best for your business or company because you are not biased and you can see the whole picture.

Private life: Your life has been good and you can look upon the trodden path without regrets. You are a good example for other people.

Health, Feelings and Social life: The look is oriented inwards. This is a moment for introspection and to reflect about what you have done along your life.

21

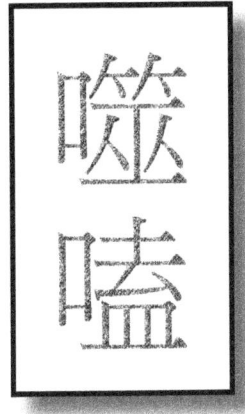

shì hé
Biting Through

Associated meanings

To bite through, crush between the teeth, consuming, union by gnawing, remove the obstacles so the jaws come together.

Judgment

> Biting Through is successful.
> It is favorable to administer justice.

This hexagram is related with criminal lawsuits, the other hexagram with a similar meaning is the number 6: **The Conflict**, which indicates a civil lawsuit.

Biting Through indicates that energetic measures must be applied to correct a wrong. There is some obstruction, some dysfunctional element that should be punished or removed. The bite indicates a fast and energetic action, applying justice with strength to fix some issue. It also indicates that this is the time to take a stand and fight for what you believe in.

The first and last lines are those who receive punishment, the other lines are the ones administering justice.

The Image

> Thunder and lightning: The image of the Biting Through.
> Thus the ancient kings applied punishments with intelligence
> and enacted laws.

21 - Biting Through

Thunder is shocking and represents the force of the law in action, lighting indicates clarity: laws should be clearly defined to make it clear what is lawful and what is not and should have real force behind them.

The ancient kings symbolize a pattern or model of good governance, which we should strive to follow.

To apply punishment with intelligence means to not act arbitrarily and to measure carefully the kind and degree of the punishment to be applied, on a case by case basis.

To enact the laws means to put the laws in action without delay and to be ready to do what is needed to restore justice.

First Nine

> His feet are trapped by fetters
> and his toes are mangled.
> No defect.

Being the first line the movement is only starting here, hence the punishment is applied as a preventive action, trapping the feet means to prevent a transgression. The fetters indicate a punitive action that stops a first-time transgressor from continuing with his bad behavior. The first line, being in a low position, is associated with the feet in several hexagrams.

The transgressor becomes free of blame because he is stopped in his tracks and prevented from committing further transgressions.

Career: Your career will be stopped or turned back, and you may be demoted. You will think twice the next time that you are tempted to ignore the rules.

Private life: You will be punished on the onset of bad behavior; as a result you will be prevented from making worse things. You may go to jail for a short while or experiment some restrictions.

Health, Feelings and Social life: Some illness related to mobility or some problem with your feet may affect you for a while.

Second Six

> Biting Through tender flesh, the nose is destroyed.
> No defect.

Tender flesh indicates that there are no complications, the facts are clear. To destroy the nose may indicate that you you're too enthusiastic and lacking in sensibility, being too hard; or it may mean that cutting out the nose was the punishment applied in this case. In any case, the punishment is right. The line says "no defect" because there are more than enough arguments to condemn the transgressor.

Career: You need to apply punishment to a hardened transgressor. You may not have a full picture of the issues, but there are more than enough motives to punish the offender.

Private life: You may need to punish some member of your family or circle of associates, justly and deservedly.

Health, Feelings and Social life: You may be hurt physically or have minor surgery.

Third Six

Biting Through dried meat finds poison.
A little humiliation.
No defect.

You face a long time neglected problem and some things that come to the light may cause trouble. The person to be punished will not submit meekly and instead will try to get back to you. Since you lack enough power to fully correct the issues that you are facing, you will lose some face but in the end you will not make any mistakes.

Career: You will be criticized and clash with some insubordination when trying to correct long standing troubles. Although you will not be able to fix entirely the problems or to punish the wrongdoer as it should be, you will keep clear of any errors.

Private life: You will have a conflict with some of your friends or family when trying to correct some problems. Your just actions will generate resentment and may cause an embarrassing confrontation with the troublemaker. Since you are doing the right thing your conscience will be clear.

Health, Feelings and Social life: Risk of food poisoning or some kind of intoxication, but it will not be fatal.

Fourth Nine

Biting Through bone-dry meat he gets metal arrows.
Fortitude under trying conditions is favorable.
Good fortune.

To get metal arrows indicates that to overcome strong resistance and to manage an old problem, which is tough as dried meat, you need to have the proper elements (the **hexagram 40.2** also mentions getting arrows, but golden instead metallic). The arrows symbolize speed, guidance, hardness and penetration; they indicate as well that you should be very determined and tough to be able to apply the proper punishment effectively.

"Of old, in a civil case, both parties, before they were heard, brought to the court an arrow (or a bundle of arrows), in testimony of their rectitude, after which they were heard; in a criminal case, they in the same way deposited each thirty pounds of gold, or some other metal." (*Legge*)

Career: You will succeed and may even get a promotion, but only after strenuous efforts and facing strong resistance.

Private life: To manage well old troubles and chastise hardened transgressors you will need to toughen yourself up, also you will need to find some clues that will help you to find a solution.

Health, Feelings and Social life: Strong measures are required to treat a chronic illness.

Fifth Six

> Biting Through dry meat he gets yellow metal.
> The determination is dangerous.
> No defect.

This line represents the regent, but as a weak, *yin* line, he will be disposed to leniency. To get yellow metal indicates that you should take precautions. Be ready to be impartial and just, and have ready the proper means before facing dangerous situations.

"The determination is dangerous" means that it would be perilous to force the situation or to go to extremes. Keep your balance and you will make no mistakes.

Career: You will succeed and may get a promotion, but if you overdo it, you may lose all your previous achievements.

Private life: After overcoming some resistance you will have good gains, your life will improve. If you bite off more that you can chew you will have trouble.

Health, Feelings and Social life: Do not over-stress yourself. If you have an illness it will improve.

Top Nine

> He carries a yoke that make his ears disappear.
> Ominous.

An obstinate wrongdoer who doesn't heed any warnings only will have misfortune. The fact that the yoke cover his hears indicates that he is not able to hear or learn, that he will not correct his ways because he is deafened by his stubbornness.

Career: You will be keep apart and may be sanctioned if you are not able to follow the rules and don't work harmoniously with the team.

Private life: If you choose to ignore good advice and are deaf to well founded complains, you will pay a heavy price.

Health, Feelings and Social life: If you ignore reality you will be isolated from other people. Bad habits will damage greatly your health.

22

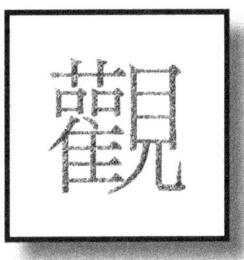

bì
Elegance / Adornment / Grace

Associated meanings

Ornate, elegant, brilliant; embellish, adorn; good manners, finesse, diplomatic maneuvering.

Judgment

> Elegance.
> Success
> It is favorable to have a goal in minor matters.

Social etiquette norms are useful to regulate the behavior of people for the benefit of the common good. Thus grace helps to keep the social order.

Applied to the current situation, it means that you should handle it with finesse and charm; this is not the proper time for assertive or bold behavior but for tactful and elegant conduct. Your relations with other people will be better if you are polite and have educated manners.

Avoid taking important decisions or handling difficult affairs.

The Image

> Fire at the foot of the mountain: The image of Elegance.
> Thus the noble regulates the crowds with enlightenment.
> But doesn't dare to decide criminal cases.

The fire illuminates and highlights the mountain, in the same way, by emphasizing the desired behavior, with charm and persuasion, a sage guides the people. This means using soft, persuasive methods, to teach and convince the people.

Nevertheless, such soft methods cannot be used to handle hardened criminals.

First Nine

He gives Elegance to his feet, leaves the carriage and walks.

To leave the carriage means to get down to essentials, to discard some things and simplify your life. To give elegance to his feet suggests to use your own means for advancing, to use your own resources instead relying on others for getting an easy ride.

Career: You will give up some privileges to be able to follow your own path. You may be demoted, but you will be your own man.

Private life: To favor your independence you will discard some privileges and make your own choices.

Health, Feelings and Social life: Instead following blindly what others say, it is time to do some independent thinking. Time to leave props back and tone up your own physical and mental muscles.

Second Six

He gives Elegance to his beard.

To gave elegance to his beard means to follow some rules or traditions required in some places. Your position is weak and dependent so you need to conform to the customs established by your superiors or by society.

Career: You should conform to the conventions in the place where you work, following the norms on behavior.

Private life: To be accepted in some circles you have to follow some rules regarding your clothing and appearance.

Health, Feelings and Social life: You care too much about your appearance.

Third Nine

Adorned with moisture.
Long-term determination is fortunate.

You have a very elegant and comfortable way of life. However you ought to keep your constancy to avoid being weakened by your opulent lifestyle. If you keep up your strength and determination you will be fortunate.

Career: Your position is very good and you have plenty of support. Do not be over-confident and keep planning long-term.

Private life: Charmed moment. Good luck and plenty of friends. Do not forget your duties.

Health, Feelings and Social life: Good health and happiness. Do not overindulge yourself.

Fourth Six

Adorned in white.
A white horse soaring.
He is not a robber, but a suitor.

The sudden appearance of a newcomer –adorned with simple white elegance, but with soaring thoughts and objectives–, may cause some doubts, but his sincere wish is to cooperate. In time, he will be accepted and the obstructions will disappear.

You may hesitate before taking an important decision. May be somebody offered you something or asked for your friendship or love.

Getting the trust of another person will take some time.

Career: You will face temporary obstructions, but in the long run you will have good prospects.

Private life: Other people may misunderstood your good intentions but at last you will be accepted.

Health, Feelings and Social life: You health may not improve for a while but your mind is sound and clear. A delayed union with a friend or lover.

Fifth Six

Elegance in hills and gardens.
The silk bundle is meager.
Humiliation, but good fortune at the end.

Hills and gardens also can be translated as "native forest" or "wild park". In any case it indicates a quiet place, outside the active city life. It symbolizes a secluded circle where you want to enter, a natural and spiritual place. But you don't have much to offer, your material resources are meager, and you may feel humiliated because that. In the end such things will not matter because you will be accepted.

To look for the hills and gardens also may indicate a search of peace, to move away from the mundane noise.

22 - Elegance / Adornment / Grace

Career: You will face new work opportunities in a new environment. You may not feel confident, but you will succeed at the end.

Private life: This may be a good moment to retire and start a more contemplative life in the country.

Health, Feelings and Social life: The hills and gardens symbolize the entrance to a new spiritual level, where material things are not important.

Top Nine

Simple elegance.
No defect.

Many times the sixth line is beyond the situation. In this case it is beyond adorning.

Simplicity is the only thing that you need. By being completely sincere you will make no mistakes.

Career: You have no need to embellish reality; be simple and forthright and you will not fail.

Private life: An authentic person needs no postures or adornment.

Health, Feelings and Social life: Excellent physical and spiritual balance.

23

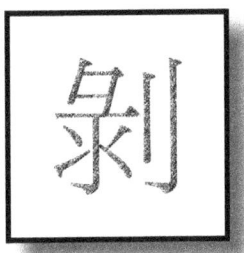

bō
Splitting Apart / Decay

Associated meanings

Flay, strip, peel; pluck, lay bare, strip (as clothes or badges of office); split, slice, crack; disintegration.

Judgment

> Splitting Apart.
> It is not favorable to go anywhere.

This is a time of decay, when evil men prosper and destroy the support that good people have. Interpersonal relations are hampered, each person is for himself; trust is scarce and people don't cooperate between them any longer. This declination process cannot be stopped, so instead wasting time and energy in fighting it, the best course of action is to remain calm and stay out of trouble until it ends.

The Image

> The mountain lies on earth: The image of Splitting Apart.
> Thus by means of being munificent with those below them,
> the superiors secure the peace and stability of their own position.

To keep your position safe you have to secure your foundations. Make sure that you keep the support of the people from whom you depend for your needs. Be ready to make concessions to others instead fighting and keep a low profile.

23 - Splitting Apart / Decay

First Six

> Splitting Apart the legs of the bed.
> Determination leads to destruction.
> Ominous.

A bed that is disintegrated bit by bit symbolizes how the situation is undermined gradually by evil men, from the periphery (the legs) up to the center (the skin, in the fourth line).

Splitting apart the bed's legs indicates a systematic plan of action for depriving you of your support. Also, since the bed is a place for resting, your tranquility and peace are threatened as well.

There is nothing you can do except to be alert and wait. Any offensive action will only make worse your plight.

Career: Somebody is plotting to undercut you. Be wary of the people around you. It would not be wise to start any business now or to fight your enemies openly. Wait and see.

Private life: Quarrels in the family or between friends. You may be betrayed. Try to stay quiet and calm.

Health, Feelings and Social life: Problems with your foot. Mental confusion.

Second Six

> Splitting Apart the bed's frame.
> Determination leads to destruction.
> Ominous.

The situation worsens and the attack is affecting the very frame that supports your position. You will be left without supporters and defenseless.

Be flexible; try to see a way to retreat to a safe place. If you try to fight to maintain your position you will be crushed.

Career: Your influence and the strength of your position are waning. Do not be stubborn and look for a way out of your predicament before it is too late.

Private life: Bit by bit you are becoming isolated and left devoid of support by people who look to take from you what you value most. Do not be self-righteous and obstinate. It is better to retreat and accept some losses now that to lose everything in the end.

Health, Feelings and Social life: Confusion and lack of points of reference. Problems with your knees.

Third Six

> Splitting Apart them.
> No defect.

Do not let others sway you from your principles. You are surrounded by bad people, but if you break your bond with them you will make no mistakes.

Career: Preserve your independence at all costs. Do not follow the crowd.

Private life: Do not lower your standards following blindly the people around you. It is better to keep aloof instead being dragged down into some wrongdoing.

Health, Feelings and Social life: It is time to reassert your will and reaffirm your personality, disregarding what other people say.

Fourth Six

> The bed is peeled down to the skin.
> Ominous.

In ancient times the bed mattress was an animal skin stretched across the frame. If that skin was destroyed the bed became useless.

The bad times are at its worst. Decay affects you directly; you have no support and nowhere to rest. There is no way to escape from the trouble now.

Career: Danger; calumny and possible demotion.

Private life: You have no place to rest and you may be betrayed. There is not a thing that you can do about it.

Health, Feelings and Social life: You have reached the lowest point in this cycle. Keep your strength up and hope for the best.

Fifth Six

> A string of fishes.
> Favors by means of the ladies of palace.
> Nothing that is not favorable.

Decay is ending. The string of fishes symbolizes people that are starting to cooperate following a good lead. The ladies of palace are symbolized by the five *yin* lines that are now stopping their hostility and instead cooperating for the good of all. Receiving favors by the ladies of palace means to be endorsed, to be introduced to the center of power. New opportunities for moving things forward will appear.

23 - Splitting Apart / Decay

Career: Supported by influential friends, you will prosper.

Private life: The social fabric is restored. Conflicts with your friends or family will be left behind. A new period of peace and cooperation is dawning.

Health, Feelings and Social life: Your health will improve.

Top Nine

> A large fruit still uneaten.
> The noble gets a carriage; the petty man shelter is split apart.

The large fruit symbolizes great achievements and indicates a great person among many others who are inferior.

Also, the large fruit is the symbol of the new opportunities for advancement that will open up.

The noble getting a carriage indicates that capable persons are now in power, with plenty of support and moving ahead. On the other side, the petty people that thrived in the bad times will lose all their ill-gotten gains.

Career: You will be promoted and will get new business. Plenty of support will allow you to carry on successfully you projects.

Private life: Your position as head of the family is restored. Those who created trouble will be shamed.

Health, Feelings and Social life: Excellent health. Your spiritual horizon will expand.

24

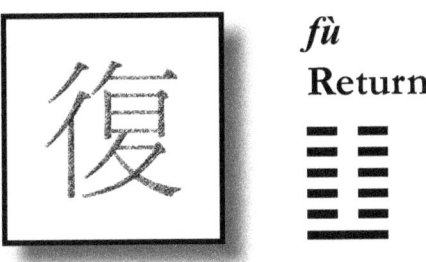

fù
Return

Associated meanings

Return, turn back; repeat; restore, revert, renewal.

Judgment

> Return.
> Success.
> Exit and entry without harm.
> Friends come.
> No defect.
> Back and forth along the way.
> In seven days will return.
> It is favorable to have where to go.

This hexagram is related with the month of the Winter Solstice, the time in the year when days start to grow longer and the *yang* power, symbolized by the thunder and the first line, returns.

The "seven days" reference may refer to a short time or to the start of a new cycle, like the seventh day when the moon reaches a major phase after the new moon. Besides this hexagram, the Chinese character for seven only appears in the hexagrams 51 and 63, in the second line in both cases. Here it indicates the beginning of a new cycle and a return. It is related with the return of money in the hexagram 51 and with the return of a curtain in the hexagram 63.

24 - Return

The return is a natural occurrence, the days will be getting longer at the winter solstice, but spring still is several months off. For this reason it would be useless to try to force matters, since the situation will develop at its own pace.

Exit and entry without harm means that after a period of stagnation, there will appear opportunities and things will start to move ahead. People will join in groups to collaborate spontaneously.

Since the *yang* energy still is not firmly established, there will be adjustments to be done and you may have to try different ways until finding the proper one, but in the end you will find a worthy goal, which is the reason the text says "it is favorable to have where to go".

The Image

> The thunder in the middle of the earth: The image of Return.
> So on the day of the solstice, the ancient kings closed the border crossings.
> Merchants and travelers did not travel
> and the ruler did not visit his dominions.

The ancient kings closed the entry points of the realm at the winter solstice to allow people rest.

The return is a period of renewal, a recovery after a time of weakness or estrangement. At the beginning of such moments it is important to rest for a while, to halt all activity to nourish the returning energy (*yang* principle) in order to allow it to grow, to be ready for intense activity at the proper time, later.

First Nine

> Returning before going too far.
> There will be no need for repentance.
> Outstanding good fortune.

Mistakes should be corrected before they complicate the situation further. When an error is corrected without hesitation, reacting on time, there will be no cause for shame and you will secure a good result.

Career: Correct any false start before it damages your position or reputation.

Private life: It is better to recognize your mistakes soon, before they grow into further trouble instead ignoring them. Do not hesitate in saying "I'm sorry" if you did some wrong to other person.

Health, Feelings and Social life: No harm will be done if you correct your mistakes on the spot.

Second Six

> Quiet return.
> Good fortune.

The Chinese character translated as "quiet" also means "resign, release, let go". This means that you will be able to relax, reconsider and finally go back. It also indicates avoiding trouble and to be happy with the outcome of the situation.

Career: Be ready to reevaluate your choices when a wiser person gives you advice. You may be overextending yourself.

Private life: Relax, stop for a moment and think again. Take the time to evaluate where you are going and to make some adjustments.

Health, Feelings and Social life: Be ready to make any changes that are necessary to reduce the stress in your life.

Third Six

> Repeated return.
> Danger.
> No repentance.

Insecurity and vacillation will make you to waste your time, but at least, if you see and correct your mistakes you will avoid having further trouble, hence there will be no reason for repentance.

The Chinese character translated here as "repeated" also means "on the brink of, river bank, shore", so the line may alternatively read "returning from the brink of water". The meaning in such case is to return from a dangerous position, to step back from the brink of a dangerous body of water, since moving water is a symbol of danger in the *Yijing*.

Career: Your position is unstable. Take all the time you need to evaluate properly your actions before committing yourself, but do not procrastinate.

Private life: Focus in every single thing that you are doing at a time. Dilly-dallying will slow you down. Consider carefully what you have to do, but once you take a decision stick to it.

Health, Feelings and Social life: You lack will power and because that you will find difficult to make out your mind. If you follow a medical treatment stick to it until it is fully finished.

Fourth Six

> Returns alone by the middle of the road.

24 - Return

You are subjected to different influences, but you will choose to follow your own course, and as result you will return alone. The line doesn't say if your new course is good or bad, but walking by the middle of the road (avoiding the extremes) indicates good balance and composure, which can never be a bad thing.

Career: If you want to reach your true goals you will have to split with the people around you. Follow your vocation.

Private life: Do not let others to sway you from your purpose. It is better to be alone and to be true to yourself than submit mindlessly to the wishes of the flock.

Health, Feelings and Social life: Follow your own heart. Good physical and spiritual balance.

Fifth Six

Earnest return.
No defect.

The Chinese character for "earnest" also means "honest, solid, and sincere". It indicates that the return is a true one and that it is done without doubts, with full commitment.

Career: You have very good reasons for returning because you know that a sincere reform is the only viable option.

Private life: If you follow your heart you will not miss the mark.

Health, Feelings and Social life: After you find the right course, follow it without hesitation.

Top Six

The return goes astray.
Ominous.
Calamities and errors.
If he puts armies on the march, in the end will suffer a great defeat, whose misfortune will extend to the ruler of the state.
For ten years he will not be able to attack.

Being the last line in the hexagram, the return here is done from the most distant point. Because you are confused and have advanced too far in the wrong direction, you will miss the proper moment and the right path for returning.

Putting armies in the march means to put considerable resources in the wrong place. If you insist obstinately in such aggressive and wrong behavior you will suffer big losses.

Ten years indicates a long period, like in hexagrams 3.2 and 27.3, but in this case it also means that you will be powerless for a long time after suffering a resounding defeat.

Career: Your stubbornness will cost you dearly. You will be stripped of rank and your errors will damage your entire organization in a bad way.

Private life: If you follow your own and wrong way for too long you will damage your whole family and will loss the respect of everybody.

Health, Feelings and Social life: Pride, confusion and obstinacy will keep you in the dark for a long time. Your bad choices may cause acute health problems followed by a chronic illness.

25

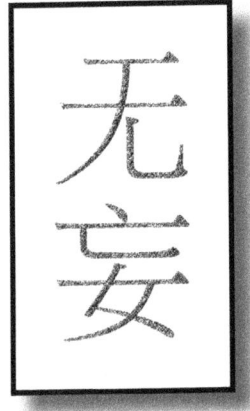 *wú wàng*
Innocence /
No expectations

Associated meanings

Innocent behavior, no expectancy, acting spontaneously, wholehearted sincerity; unexpected happenings.

Judgment

> Innocence.
> Outstanding success.
> The determination is favorable.
> If he is not honest he has misfortune.
> It is favorable to have a goal.

Innocence means genuine, without fakery, without guile or pretensions. Innocent action signifies following your natural instincts when facing the unexpected. Doing what you really want to do, without expectations, just for the sake of it.

Being in touch with the time is the key point here. The time of innocence requires intuition, sincerity and adaptability to the changing circumstances, not following a script.

This is one of the few hexagrams that mention the "four cardinal virtues": *yuan*: outstanding (fundamentality, primal, originating, spring season, head, sublime, great, grand); *heng*: success (prevalence, growing, penetrating, treat, offering, sacrifice); *li*: determination (perseverance, constancy, correct and firm) and *heng*: favorable (advantageous, suitable, beneficial, lucky). One or

25 - Innocence / No expectations

more of the cardinal virtues appear in 50 different hexagrams, but only the hexagrams 1, 2 (with some modification), 3, 17, 19, 25 and 49 have the four virtues in its Judgment. Since the *Han* Dynasty onwards they have become keywords of Confucian thought, four qualities or virtues applicable both to Heaven and to the noble-minded person.

Any oracle encompassing the four cardinal virtues indicates that success is granted, but only if you don't stray from the good; for this reason determination in the right way is the key to success.

The Image

> The thunder moves under heaven and all things partake of innocence. Thus the ancient kings, in excellent harmony with the seasons, nurtured all beings.

The thunder under the heavens means power and creativity.

The ancient kings symbolize a pattern or model of good governance, in tune with the rhythms of nature.

In the same way, you should be in harmony with the tides of change, accepting people and the ever changing world on its own terms.

Do not try to adapt people and reality to your own conditions; you should be flexible enough as to perceive intuitively the best way to relate with the changing circumstances around you.

First Nine

> Going forward with innocence brings good fortune.

Acting with spontaneity, following your natural impulses will be lucky. Do not repress yourself, be flexible and open to change.

You will accomplish your wishes.

Career: The first line is associated with beginnings. Do not be stifled by routine, if you go ahead spontaneously the events will unfold naturally in a fortunate way.

Private life: Do not stop your creative impulses. This is a good time for following your vocation and the true wishes of your heart.

Health, Feelings and Social life: Opportunity for spiritual growth. Be open-minded.

Second Six

> Harvest without plowing.
> The fields are ready for use without having been prepared.
> It is favorable to have a goal.

To harvest without plowing and having the fields ready without preparing them beforehand indicates that you work on behalf of another and you don't initiate the action yourself. But you will do what you are asked for because you want to do it, not because of greed or blind obedience.

Another alternative translation would be "not doing the plowing for the sake of the harvest, nor doing the clearing for the sake of having a mature field", meaning that you will do what you have to do, without caring for the possible benefits, without expectations, simply taking pride in doing a good job.

The line also means to get good rewards after little effort or simply getting lucky, but it is important to focus properly in your goals.

Career: By simply doing your duty you will benefit greatly, since you will find that most preparatory jobs were already done.

Private life: This is a lucky moment for investments and good bargains. You will prosper easily with not much effort.

Health, Feelings and Social life: Your inner self is ready for a major development. Your health will improve.

Third Six

> Unexpected disaster.
> The cow tied by someone, is the traveler's gain and the villager's misfortune.

The loss of somebody is the gain of other person. Good time for the wanderer and losses for the sedentary person.

Some may benefit from your bad luck, but your troubles are not your fault. Alternatively you may have gains at the expense of other people.

Career: Arbitrary gains and losses. Somebody may benefit unintentionally from your disgrace or vice versa.

Private life: Profit and loss. Unexpected troubles. Be open to new sudden opportunities.

Health, Feelings and Social life: The situation is unstable, you will have ups and downs.

25 - Innocence / No expectations

Fourth Nine

If you can keep your determination there will be no defect

An alternative translation would be "can be determined", or "an augury can be made". The meaning is that you choose what to do you should stick to your own decision and do not let it waver. Stick to your own vocation and advice, be true to yourself.

Career: If you keep your course without being swayed for others you will have no trouble. Do not expect changes.

Private life: Do not follow the wishes of other people blindly. Stand by your vocation and beliefs.

Health, Feelings and Social life: Be careful; do not change your plans or lifestyle only because other people tell you to do so.

Fifth Nine

Unexpected illness.
Do not take medicine and you will rejoice.

Unexpected trouble unfolds. Let the situation take its own course, do not interfere and the problems will improve by themselves.

Career: Do not get involved with things that are not your own responsibility, do not bear the blame for things outside your control. Wait and see what happens, do not hurry to correct problems that you have not originated.

Private life: Do not try to regulate everything or to fix all troubles around you. A hands-off approach is the best option. Let things and people take care of themselves.

Health, Feelings and Social life: Your body will heal itself, interfering with it only will make things worse. Some diseases should be left to run its own course, until they disappear naturally.

Top Nine

Innocent action brings misfortune.
No place is favorable.

Stop right now. Following your natural impulses only will get you into trouble. The time for innocent behavior is gone. Wait until new opportunities arise, until then do nothing.

Career: There is no way you can do anything to improve your position now. Keep a low profile and be still, in that way you will minimize your losses.

Private life: You cannot do anything more. Try to keep to yourself; further actions will produce only trouble.

Health, Feelings and Social life: Time for meditation and stillness. Stop and wait.

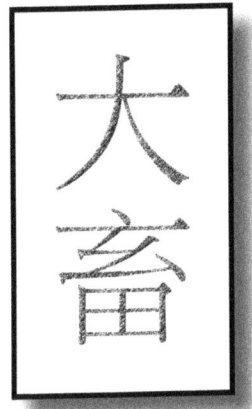

dà chù
Great Accumulation

Associated meanings

The taming power of the great, controlled power, great domestication, great restraint (what is restrained accumulates its strength), big accumulation, great nurturing, gathering up and developing resources for future use.

Judgment

> Great Accumulation.
> The determination is favorable.
> Not eating at home brings good fortune.
> It is favorable to cross the great river.

Before accomplishing great achievements, you should muster your resources. Do not act before making appropriate preparations.

To leave your own home in order to look for sustenance means to expand, to overcome your current limits.

In ancient China, crossing rivers, either at a ford or when the river was frozen, was not an easy task. It implicated dangers and hardships; hence crossing the great river means to carry out a difficult undertaking.

26 - Great Accumulation

The Image

Heaven in the middle of the mountain: The image of Great Accumulation. Thus, the noble is acquainted with many words and deeds of the past and cultivates his character.

Heaven in the middle of the mountain symbolizes hidden treasures. Knowledge from the past is a valuable treasure that not only has intellectual value but also can be applied to the present. Before embarking in a new venture gather as much information as possible about it and also look at how similar projects have fared in the past.

The Chinese character translated as "character" also means "ability, aptitude, quality"; increasing your knowledge will surely make you more able and confident. Also, the deeds of other people in the past will provide you with good role models to follow.

First Nine

> Danger.
> It is best to halt.

It should be better to wait for a change in the current conditions, because there are dangerous obstacles ahead blocking your path.

Career: Do not take any risks nor invite any conflicts. Stop now.

Private life: This is not the proper time to starting anything new. Wait until things improve.

Health, Feelings and Social life: Do not try anything new. Be conservative.

Second Nine

> The axle brackets are removed from the carriage.

The axle brackets are two pieces of wood underneath a cart, which hold the axle firmly on both sides. If they are removed the carriage will not move, no matter how much power is applied to push or drag it.

You will not receive any warnings before your are stopped, and your advance will be completely checked since the repressing power is incontestable. It is time to submit and wait, storing up resources for future usage.

Career: Use self-restraint and wait patiently until you have a good opportunity.
Use your time constructively, increasing your knowledge and resources.

Private life: Protracted conflicts in the family. Wait patiently.

Health, Feelings and Social life: Time of impasse.

Third Nine

> Good horses that run one after another.
> Fortitude under trying conditions.
> Exercise every day with chariots and defensive measures.
> It is favorable to have a goal.

The blockage is removed and you can advance along with other people of the same mind, like horses running together.

Danger and further difficulties lurk ahead, do not be reckless. Your determination will be tested.

To make your plans work, mobility, speed and good defensive measures will be required.

It is imperative that you take precautions and every conceivable defensive measure. Training with chariots indicates that you should check and recheck your plans, make sure that they will work as intended, and also to be ready to make adjustments on the go.

Career: A promotion and some challenges lie ahead. Prepare yourself and don't let your guard down, you may have to defend yourself. You will need to acquire new abilities to face your new responsibilities.

Private life: You will have new opportunities, and with the collaboration of your friends or family, you will make the most of them. But you are in danger, advance with caution and firmness. Be open to learn new things to improve yourself.

Health, Feelings and Social life: If you have health problems, they will improve. Do not be reckless, take all the time you need to adjust your body to the new circumstances.

Fourth Six

> The protective covering of the horns of the calf.
> Outstanding good fortune.

Preventing a young bull from goring anyone with his horns before they have grown indicates that precautionary measures should be applied long before real danger is present, to prevent trouble in advance. Also it means than you should control the people under your responsibility to avoid potential trouble.

In the same way, applying this to you inner self, you should exercise self-control and avoid taking any action before you are ready for it.

26 - Great Accumulation

The main theme of this hexagram is to accumulate power by restraining and channeling properly your strength without wasting it prematurely, and in that way avoiding falling into danger.

Career: Good fortune comes from biding the right time. Do not make a false start; discipline yourself and those under your command. If you act in the right moment you will be very successful.

Private life: Hold back for a while until you can handle things better, without making a costly mistake.

Health, Feelings and Social life: Time for restraint and learning.

Fifth Six

> The tusks of a castrated boar.
> Good fortune.

The raw power has been tamed; the energy is sublimated and now it can be used without danger.

Danger can be external, coming from other people; or internal, if you lose control of your passions.

Here the danger is neutralized in his source and at last you can apply the power successfully.

Good fortune is the result of regulating effectively your energy and using it for the good.

Career: Excellent options for advancing your career or business, but you should exercise firm discipline.

Private life: If you can prevent the situation from getting out of control you will be lucky. Keeping yourself cool and controlled is essential to avoid trouble.

Health, Feelings and Social life: You are your own master. Excellent balance and stamina. Good health. Not good for romantic love.

Top Nine

> Attains the way of heaven.
> Success.

An alternative translation would be "receives the blessings from heaven". At this point all obstacles have been overcome and you will find the appropriate way of expression to fulfill your potentialities. The way of heaven means to have a very broad scope of action.

The "way of heaven" also may indicate that you will fulfill your destiny and that you are following commands from above. The Chinese character translated as "heaven", *tiān*, only appears three times as a religious concept (instead the physical sky) in the Judgment and lines, once in this hexagram and two more times in the hexagram 14. In this context it means "divine, power above the human".

Career: Great success in all your endeavors.

Private life: A very good moment. You will make no mistake and all will proceed according to your plans.

Health, Feelings and Social life: You will achieve an authentic spiritual realization.

27

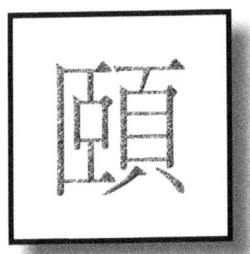

yí
Nourishment / The Jaws

Associated meanings

Nourish, feed, to care for in the early years of life; the jaws, the chin, the cheeks, jawbones.

Judgment

> Nourishment.
> Determination brings good fortune.
> Watch what you nourish
> and what you are looking to fill your mouth with.

This hexagram is related to nourishment, which includes not only material food but emotional and spiritual nourishment as well.

The three lower lines nourish themselves (material nourishment) and the three upper lines nourish other people (spiritual nourishment).

Choosing the right source of nourishment for your spirit is important, since it will determine the kind of people that you will become.

To watch the nourishment means not only to select the right values for your spiritual nourishment, but also the right food for your table. Also you shouldn't take your nourishment at the expense of other people.

The Image

> Under the mountain is the thunder: The image of Nourishment.
> Thus the noble is careful with what he says,
> and restrained in his drinking and eating.

27 - Nourishment / The Jaws

Your words affect the people around you, they can nourish others emotional and spiritually or damage them. The kind of food you incorporate into your body may damage you if you are not temperate. In both cases the jaws are used either for taking food or for saying words. Also, the things you watch and hear are part of the nourishment of your spirit.

First Nine

> You let your magic turtle go and look at me with your jaws hanging. Misfortune.

Losing the magic turtle indicates that you are not taking care of your responsibilities as you should. The magic turtle symbolizes your intelligence and initiative. You should be able to take care of yourself easily; you have the means to do that. But instead you look at other people with envy. Such dependent attitude will be bad for you.

Take control of your own life and accept responsibility for your own decisions.

Turtle shells were used as an oracular medium long before the *Yijing* was in use. During the *Shang* and *Zhou* dynasties, ox shoulder blades and turtle's shells were used to divine. With time, the *Zhou* dynasty replaced that method by yarrow stalks to query the *Yijing*. Hence, the magic turtle indicates oracular powers and spiritual insight. Also the turtles were a symbol of longevity.

Career: You may get demoted because your mistakes or you can lose an important business.

Private life: If you don't take care of your own interests and instead expect others taking care of you, such attitude will cause you plenty of trouble.

Health, Feelings and Social life: Take care of your health, do not neglect it.

Second Six

> Forages in the summit.
> Turns away from the path and goes to the summit for Nourishment. Going forward brings misfortune.

You are seeking nourishment in the wrong place instead doing the job of providing for yourself as you should do. If you continue on the wrong path you will face misfortune.

The Chinese word translated as "summit", in this context also indicates danger of falling down or being overthrow. If you do not know any limit and measure and take excessive risks, you will fall down.

Career: If you invade other's people turf or try to take what is property of others you will get in trouble. Do your job instead taking advantage of the efforts of other people.

Private life: You are breaking the rules for personal profit and convenience, but your designs will only work for a short while. At the end you will pay dearly for it.

Health, Feelings and Social life: Abusing your health will damage your body.

Third Six

Rejects Nourishment.
The determination brings misfortune.
Do not act for ten years.
Nothing at all is favorable.

Seeking the wrong nourishment with persistence will trap you in a vicious cycle that will damage your health.

Ten years indicates a long period, like in the hexagrams **3.2** or **24.5**.

Career: You may be tempted to go the wrong way, but if you do that your career or business will be become stagnant for a long time.

Private life: Taking the wrong turn, seeking for nourishment in the wrong places will cause long lasting damage to your life.

Health, Feelings and Social life: If you nourish yourself with the wrong food you will damage your health, both physically and spiritually.

Fourth Six

Forages in the summit.
Staring like a tiger, with greed and insatiable desire to chase.
No defect.

The summit is a high place which allows a clear view all around, it indicates clarity of mind and intent. The tiger is a symbol of extreme *yang*, powerful and energetic, but in this case such strong desire is oriented toward nourishing others in the right way, for that reason there you will make no mistakes.

The fourth line symbolizes a minister who is working for his king, looking out for reliable helpers.

Career: You may be a recruiter of personnel or somebody who is looking for the right people for a job. You will do your work properly because your strong desire is oriented towards following your duty.

27 - Nourishment / The Jaws

Private life: You will receive help from other people to help you to fulfill your duties.

Health, Feelings and Social life: If you have some illness, this is a good moment for searching the proper treatment for it.

Fifth Six

> Moving away from the path.
> The determination brings good fortune.
> He cannot cross the great river.

To move away from the path indicates that you cannot find a way to help and nourish others under the current circumstances and you will have to look for unconventional ways to comply with your responsibilities. You will need the help of a wise person (the sixth line) who will guide you with his experience and knowledge.

Not crossing the river means to recognize your own limitations and to avoid doing dangerous things that are beyond your means, but instead to seek guidance.

Career: Do not take over more that you can manage on your own. If you are insecure, ask for guidance from experienced people.

Private life: You are in a good position but you are facing some issues that you cannot handle by yourself. Do not hesitate in asking for help form other people who know best than you.

Health, Feelings and Social life: Seek guidance outside the conventional path. Be open to alternative treatments.

Top Nine

> The source of Nourishment.
> Danger, but good fortune.
> It is favorable to cross the great river.

You have the power to educate, guide and nourish other people. Do not take your responsibilities lightly, if you are careful you will have success.

In ancient China, crossing rivers, either at a ford or when the river was frozen, was not an easy task. It implicated dangers and hardships; hence crossing the great river means to carry out a difficult undertaking.

Career: You are ready to carry on difficult tasks, guiding and educating other people. If you are cautious you will be successful.

Private life: This is an auspicious moment. You can help other people and accomplish a great deal of good. If you realize the dangers involved and act with prudence you will not fail.

Health, Feelings and Social life: Crossing the great river means attaining an increased level of conscience, but you should take precautions to avoid the danger.

28

dà kuo
Great Excess

Associated meanings

Overload, critical mass, excess of the great, major superiority, preponderance of the great, inner preponderance.

Judgment

> Great Excess.
> The main beam sags.
> It is favorable to have a goal.
> Success.

The four internal *yang* lines in this hexagram symbolize a supporting beam that is overloaded. The *yin* lines on the bottom and the top are the weak support of the inner *yang* lines. The text says "the main beam sags", it means that the load is too heavy for the supporting beam, which is straining beyond its endurance.

The *yang* lines symbolize power, energy that is reaching the breaking point. This is an extraordinary time because the abundance or *yang* energy, but it also requires extraordinary measures to avoid trouble and balance the situation because the foundation is not stable.

You are overburdened and stressed; to be successful you should decide what to do and then advance towards your goal without wasting any time. It is time to take prompt action, but with utmost care and without violence.

28 - Great Excess

The Image

> The lake covers the trees: The image of Great Excess.
> Thus the noble remains alone without fear
> and retreats from the world without regret.

The lake covering the trees symbolizes a situation that has reached a critical point, that is no longer under control.

The threes under water also indicate that you are isolated and cannot act effectively. Actually you should stop and take distance from your daily troubles for a while; you cannot deal with all the obligations that are wearing you down.

You should decide what you can do and discard what you cannot handle anymore; no matter if that means that you have to leave things or some people behind or if you defy conventional wisdom or political correctness.

First Six

> Use a white reeds offering mat.
> No defect.

The first line is where the movement starts but it also indicates a humble position. Poor people used to place their offerings on mats of grasses, while wealthy people used bronze ritual vessels for that.

The mat or reeds symbolizes taking careful precautions before doing anything. If you advance with caution and sincerity you will make no mistake.

"To place the things on the ground might be considered sufficient; but when he places beneath them mats of the white grass, what occasion for blame can there be? Such a course shows the height of carefulness. The white grass is a trivial thing, but, through the use made of it, it may become important. He who goes forward using such careful art will not fall into any error." (*Ten Wings, Xiaoxiang I*).

Career: You should be frugal and take attention to every detail in your business and expenditures, but do not cut corners.

Private life: Be careful and modest. Take care of your tasks earnestly and carefully.

Health, Feelings and Social life: The sincerity and devotion of your heart is the best offering you can present.

Second Nine

    New shoots grow from a withered willow.
    An old man gets a young wife.
    Nothing that is not favorable.

This line indicates that something that looked withered is being renewed; an unusual alliance is putting new energy into your life.

Also it may indicate that you will look at your life with new eyes and new interests after forming a partnership with a younger or inexpert person.

Career: If you are open to new ideas and are ready to accept new good people you can prosper and revitalize your business. Value people for what they are and what they offer; it doesn't matter if they are beginners or people with a humble résumé.

Private life: Good time to make alliances with young people or people outside your current sphere. Be open to unconventional thinking and look for unexpected opportunities.

Health, Feelings and Social life: If you are ill your health will improve. Be flexible and open-minded. You may get help and support from unexpected quarters or get a new younger partner.

Third Nine

    The main beam sags.
    Misfortune.

If you go too far and are stubborn and inflexible; the price for your arrogance will be failure.

Know your limits and ask for help when needed, otherwise you will struggle with more than you can manage.

Career: Your position is not strong because you did not secure your advance. You may be demoted or your business can go down because your stubbornness and lack of adaptation to new challenges.

Private life: If you are not flexible enough to handle the needs of the moment and are deaf to good advice, you will have trouble.

Health, Feelings and Social life: Pride and arrogance will get you nowhere. You may have trouble with your health because of excessive stress.

Fourth Nine

> The main beam bulges upward.
> Good fortune.
> If there is something else, it will be regretful.

The main beam bulges upward because it is supported from below. It forms an arch and in that way it can support more weight than before.

If you make good use of your current position of strength you will have good fortune, but if you misuse your resources trying to get advantages only for yourself, forgetting your supporters, you will be sorry. Know your limits or you will have trouble.

Career: You will be promoted and your business will prosper. Do not forget those who made possible for you to reach your actual position or you will be shamed.

Private life: You will have plenty of support. You may improve or build your house. Do not be ungrateful.

Health, Feelings and Social life: Your health will improve.

Fifth Nine

> A withered willow produces flowers.
> An old woman gets a young husband.
> Neither failure nor praise.

An old man can have children with a young wife (like the second line suggests), but an old woman cannot do the same with a young husband.

The union described in this line cannot generate good and lasting results, only something evanescent as flowers, which symbolize temporary pleasure. If you try to fix your problems only on the surface, for show, in the long run you will get nowhere.

This line occupies the place of the ruler; a decadent ruler cannot fix his problems by getting help from a strong subject.

Career: You waited for too long. Now it is too late to fix your troubles. Doing things just for show will not help you.

Private life: You may try to renovate your life, but besides having a good time, you will not be able to change anything important.

Health, Feelings and Social life: Wasting your energy, keeping up appearances will not help you in the long run.

Top Six

> Excess when fording the river.
> The water covers the top of the head.
> Misfortune.
> No defect.

If you cope with a dangerous endeavor at any cost (like wading a river that is too deep) it will cost your dearly. You may have to sacrifice too much, because you are not up to the task and you will not be able to finish it successfully.

It is only you who can decide if the sacrifices that you are facing are worthwhile.

Career: You may sacrifice your career for a cause or because you are following your duty regardless of the difficulties or the cost.

Private life: If you continue pushing ahead you will experience heavy losses, but nobody will have anything to say against you.

Health, Feelings and Social life: You may suffer a serious illness or have an accident. Danger of drowning.

29

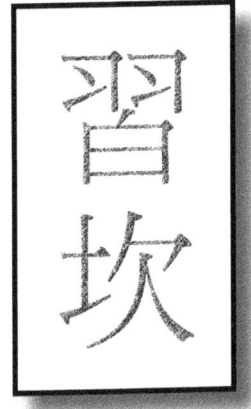

xí kǎn
Pit doubled /
Pit within a pit

This is one of the eight hexagrams that are comprised by the same trigram repeated twice, in this case *kun*, The Abysmal. Please see **The Eight Trigrams** for more information.

Associated meanings

Entrapment, perilous passage, danger, critical time, sinking, pit, trap, snare, pitfall, mastering pitfalls. The meanings are intensified because the first character in the hexagram tag means "repeated", hence it gives the idea a of a long stretch of danger. Pits were dug in the ground to keep prisoners jailed in ancient China.

Judgment

> The Pit doubled.
> If you follow what you feel in your heart you will succeed.
> Moving forward brings rewards.

The situation is dangerous and difficult. To be successful in these critical times you should emulate water, which is the symbol of danger but also tells us how to overcome perilous times. Water flows unceasingly and always is true to itself, it fills every crevice following its course, without ever turning back.

To ride successfully this time you should not retreat, but to advance unceasingly like flowing water, facing every turn of the way with resolution. Follow what your heart tells you and be true to yourself.

29 - Pit doubled / Pit within a pit

You may make mistakes and will be exposed to danger, but if you keep your determination and continue pushing ahead with determination, you will prevail against the odds.

The Image

> The water flows to reach the goal: The image of the Pit doubled.
> Thus the noble maintains constantly his virtuous conduct,
> and practices the job of teaching.

Like the water flowing non-stop, filling all holes in its way, you should take care or every detail. This is not a good time for cutting corners, but to act earnestly and with devotion to the task or duty that you are committed for.

Water flowing unremittingly also symbolizes teaching by example, by repetition.

First Six

> The Pit doubled.
> One falls into a pit at the bottom of the cave.
> Misfortune.

After losing your way you have fallen into a pattern of repetitive mistakes that have trapped you like if you were in the bottom of a double pit. The situation is very serious, if you do not realize how bad it is and do something about it, you will have serious trouble.

Career: Repeated mistakes will put you in dire straits.

Private life: You are trapped by your bad decisions. If you do not correct your behavior you will fall into further danger.

Health, Feelings and Social life: You are harming your health with your bad habits. You may have a chronic illness or even die.

Second Nine

> The Pit is dangerous.
> You can only get small gains.

When confronting dangerous obstacles you can only do small things. Do not try to solve all your problems in a hurry. For now you only can manage to improve a few things, making your situation safer by small steps.

The Chinese word translated as "dangerous" also means "steep, a precipice". Hence the danger of falling down the abyss.

Career: Try to work on the issues that you can handle safely, one at a time. Avoid taking risks.

Private life: You are blocked. The only way to ease your situation is by gradual improvements. Be careful.

Health, Feelings and Social life: Your health will improve slowly and gradually.

Third Six

> Coming to the Pit.
> Deep and dangerous Pit.
> Enters a pit in the cave.
> Do nothing.

You are trapped in a dangerous situation which you do not understand completely. Anything that you try to do to extricate yourself only will worsen your position. You cannot leave from where you are without external help, so until you get it just relax and wait.

Career: You will be stuck in your present bad situation for a while. Wait until you have a good chance to do something positive. If you act now you only will entangle yourself even more deeply in trouble.

Private life: You are stopped in a cul-de-sac, in the middle of trouble and family disputes. Anything that you do only will infuriate more your antagonists. The only way to alleviate your plight is to stop, stay quiet and let things work by themselves for a while until some new factor opens a way out of your troubles.

Health, Feelings and Social life: Anything that you may do to improve your health now may have unintended consequences. Do not try anything new for the time being.

Fourth Six

> A jug of wine over a bowl of rice.
> Using clay pots, delivered jointly by the window.
> At the end there will be no defect.

Proceed with utter simplicity, directness and honesty. You may feel that what you have to offer is not much, but the important thing is to be truthful, that will be enough to avoid making any mistakes.

In another interpretation level, pits were often used as prison cells and this line shows somebody giving help to a person that is imprisoned or trapped in a bad situation, nourishing the prisoner with material or spiritual food.

29 - Pit doubled / Pit within a pit

Career: You will be given a chance to meet an influential person and form with him a mutually beneficial relationship. Focus in the real things that you can offer and be truthful and straightforward.

Private life: You may give or receive help from another person. The important thing are your good intentions no the appearances. Keep it simple and true.

Health, Feelings and Social life: Be sincere and share your feelings.

Fifth Nine

> The Pit does not overflow.
> Only is filled to the brim.
> No defect.

You will get out of your current difficulties. The situation will worsen only up to some point, an then it will stabilize and improve by itself.

Be careful to avoid any excesses, do not overextend yourself.

Career: You will overcome the impediments and then you will be safe. This is not a good moment to start ambitious projects.

Private life: The situation will improve with time. Be careful and keep your balance.

Health, Feelings and Social life: Your health will improve. Have a period of rest.

Top Six

> Tied with a braided rope and a black cord.
> Abandoned in a thorny bush.
> For three years you get nothing.
> Misfortune.

If you insist in going the wrong way you will be punished and trapped by your own folly. You will be stopped and immobilized for a full period because you have broken the law.

The thorny bush suggests that you will be kept captive or trapped in some bad situation (the two Chinese characters translated as "thorny bush" also mean "to keep a prisoner captive in a place").

Three years indicate a full period of stoppage.

Career: You may be arrested or restricted to a bad position until you reconsider your bad ways.

Private life: You will be isolated and stopped in your tracks. You may even be incarcerated.

Health, Feelings and Social life: You may suffer chronic health problems.

30

lí
The Clinging / Fire

This is one of the eight hexagrams that are comprised by the same trigram repeated twice, in this case *lí*, The Clinging. Please see **The Eight Trigrams** (p. 369) for more information.

Associated meanings

Brightness, radiance, clarity; attach, cling, a net, allegiance; name of a bird (oriole or some kind of owl), bird of omen. The modern meaning is to leave.

Judgment

> The Clinging.
> The determination is favorable.
> Taming a cow brings good fortune.

Enlightenment and allegiance are the main themes of this hexagram.

A tamed cow indicates docility and compliance; also it means to know when you should be ready to make concessions.

To have determination but to be compliant as well means that you should do what duty demands, to adhere closely to what is the correct thing to do.

The Clinging also depicts the ability to catch insights and perceptions, like a net, using them to follow the proper path of enlightenment.

30 - The Clinging / Fire

The Image

> Brightness duplicated: The image of The Clinging.
> Thus the great man maintains its clarity,
> illuminating the four cardinal points.

The lower trigram symbolizes clarity within, and the upper external clarity. The meaning of this, applied to human life is that, only having internal insight, knowing yourself well (as indicated by the lower trigram), you will be able to shed light over the world around you (symbolized by the upper trigram) and to understand it in depth.

Fire is consuming, and consequently this hexagram speaks about the transience of life. Only if the fire of enlightenment clings to your life, you will make sense and a good use of it.

First Nine

> Walking with hesitant and cautious steps.
> If you take care there will be no defect.

This line symbolizes sunrise time and the start of a day or a journey through life.

You are beginning your journey still ignoring your destiny and your path. For that reason it is only natural to be cautious and to hesitate for a while. The important thing is to have proper care, if you take reverent attention to the task at hand you will not fail.

Career: Take all the time you need to get a good understanding of the situation before taking any action.

Private life: Do not act with haste. You may try different approaches until you find the best way to proceed.

Health, Feelings and Social life: Be careful with your steps or you may get injured by a fall. If you are convalescent, do not push your recovery, be patient.

Second Six

> Yellow glow.
> Outstanding good fortune.

This line symbolizes the middle of the day when the Sun shines.

You have reached a good understanding. The yellow color symbolizes taking the proper way, the middle path between the extremes, indicating good balance.

Career: You excel at your work and know well what you should do to succeed.

Private life: A propitious moment with good luck and clarity.

Health, Feelings and Social life: Excellent health and spiritual insight.

Third Nine

> In the light of the setting sun, if he does not drum the pot and sing, he will regret the approach of old age.
> Misfortune.

This line symbolizes the setting Sun and the end of a cycle.

A moment of splendor is fading; you can either enjoy the present or be sorry because the good times are going to end soon.

It doesn't matter what you do, you will lose something, but if you accept your fate with docility you will suffer less.

Career: You may experience some losses or possibly retire.

Private life: A cycle of your life is ending. It is a natural occurrence; try to accept it and be happy with what you still have.

Health, Feelings and Social life: You should learn how to cope with losses. Your health may decline.

Fourth Nine

> Comes abruptly, as with fire and death and thus is discarded.

This line describes a rapid ascension, propelled with violence and extreme brightness. Such an accelerated process will not have enough time to consolidate, it will burn quickly, like a straw fire, and extinguish itself with the same velocity.

The person described here will be discarded because he didn't take the proper measures to get support. At the end he will be isolated and forgotten.

Career: If you get quick gains using extreme methods your triumph will not last and finally you will lose all your winnings or your job.

Private life: You will clash with other people because you are too hasty and aggressive. At the end you will be alone.

Health, Feelings and Social life: If you are not more temperate you will ruin your health.

Fifth Six

> Torrents of tears with sorrow and lamentations.
> Good fortune.

30 - The Clinging / Fire

Looking over your past mistakes you will regret bitterly them when you see the things that you have done with a new clarity.

After the darkest hour a new dawning is coming.

Career: Only after you recognize and feel sorry about your past mistakes you will be able to turn defeat in triumph.

Private life: This is a turning point. Regret and shame are the prelude to experiencing new opportunities in your life.

Health, Feelings and Social life: After a time of sorrow your health will improve.

Top Nine

> The king sends him to attack.
> It is worthwhile to execute the leaders and capture those that are not of the same evil sort.
> No defect.

Some problems should be taken care off. To be sent by the kind means that you have real authority and no doubts. Executing only the leaders means to get to the root of the problem, and avoids wasting time with small details.

Killing the leaders may be also translated as "sever the heads"; this phrase emphasizes the need to deal with the cause of the problem, not its manifestations.

Career: Your worth will be recognized and you will be given an important disciplinary task.

Private life: You will put order in your family.

Health, Feelings and Social life: When trying to overcome your own weakness you should stop your bad habits immediately, but avoid mortifying yourself too much. Be strict with yourself, but do not become a masochist.

xián
Influence / Reciprocity

Four hexagrams are related with marriage and the preliminary steps leading to it: 31-Influence, depicts the initial attraction and courtship in a couple; **32-Duration**, indicates the institution of marriage; **53-Gradual Development**, shows the steps and ceremonies leading to marriage and **54-The Marrying Maiden**, describes a young maiden entering an older man's house as a secondary wife.

Associated meanings

Influence, wooing, joined, together, reciprocity, mutual attraction, to unite, feelings, sensitivity.

Judgment

>Influence.
>Success.
>The determination is favorable.

Taking a wife brings good fortune.

Influence is reciprocal; it involves not only influencing others, but also being open to influences from other people.

In this context determination means to be ready to follow the natural course of development of the relationship, without having any secret designs about it.

"Taking a wife" not only means marriage but also may refer to many other kinds of long lasting relationships based on mutual openness, like friendships, family relations, business relations, etc.

31 - Influence / Reciprocity

The Image

A lake on the mountain: The image of Influence.
Thus the noble is open-minded and welcoming for people.

In the same way that water collects in a mountain lake because it is concave, leaving space for storing water, being open-minded will attract people to you. The word translated as "open-minded" also means "humble, modest, pure, unprejudiced".

Such forgiving and receptive attitude will allow you to connect deeply and sincerely with other persons.

First Six

Influence in the big toe of the foot.

The big toe alone cannot move the rest of the body.

At this point your influence is hardly noticeable. You may want to establish a relation with other person who seems to be agreeable, but nobody has made yet any concrete move.

Career: The time to achieve your expectations is not yet ripe.

Private life: You are at a planning stage. You wonder what you may do to reach the other person but until now you have not done anything.

Health, Feelings and Social life: Nothing much will happen since you have not yet decided what to do next. For now stick to conventional methods.

Second Six

Influence in the calves.
Misfortune.
Keeping still brings good fortune.

Advancing before the proper time would cause trouble.

Keep your independence and stay in your own place. Do not let others involve you in a course of action that will compromise you.

Career: This is not the proper time for changing anything. Stay in your position and ignore those who may try to misguide you.

Private life: Wait until you are sure about what you want. Do not let other's opinions to sway you.

Health, Feelings and Social life: This is not a good moment to innovate or to follow the advice of others.

Third Nine

> Influence on the thighs.
> He holds close to what he follows.
> Going ahead causes humiliation.

Do not act rashly. Take enough time to evaluate the situation before doing anything.

Being open to influences is good, but losing your self-control and becoming a puppet of other people or being enslaved by your own desires would be humiliating.

Career: You are a subordinate in a precarious position. Do not let your ambition blind you to the fact that others are taking advantage of you.

Private life: If you do no exercise self-control you will be played as a fool.

Health, Feelings and Social life: Emotional imbalances may affect your health. Try to calm yourself.

Fourth Nine

> The determination brings good fortune.
> Regret vanishes.
> Restless and indecisive comes and goes.
> Only is friends can follow his plans.

Your doubts and lack of resolve are stopping you. This is the proper time to act with determination, choose the path to follow and keep to it.

Since you do not have a wide sphere of influence, only those closely associated with you will support your actions.

The word translated as "follow" also means "adhere, obey, pursue".

Career: Seize the opportunity. You will have support from your close associates.

Private life: After you decide what to do, stick to your plans. Your family and close friends will follow your lead.

Health, Feelings and Social life: Good health. You are insecure but your friends will support you.

Fifth Nine

> Influence in the back of the neck.
> There is no repentance.

The back of the neck can also be translated as "the flesh along the spine above the heart". In either case it means that the influence comes from the

31 - Influence / Reciprocity

heart, from a true source. You have reached a firm decision and have clarity of mind. Such firmness of purpose will allow you to expand your influence steadily.

Career: You are sure about yourself and your goals and hence you can exercise a good influence on others. Your position is secure.

Private life: Your firmness of purpose and sincerity will earn the trust of the people around you.

Health, Feelings and Social life: Excellent physical endurance and good emotional balance.

Top Six

Influence in the jaws, cheeks and tongue.

If you try to influence others only using words with no substance behind them, you will not make any lasting effects.

Career: Empty rhetoric will not benefit you. Your influence will be negligible.

Private life: Actions speak louder than words, if you words are not supported by anything real they will be useless.

Health, Feelings and Social life: The less you speak the more valuable your words will be.

32

héng
Duration / Constancy

Four hexagrams are related with marriage and the preliminary steps leading to it: **31-Influence**, depicts the initial attraction and courtship in a couple; 32-Duration, indicates the institution of marriage; **53-Gradual Development**, shows the steps and ceremonies leading to marriage and **54-The Marrying Maiden**, describes a young maiden entering an older man's house as a secondary wife.

Associated meanings

Duration, persistence, endurance, steadiness, constancy, continuity, for a long time, perpetuation.

Judgment

> Duration. Success.
> No defect.
> The determination is favorable.
> It is favorable to have a place to go.

You should not try to change your status, continue doing the same thing; keep to the right path, focused on your objectives.

To achieve duration you should be ready to adapt to the changing times, but always being true to your goals and commitments.

Traditionally this hexagram is related to marriage, as a long lasting relation that requires constant care and adaptation to endure through the years. Long term relationships require shared goals and constant commitment to be workable.

32 - Duration / Constancy

The Image

Thunder and wind: The image of the Duration.
Thus the noble stands up and does not change its course.

Duration is a dynamic process; keeping still would mean stagnation, but being steady following your goals is the way to achieve duration.

Being flexible and yet persistent you can maintain constancy for a long time. You should keep focused on your objectives but be ready to make any necessary adjustments along the way.

First Six

He goes too far.
The determination brings misfortune.
No target is favorable.

The Chinese word translated as "too far" also means "ask too much, overstep, go beyond". It describes an individual that is too hasty and overzealous.

You are in a low position and you want easy and fast results, but if you don't wait for the right moment and know no boundaries you will commit mistakes that will land you in plenty of trouble.

Career: If you are too impetuous and act without due preparation you will fail. Don't go beyond your area of responsibility or you will clash with other persons in your work.

Private life: Your stubbornness and lack of limits will produce very bad results.

Health, Feelings and Social life: Lack of self-control can affect your health for the worse. Be careful, you may have an accident.

Second Nine

Regret disappears.

If you learn how to be steadfast and keep committed to your goals without making mistakes, you will have no regrets.

You have a strong character but your position still is low, hence prudence and self-improvement are required. You know that you will have a chance to succeed, but it will take some time.

Career: You will prosper in the long run if you are prudent and take care of doing a good job.

Private life: You will not make any mistakes because you know well how to handle yourself and because that you will be free of trouble.

Health, Feelings and Social life: By exercising self-control you will be healthy, both physically and spiritually.

Third Nine

> His character is not constant.
> He may have to bear the shame.
> The determination is humiliating.

To be unhappy with the present situation, dreaming with unrealizable goals and to be dependent of external approval, weakens the character and humiliation is the logical consequence.

If you do not have constancy and fail to meet your commitments you will not achieve anything of value and will be shamed.

Career: If you do not fulfill your duties, your reputation will be ruined and you may be even fired.

Private life: If you do not keep your obligations or your word you will be sorry and your reputation will be in shambles.

Health, Feelings and Social life: An unbalanced state of mind will cause distressing situations.

Fourth Nine

> No animals in the hunt.

Not finding game in the hunt means that your efforts are misplaced or your expectations are out of touch with reality. As a result you will fail.

Perseverance is not enough, you should be flexible enough as to change your approach when you see that what you do is not working properly.

Career: You will expend your energy and resources in failed attempts because your goals are unrealizable, may be for the reason that you are using the wrong methods.

Private life: Your projects will fail because you are looking for non-existent things or you are searching in the wrong place.

Health, Feelings and Social life: Unrealistic dreams will generate frustration.

Fifth Six

> Perseverance in constancy is auspicious for a wife but wrong for a master.

The wife symbolizes a person in a subordinate position, as wives were in ancient China.

32 - Duration / Constancy

This means lack of character or initiative. Also indicates incapacity to adapt to new circumstances.

If you are following the lead of others, not having much character or initiative wouldn't be a fault, but if you are expected to take decisions or you have responsibilities over other people, such deficiency would be wrong.

Career: For a subordinate, absence of initiative may not be wrong, but for a manager this would be a mistake. You may lose an opportunity because you are too rigid or too slow to react to new situations.

Private life: Lack of flexibility or a rigid following of traditions may cause trouble for you if you are the head of the family.

Health, Feelings and Social life: Your beliefs may stop your spiritual evolution making you blind to new thoughts and possibilities.

Top Six

Constantly agitated.
Misfortune.

If you do not calm down and stop your agitation for a bit, your anxiety will bring you misfortune.

To be agitated constantly indicates lack self-control and being reckless.

Career: Uncontrolled and careless actions will land you in trouble.

Private life: Rash actions will cause accidents and mistakes.

Health, Feelings and Social life: You are overstressed. If you do not calm down you will damage your health.

33

dùn
Retreat

Associated meanings

Retreat, escape, evade, strategic withdrawal; hide away, skulk.

Judgment

> The Retreat.
> Success.
> Determination in small matters is favorable.

The two *yin* lines on the bottom of this hexagram represent petty persons that are advancing and forcing better people to retire.

In this time, the only way to avoid losses –for good people– is to withdraw, to stop advancing and retiring to a secure position. By retreating you will avoid failure and also will save face. Retreat also means to keep a low profile, to stay in the background.

Retreating is not the same thing than giving up. Retreating is a strategic move that preserves your strength and lets you plan your future comeback at the proper time.

Determination in small matters means that ambitious goals cannot succeed now, only small things can be done.

The Image

> Mountain under heaven: The image of Retreat.
> Thus the noble keeps the petty afar,
> not with hatred but with reserve.

33 - Retreat

Stern reserve will prevent undesirable people from coming near you. Avoid open confrontations but keep them away by staying out of reach. Do not let them involve you in their petty schemes.

First Six

> At the tail of the Retreat.
> Danger.
> Do not try to undertake anything.

It is too late to retreat safely. By being at the tail of the retreat you are in direct contact with your pursuers and in danger.

You waited for too long, now you must stay quiet until you can see clearly what has to be done. Retreating hastily only would worsen your problems.

The trouble following you may be some unsolved conflict from the past.

Career: Keep a low profile and wait. This is not a good moment for taking risks or fighting.

Private life: Do not draw attention on yourself. Be content with what you have and do not ask for more.

Health, Feelings and Social life: Rest and do not change anything.

Second Six

> Clutching a yellow ox leather no one can remove.

Yellow symbolizes balance, it is the color of the middle and in this case it indicates that you are following the right path and you will stay firmly in it.

This line also indicates that a person in an inferior position (the second line) holds strongly to someone in an elevated position (the fifth line).

Following this idea you should get help from a person more experienced and powerful than you and hold loyal to him.

Career: You will need help from your superiors to get good results.

Private life: By cooperating with other people you will escape from danger.

Health, Feelings and Social life: If you seek guidance for your spiritual development, you will get it.

Third Nine

> An entangled retreat is stressing and dangerous.
> It is favorable to take charge of servants and maids.

An entangled retreat means that your choices are limited. Your freedom is severely restricted by the sentimental attachments or obligations that you have with inferior people.

Until you recover your freedom only small things can be done.

Career: Your choices are limited by the associates that cling to you. If you cannot get rid of them, take the initiative and keep them under your domain.

Private life: Choose wisely your companions. If you have people under you, keep them well disciplined.

Health, Feelings and Social life: Your low desires will prevent you from growing spiritually.

Fourth Nine

Retreats from what he is fond of.
Good fortune for the noble, decline for the vulgar.

To retire from what one likes is not easy. A vulgar man, attached to his pleasures would not be able to do so, since it requires a strong will and commitment to duty to detach yourself from something enticing.

This kind of retreat should be performed with courtesy, without bitterness but with resolve.

You will be able to live well without the person that you are leaving behind, but it is the vulgar who depends on you who will not be able to prosper after you leave.

Career: You should retire and take distance from the people that are taking undue advantage from your work. Do not let them sway you from your purpose.

Private life: Do not let inferior people to exploit you. Let them fend by themselves.

Health, Feelings and Social life: Break-off with bad habits and vices to protect your health.

Fifth Nine

Excellent retreat.
The determination is favorable.

The word translated as "excellent" also means "joyful, happy", meaning that this a friendly retreat, performed in the right moment, without causing any

33 - Retreat

conflicts and with firm determination. In that way you will leave behind no enemies, but people with good will.

Notwithstanding such friendly retreat it is favorable to keep firm your determination.

Career: Plan carefully your retreat and wait until it is the right time. By retiring properly you will leave an open door in the place that you are getting away from.

Private life: By withdrawing from personal relations with good timing and finesse you will be able to avoid generating further conflicts.

Health, Feelings and Social life: If you are ill your health will improve.

Top Nine

Fruitful retreat.
Nothing that is not favorable.

You will be able to retire happily and successfully. Your future prospects are excellent.

Career: You can retire honorably from your work.

Private life: Finally you can withdraw easily from a situation or person that was bothering you. Expect a very successful time.

Health, Feelings and Social life: You are free from material temptations and vices. Very good health.

34

dà zhuàng
Great Power

Associated meanings

Power, strength, strong, robust, big, full grown male, in the prime of life.

Judgment

> Great Power.
> The determination is favorable.

Having plenty of strength any action that you take will have strong effects. But having power and knowing how to use it are two different things.

Determination here means to persevere in the right path, to apply your power in a wise manner, only in that way you will be successful.

The Image

> The thunder at the top of the sky: The image of Great Power.
> Thus the noble does not tread any path that deviates
> from the established order.

Great Power can be really useful only when you are able control it, without causing damage to others or to yourself. Without wisdom and self-control Great Power only causes trouble.

Only by avoiding straying from the correct path and abusing your strength, you will perfect your power; otherwise you will complicate your life and create unending conflicts with other people.

34 - Great Power

First Nine

> Power in the toes.
> To push ahead brings misfortune.
> Have confidence.

The toes indicate the first stage of development. You are in no condition to apply your strength effectively, because you have no connections and you still lack self-control.

Use your power to improve yourself, resist the urge or use your power before you are ready for handling it, or it will be wasted. Be aware of your limitations and wait for more propitious circumstances.

Career: You are still in a preparatory stage. Do no act before you are ready, without having the necessary support.

Private life: Do not be aggressive or reckless. Wait until the situation offers you a good chance to advance without friction.

Health, Feelings and Social life: Do not overexert yourself, be patient. If you are not careful you may hurt your feet.

Second Nine

> The determination is favorable.

The obstacles to your advance are vanishing. At this point it is important to avoid being over-confident but instead exercising moderation.

By avoiding excesses you will have long-standing success.

Career: Your responsibilities and influence will grow. If you use your new resources wisely you will prosper.

Private life: You can begin to apply your power successfully. Be careful and keep a balanced lifestyle.

Health, Feelings and Social life: Your health is improving and you have plenty of energy. Do not be self-indulgent.

Third Nine

> A common man uses the power.
> The noble does not act like that.
> The determination is dangerous.
> A ram butts the fence and his horns get stuck.

Power should be used with moderation to avoid trouble.

To persist in blatant use of power would be dangerous, because when you try to fix a problem with brute force you will cause unnecessary resentment among people.

This hexagram uses the image of a ram as a symbol of abuse of power and lack of self-control, since the shape of the six lines, with two broken lines at the top suggest a ram with its horns at the top.

Getting stuck in the fence means that you will create unforeseen complications if you wield power with arrogance and show disregard for others

Career: By reckless acting you will get trapped in trouble. Do not flaunt your power, keep it hidden.

Private life: If you try to impose your views you will generate disputes and troubles with others.

Health, Feelings and Social life: Arrogance will get you into trouble. You may have mobility issues.

Fourth Nine

> The determination is favorable.
> Regret vanishes.
> The fence is broken and will not entangle you anymore.
> The power lies in the axle-brace of a great carriage.

The mention to "determination" and the fact that "regret vanishes" indicates that you will make no mistakes and will progress with ease in the correct path.

In the same way that a carriage rolling smoothly, supported by its axle, you can move forward with your plans without anything hindering you, because there are no obstacles stopping you any more.

Career: You may get promoted in your job or advance in your business. Your efforts will be rewarded.

Private life: You will be able to use your abundant resources effectively and without glitches.

Health, Feelings and Social life: Any mobility issues will be resolved. Your health will improve.

Fifth Six

> Loses the goat at *Yi*.
> There is no repentance.

34 - Great Power

Yi was the name of a place. Losing the goat at *Yi* means to overcome bad character traits as stubbornness and arrogance although there is also the idea of losing strength or power.

Now you can handle the situation with proper balance and harmony, making no mistakes, because you are strong but flexible.

Career: You will be able to solve any issues peacefully and with ease.

Private life: Because you are polite and tactful you will have no trouble with you relationships.

Health, Feelings and Social life: By sublimating your lower desires your will achieve internal peace. You may die.

Top Six

> The ram butts the fence.
> Cannot retreat and cannot push through.
> Nothing is favorable.
> Fortitude under trying conditions.
> Good fortune.

You have reached a standstill. You went too far and got stopped, now you cannot advance more but neither can retreat.

Stop trying to fix your troubles using force, reconsider the situation and accept your limitations. Try to see the different sides of the issue and look for a new approach.

Career: Your frantic efforts will get you to nowhere. Until you rethink the situation and find a new way, you will be at an impasse.

Private life: Impatience and stubbornness put you into trouble. Stop pushing things hard and reconsider your methods.

Health, Feelings and Social life: Time for a change of heart. Your arrogance put you in a quandary.

35

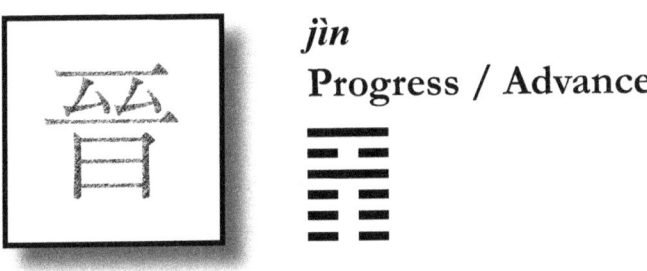

jìn
Progress / Advance

Associated meanings

Progress, advance, promotion, flourishing, increasing.

Judgment

> Progress.
> The Marquis of *Kang* is honored with numerous horses.
> On the same day he is received three times.

The Marquis of *Kang* symbolizes a person whose importance is recognized by the authorities, who support him. Being received three times indicates that he works closely with his superiors and that his progress is continuous.

You should wait for the sanction of the authority before advancing, because albeit you have a high position, it is a dependent one.

The horses symbolize power and means for advancing. The most valuable means that you can have are the people at your service. Hence you should cooperate with other people, for the good of the organization to which you belong.

Kang Hou, the Marquis of *Kang*, was the title of *Feng*, the ninth son of King *Wen*. His name only appears in the Judgment of this hexagram. Most possibly, by the time the text of the this hexagram was written, *Feng* still was the Marquis of *Kang*. Afterwards he was bestowed the fief of *Wei*, since then he was known as the Marquis of *Wei*, and his previous title was forgotten from history. Many *Yijing* versions, following Wilhelm, translate *Kang* as "vigorous", because in Wilhelm time it wasn't know that *kang hou* was the title of *Feng*.

35 - Progress / Advance

The Image

> The brightness of the sun rises over the earth: The image of Progress. Thus the noble himself makes clear his talents.

After you perfect yourself and establish a reputation you will be in condition to get support from the authorities in your field of activity.

Once you have gained some recognition from your superiors, your talents will serve to illuminate not only your way but also to help other people.

On other interpretation level, to "make clear his talents" indicates that before having any repercussion in the world you need to have a clear view of your strengths and weaknesses, know what you want and what are your chances of getting it.

First Six

> Progressing but repressed.
> The determination is favorable.
> Be tolerant of lack of confidence.
> No defect.

At the beginning of the progress you will not have yet earned the confidence of others. Possibly you lack enough experience and because that you cannot get enough support.

Be faithful to your own expectations. Continue working with determination to turn your vision into reality.

Career: You will not receive support and you may be even stopped in your progress by others. Be confident in yourself and continue to move toward your goal. Do not blame others for not believing in you. You will have to earn the trust of other people with hard work.

Private life: You cannot advance at the present moment because people are not helping you. Avoid conflicts with others and continue developing your plans. Have faith in your own potentiality and ignore what others say about you.

Health, Feelings and Social life: You are isolated but nevertheless you are improving yourself. If you continue doing that you will make no mistake.

Second Six

> Progressing with grief.
> The determination is favorable.
> Receives a great blessing from her ancestor.

Progressing with grief means that you have to make some sacrifices to continue advancing forward.

Your progress is difficult because you are still alone, not receiving any help or cooperation from others.

At some time you will receive help, may be from a woman or a motherly figure. Also the "great blessing from her ancestor" may indicate that you will get an inheritance or will receive recognition from your predecessor.

Career: Your work is not easy and your efforts are not recognized yet because you have not found the right approach. You may get help and advice from somebody in your past or perhaps from a colleague who occupied your same position before you.

Private life: You are anxious or in mourning. Have faith in yourself and be patient. You may inherit or receive support from a motherly figure from your past.

Health, Feelings and Social life: You have not found your way yet because you don't know yourself. After you understand your true feelings you will know what you have to do.

Third Six

All agree and trust.
Regret disappears.

You gained the trust and cooperation of your peers. By working with other people you will be able to carry out your goals successfully.

"Regret disappears" means that all involved people share the same objectives and that they have no doubts about them.

Career: You will get support and will advance in your career, not alone but within a team.

Private life: Your friends and family will trust and help you because all them share the same commitment than you.

Health, Feelings and Social life: Your internal conflicts have been overcome. You know clearly what you want to do.

Fourth Nine

Progressing as a squirrel.
The determination is dangerous.

35 - Progress / Advance

The word translated as squirrel indicates a rodent of some sort. Such animals were seen as a plague since they destroyed the crops. The squirrel symbolizes a dishonest and aggressively greedy behavior.

The sense of this time is to progress along with other people, not to monopolize all goods for yourself. If you continue behaving rapaciously you will be punished.

Career: If you only care for immediate gains for yourself, without thinking about other people, you will be disciplined and may be even fired.

Private life: If you do not control your greed, your avaricious conducts will cause many disputes that will put you in trouble.

Health, Feelings and Social life: Ambition and recklessness have made you blind to the spiritual values.

Fifth Six

> Regret disappears.
> Do not worry about loss or gain.
> Going forward brings happiness.
> Nothing that is not favorable.

"Regret disappears" indicate that you have no doubts; you are fully focused in your duty, without being obsessed with the chances of gain or loss, victory or failure.

Your commitment and fine balance will make you happy and successful. You will make no mistakes.

Career: A humble attitude which is able to delegate tasks to the subordinates, not superseding them, and also to heed the advice from the experts –the sixth line–, will make you successful.

Private life: Do not worry about minor details. You really enjoy what you do and you do it superbly, because that you will be both happy and successful.

Health, Feelings and Social life: Excellent health. You have a very good physical and spiritual balance.

Top Nine

> Progressing with the horns.
> Use them only to punish your own city.
> Danger, but there will be good fortune.
> No defect.
> The determination is humiliating.

Punishing your own city means to discipline yourself and the people under your leadership.

The time for progress is ending. Since you cannot advance more, use your energy to put in order your own sphere of influence.

This is the last line of the hexagram, so there is danger of matters getting out of hand, but that would not justify you to use extreme measures to punish others. If you do that you will be humiliated.

Career: Focus in your own self-control first and the discipline of people under you command after. You can still be successful, but only if you keep a proper balance.

Private life: You may discipline yourself harshly, but do not apply the same hard methods to other people.

Health, Feelings and Social life: Self-control and discipline are good things, but only in the proper measure. Do no overexert yourself or your health will suffer.

36

míng yí
Suppressed Light

Associated meanings

Darkening of the light, hiding the light, brightness dimmed, light suppressed, hiding one's brilliance; censorship.

Judgment

> Suppressed Light.
> Fortitude under trying conditions brings good fortune.

You are coping with adverse circumstances. Neither your words nor your deeds will be appreciated by others.

Lowly people will harass and keep grievances against you. Avoid attracting attention to yourself; do not exhibit your knowledge or your talents, since that would draw hostility upon you.

Do not tell other people about your opinions or plans; keep true to your objectives and continue ahead following your own way, firmly, but quietly.

Suppressed Light also may indicate that the situation is not clear or your perception is clouded.

The Image

> Light has come into the earth: The image of the Suppressed Light.
> Thus the noble deals with the masses, concealing his talents,
> but still illuminating.

36 - Suppressed Light

Keep a low profile. Light hidden under the earth means that in times of intellectual decadence it is dangerous to show your brilliance.

Bear with patience the ignorance of others and do not try to correct or criticize them. It is preferable that they take you for a fool rather than antagonizing them. The important thing is to keep your clarity of mind for yourself.

First Nine

> Suppressed Light during the flight.
> He lowers his wings.
> The noble goes along the road for three days without food,
> but has somewhere to go.
> The host gossips about him.

Some danger or an unexpected contingency will compel you to scale down your plans. Lowering the wings indicates that you cannot advance for the moment and you have to descend, avoid attracting attention and resigning some ambitions.

You will not abandon your objectives. The three days on the road without food indicate that you will persevere in spite of the lack of resources, being faithful to your goals.

People will not understand and will criticize you, that is other reason for keeping a low profile.

Career: Decrease your exposure and avoid drawing attention to yourself. You will have to postpone some things, but with some sacrifices you will get along. You will lose the trust from your superiors and peers for a time, because they do not understand you, and may even conspire against you. Do not lose faith in yourself and your goals.

Private life: People around you have their minds clouded; they will misunderstand and resist you. You must to continue ahead by yourself, with decreased means. Do not abandon you goals, if you are strong, in the long run you will be successful. You may have trouble with your landlord.

Health, Feelings and Social life: Possible slight injury to your hands or feet. You may have limited mobility for a time.

Second Six

> Suppressed Light.
> Wounded in the left thigh.

> Rescued by a powerful horse.
> Good fortune.

To be wounded in a leg means that resistance against you is mounting; it will decrease your means and hurt your capacity for advancing, but it will not disable you entirely.

The left is the direction of retreat, hence to be wounded in the left thigh may indicate that you are wounded from your back, that you didn't see the blow coming.

The horse is a symbol of courage, spirit and moral strength to resist opposition; it means that if you keep up your resolution you will surmount the difficulties and will even help those under your responsibility. The horse also indicates that you will improve your mobility and capacity for advancing.

Career: You career and plans are hindered by some serious opposition. Do not let them stop you; keeping your mobility and your spirit up is the proper way to overcome your troubles.

Private life: Remain confident in the face of opposition, do not lose your calm and carry on. If you do not give up you will have good fortune.

Health, Feelings and Social life: You are in the right path; do not let others discourage you. You may have an accident and hurt your lower extremities.

Third Nine

> Suppressed Light during the hunt in the south.
> The great leader is caught.
> Cannot be hurriedly determined.

The hunt means to search for a way to solve the present difficulties. In ancient China the south was placed at the top of the maps, thus this indicates that you are hunting for a person in an elevated position, who is the source of all the troubles.

Only when the "Lord of Darkness" (the sixth, top line), is finally uncovered you will find a way to fully understand and control the situation.

To solve the current bad situation you should not be too hasty, the problems that you are trying to fix have existed for a long time and they should be corrected gradually.

Career: Your task will be to clean up a complicated and obscure situation. You may be an investigator or somebody who is looking for clues to find where is the origin of the current troubles.

36 - Suppressed Light

Private life: You will face conflicts and suspicion until you discover who is the source of your troubles. Take your time to determine the best way to fix your problems.

Health, Feelings and Social life: The cause of your ailments will be found, but it will take some time to restore hour health.

Fourth Six

> Enters the left side of the belly.
> Grasps the heart of the Suppressed Light.
> Leaves the gate and courtyard.

You will get to the bottom of the matter; the heart of darkness is the central point, from where you will know everything. The mention to the "heart" and "the left side of the belly" indicate that you have access to the inner machinations of the one that is the source of all darkness. You are close to a dangerous and evil person and even may have his confidence.

At that point you will know that there is nothing more to do there, it is time for a new stage. Leave your position (the gate and courtyard) and escape from there.

Career: You may be assigned to a new position or place or you may leave voluntarily your position to avoid troubles.

Private life: There is no chance of improving matters. Your best option is to make a clean break and start anew.

Health, Feelings and Social life: You should rest to restore your health, take it easy, but do not stand still. According to traditional Chinese beliefs, *hún*, the light spirit normally occupies the area above and behind the space between the eyes. During rest it goes to the liver, which is inside the belly.

Fifth Six

> Suppressed Light (as) Prince *Ji*.
> The determination is favorable.

Prince *Ji* was the minister the last *Shang* king, a tyrant who allowed no opposition. Because of his family connections he couldn't withdraw from the court and instead feigned madness to avoid being involved with the evil king, but remain safe.

Your situation is very complicated; you cannot withdraw from a dangerous situation and making public what you really think should put you in danger.

Following Prince *Ji* example, the best way out of danger is to conceal your brightness under a dull or crazy exterior.

Be cautious and do not enter in conflict with other people, let them think that you are inoffensive and clueless. Stay clear from involving yourself with any evil doings.

Career: Keep up your principles and avoid becoming part of illegal or immoral actions. It is better to remain aside, without taking intervention.

Private life: You family life will be troublesome. It would be better for you to pretend ignorance; do not involve yourself with the current troubles, but do not abandon your principles.

Health, Feelings and Social life: You cannot express yourself, but you will keep your mind clear and strong.

Top Six

No light, but darkness.
First ascended to heaven.
Later sank into the earth.

After darkness reaches its climax it will begin to fall. This describes a person who achieved a high position but used his power wrongly to suppress the truth.

The situation was totally wasted because lack of vision and wrong handling, and for that reason it now starts to disintegrate.

The fall of the dark forces, in turn, will open the road for progress.

Career: The situation is unstable. Those in power will fall and their business may collapse.

Private life: The situation went too far and now it will fall by its own weight. You may have some losses.

Health, Feelings and Social life: Health set-back. Risk of death.

37

 *jiā rén*
The Family / The Clan

Associated meanings

Family, house people, household, home, to keep a home; clan, close-knit group.

Judgment

> The Family.
> The determination is favorable for a woman.

In ancient China all members of a household subordinated themselves to the head of the family, hence this hexagram describes a hierarchical structure, where all members cooperate between them and obey the leader of the group. It can describe any close-knit group or hierarchical human association.

The determination of a woman refers to the proper conduct of a subordinate, as women were in ancient China; it means to take care of supporting, preserving and nurturing the members of the group or family. The duties of a subordinate are oriented towards the inside of the group, since it is the household's head the one who will take care of the group's interaction with the outside.

The Image

> The wind comes from the fire: The image of The Family.
> So the noble's speech is anchored in reality and his actions have duration.

37 - The Family / The Clan

Following traditional Confucian thinking, the relationships within a family mirror the human connections in larger groups, like a business or a country. Also they are analog to the internal workings of the psyche, where the conscience is the master and our passions are the household people.

Making your words true and your behavior consistent is very important inside the family because you cannot influence in a good way your family if you are not steady and trustworthy.

People who lead another people, either in a family, or in any other kind of human group need to keep good discipline in the group. If you are not consistent or are too permissive you will not be able to lead any human group effectively.

First Nine

> With firm boundaries in The Family regret vanishes.

The first line of a hexagram always describes the first developments of a situation.

In this case clear responsibilities and limits should be established for everyone in the group from the start. This will avoid conflicts and discussions in the future. Also it is best to prevent problems than correcting them after they have got entrenched.

Career: It is very important to assign clear duties and areas of influence to everybody in your team to avoid infighting and misuse of resources.

Private life: Children should know that there are limits and rules, and that every member of the family should take care of his responsibilities, respecting the other members.

Health, Feelings and Social life: Self-discipline and restraint are required to keep you healthy.

Second Six

> Unpretentious.
> Stays inside preparing food.
> The determination is favorable.

To stay inside preparing food indicates that you have to support others and you are not independent.

Do not try to bend the rules to follow your whims. Learn to follow the rules and fulfill your duty first.

Stay in the background; do not try to call attention over yourself.

Career: You are at the center of the group, making an important contribution. Keep focused in your responsibilities; if you stray from your tasks you will damage the whole group. You will prosper only if you fulfill your duty.

Private life: Your tasks may seem boring but you support the whole family. Do not look elsewhere for excitement, people need you, your service at home will be most appreciated and will benefit the whole family.

Health, Feelings and Social life: Keep to the tried and tested and you will be fine. This is not time for foraging into the unknown. Take good care of your nutrition.

Third Nine

> A family run with stern severity will cause regrets,
> but there will be good fortune.
> Women and children chuckling and giggling will end in shame.

Women and children symbolize lack of discipline, overindulgence and disordered behavior.

Sometimes it is difficult to get the proper balance between discipline and laxity. If you are too hard with others they will complain, but if the family or group gets disorganized and chaotic this will cause sorrow in the long run.

Try to avoid the extremes, do not be too harsh or too indulgent, but when in doubt stick to the rules. The basic idea here that it is better to err on the side of discipline instead being too lax.

Career: It you are too indulgent you will be criticized, but if you are too stern you may be censured as well. In the end your best option is to keep things running smoothly by applying the rules strictly, no matter what others may say.

Private life: You will have some pleasures and plenty of troubles. Keep both your temper and the people under your responsibility well controlled.

Health, Feelings and Social life: If you alternate between over-indulgence and extreme mortification this will make you suffer; try to find a more balanced lifestyle.

Fourth Six

> A thriving family.
> Great good fortune.

The fourth line is the place of the minister, a person with important responsibilities, who runs effectively the internal side of an organization.

37 - The Family / The Clan

In a traditional family this is the place of the wife, who makes the household thriving by keeping things in order and supporting everybody.

Your service is vital; it will be much appreciated and will contribute greatly to the success of your family or group. At this point there are no conflicts, the people for whom you work for are trusting and cooperative.

Career: You work will enrich your business and you will prosper accordingly.

Private life: Happiness and prosperity.

Health, Feelings and Social life: Excellent health.

Fifth Nine

> The king approaches his family.
> Do not worry.
> Good fortune.

The king symbolizes a respected and wise person who benefits the family or group with good leadership.

In turn, the people in the family trust and welcome their leader.

Good fortune is the result of good leadership and people willing to cooperate with each other.

Career: You will be welcomed to your new post and will be able to work seamlessly together with the people under your authority.

Private life: You will be supported and appreciated by the members of your family.

Health, Feelings and Social life: Excellent health. Very good relations with other people.

Top Nine

> He inspires confidence and respect.
> At the end there will be good fortune.

Your qualities and the excellence of your work are recognized. People will follow your example without questions because they trust you.

Career: An inspirational leader is depicted here. Such people lead naturally without strenuous effort because people want to emulate them.

Private life: The whole family or group will prosper because they follow a good example. This line may depict a respected elder member of the family.

Health, Feelings and Social life: You are inspired by the right values and as a consequence you will grow spiritually.

38

kuí
Antagonism / Opposition

Associated meanings

Diverging, extraordinary, opposition, polarization, estrangement, alienation, disharmony; to look askance, as in disapproval.

Judgment

> Antagonism.
> Good fortune in small matters.

Antagonism means that people have misunderstandings and diverging objectives; as a result they are estranged, opinions are polarized and it is difficult to find common ground.

When people cannot work together only small things can be done, therefore instead trying to fix the whole problem, you should concentrate in solving small matters and finding common ground in the least contended issues.

Antagonism only can be overcame by leaving behind the misunderstandings and finding a way to cooperate. Be tolerant, avoid confrontation and make an effort to understand the point of view of your antagonists.

This hexagram mentions chance meetings, gains and strange loses in several lines. Be adaptable and open to new opportunities.

From a psychological viewpoint antagonism characterizes somebody who cannot decide what to do and has a split personality.

38 - Antagonism / Opposition

The Image

> Fire is above, lake below: The image of Antagonism.
> Thus the noble is companionable, but maintains its uniqueness.
> It is important to see the common factors for all sides of a situation.

You have your unique viewpoint, but with empathy and tolerance you will be able to understand and accept the position of other people and to share some things with them, disregarding the fact that your own opinion may be different.

First Nine

> Repentance fades.
> Do not chase the horse that got away.
> It will return on its own.
> You will find bad people, but you will not make mistakes.

Do not try to force back estranged subjects. Sometimes misunderstandings will make some people break away, but in time they will return to your side.

Hostile people should be handled with diplomacy. The important thing is to avoid mistakes that would magnify the alienation of other persons.

A lost horse also is an image of distress and loss of strength.

Career: Some people will not cooperate and others may be downright evil. Do not let them deviate you from your goals, instead ignore them. Indecisive people may reconsider in time and bad people should be disregarded. If you focus in your goals and avoid making mistakes they will not harm you.

Private life: Do not try to push your agenda over other people. If some disagree or are not friendly, do not pay attention to them.

Health, Feelings and Social life: If you keep your spiritual balance other people cannot harm you.

Second Nine

> He meets his master in an alley.
> No defect.

A fortuitous encounter will allow you to encounter a kindred spirit at an unlikely place.

You may find a valuable person in the least expected place, and receive guidance and support from him.

Good prospects.

Career: A chance meeting will allow you to get help from a person of high position.

Private life: You will receive help from a good friend.

Health, Feelings and Social life: You will find clarity and guidance.

Third Six

> He sees his cart pulled back.
> His oxen and his men arrested, marked and mutilated.
> There is no (a good) start but (a good) end.

In ancient China criminals were tattooed in the forehead or mutilated depending on the crime committed by them.

This line indicates loss of position. You will be punished and humiliated. Your projects will be stopped.

Your advance will be blocked until you get help from a superior force.

The Chinese character translated as "mutilated" literally means "to cut off the nose". The character translated as "marked" means to be branded on the forehead or to cut off the head's hair or the top knot. This knot was a symbol of status, so it means that the subject status is diminished or its pride is injured.

Career: You may be demoted, lose face and take losses, but in the end, with external help, you will prevail.

Private life: Plenty of troubles. People will mistreat and insult you. If you do not lose faith in yourself and get some help, you will be successful in the end.

Health, Feelings and Social life: Your health will take a turn for the worse; you may have surgery. At the end all will turn out well.

Fourth Nine

> Isolated by antagonism.
> One meets an outstanding man (that can become a) truthful partner.
> Danger.
> No defect.

Mistrust and alienation keep people apart, isolated.

By establishing an alliance with a very good person you will overcome the antagonism.

Breaking the distrust will not be easy, as any alliance implies risks, but the goal is worthwhile and joining will be no mistake.

38 - Antagonism / Opposition

Career: Although you are currently isolated, you will receive help and support from important people.

Private life: You will make a new friend. Be careful when starting a new relationship, it will be promising but should be handled with care. If you asked the oracle about marriage you will find a good spouse.

Health, Feelings and Social life: Your health will improve with the help of a knowledgeable person.

Fifth Six

> Repentance fades.
> In the temple of the clan they eat meat.
> How could it be a mistake to go there?

To meet in the temple of the clan means to become part of a close-knit group. To eat meat indicates abundance.

Troubles disappear when you find a good human group to belong to.

Career: You will advance in your career or business after you find trustworthy associates.

Private life: Isolation and misunderstandings are gone. You family life is harmonious and you enjoy a good prosperous time with your loved ones.

Health, Feelings and Social life: Excellent health and happiness.

Top Nine

> Isolated by antagonism.
> He sees (the other as) a pig covered with mud, a carriage full of demons.
> First tenses his bow, but then puts it aside.
> It is not a robber but a marriage suitor.
> Going forward rain falls.
> Good fortune.

A dangerous conflict will be avoided when you overcome disagreements and irrational hatreds.

Do not act rashly, think again and you will find that your apparent enemy can become a good partner.

The rain falling down symbolizes relaxation and the clearing of all misunderstandings and hatreds, but you have to take the first step forward to solve the troubles.

Career: The only way to solve the conflicts is by reaching an agreement between opposite factions. If both sides cooperate, everybody will benefit from it.

Private life: This is a good time to leave behind conflicts and divisions and start a friendship anew. If you asked the oracle about marriage you will find a good spouse.

Health, Feelings and Social life: You are not seeing things clearly. If you can leave behind your prejudices you will have a better and happier life.

jiǎn
Hampered / Obstruction

Associated meanings

Lame, hobble, stumble, limp, proceed haltingly, impasse, obstruction, impediment, obstacle; troubles, difficulties.

Judgment

> Hampered.
> The south-west is favorable; the north-east is not advantageous.
> It is favorable to see the great man.
> Determination brings good fortune.

In the *Yijing* south-west indicates retreat and north-east advance, thus the message is clear, the path forward is blocked.

The north indicates isolation and the south the community. You cannot continue alone, you will need help from somebody who has authority and is more knowledgeable than you; also you should be in touch with other persons, do not become isolated, seek cooperation with another people.

To retire means to reconsider your position and look for alternative ways to carry on your objectives. It also means to detach yourself from your current troubles. Stop struggling, relax and look for new options.

To see the great mean also indicates that you have to grow and mature before being ready for advancing.

39 - Hampered / Obstruction

The Image

Above the mountain there is water: The image of Hampered. Thus the noble goes back to himself to cultivate his nature.

When you face an insurmountable obstacle you have to change your approach. To do so you should adjust your view of the situation, to modify your perception and expectations.

The phrase "to cultivate his nature" actually means to adapt and evolve, to grow internally and learn new ways to face the world.

Indeed external obstacles will provide the stimuli for personal growth, which in turn will help you to overcome such obstacles.

First Six

>Going forward is Hampered, going back brings praise.

Advancing will put you in trouble, stay where you are or retreat. Have patience and do not be rash.

Career: This is not the proper time to get an independent position or to challenge the status quo; if you stay in your place your superiors will support you.

Private life: Carry on with your normal routine. Do not try to change what has been working well or you will get into trouble.

Health, Feelings and Social life: Do not innovate. If you are under medical treatment, do not change it.

Second Six

>The king's servant (is struggling with) difficulties.
>Not because of himself.

You are duty bound to take action, no matter the obstacles facing you. You will have to face plenty of difficulties because holding back is not a choice.

Career: You have to face a problem head-on, either because you are following orders from your superiors or because you are taking care of your responsibilities.

Private life: You will be forced to advance and confront directly the impediments ahead. You will have many troubles, but they cannot be avoided.

Health, Feelings and Social life: Severe health problems. Adversity in social life.

Third Nine

> Going forward is Hampered.
> He comes back.

Going back means to reconsider your previous decision and accept that you made a mistake.

Retreat; you do not have the resources to go forward. By going back you will escape danger and return to normality.

Career: Be ready to make adjustments to your plans and retreat when you are in danger. You may be demoted, but the change will be for the better because it will put you out of danger.

Private life: You can escape your current troubles by turning back. It is better to resign something that to lose everything.

Health, Feelings and Social life: You are following a path that goes nowhere. Go back to proven and safe ways.

Fourth Six

> Going forward is Hampered.
> Coming back meets companions.

You cannot continue forward on your own because your path is hampered and you will be isolated if you continue advancing.

Return and cooperate with other people in order to muster enough resources and strength to overcome the obstacles ahead.

Career: You will need to get more expertise and resources to fix the obstacles that are hampering your progress. Do not continue alone, get some allies and helpers or your plans will fail.

Private life: You have gone too far alone. Go back, reconsider what you have done.

Health, Feelings and Social life: You need to reestablish your connection with other people to replenish yourself. Socialize more and get some friends.

Fifth Nine

> When the Obstruction is greater, friends will come over.

The fifth line is the ruler of the hexagram; hence you are the one who is trying to correct the current troubles.

You need collaborators and friends to overcome adversity with their help.

39 - Hampered / Obstruction

Career: You will be supported by the right people and finally you will get over your troubles. Your influence will grow.

Private life: The obstruction will be overcame with the help of good friends.

Health, Feelings and Social life: With external help you will prevail over your current ailments.

Top Six

> Going forward is Hampered, coming back brings great good fortune. It is favorable to see the great man.

You are not directly affected by the current troubles, but you feel that it is your duty to help others in this time of hardship.

To see the great man indicates that you have to look for a capable helper to fix the issues.

Career: Be generous, other people need your help and advice.

Private life: Be ready to help people in need.

Health, Feelings and Social life: Use your wisdom to help others. Do not remain aloof.

40

jiĕ
Liberation

Associated meanings

Deliverance, getting free, release from adversity, untie, loosen, divide, sever, disjoin, untangle, untie a knot, unravel a complication.

Judgment

> Liberation.
> The south-west is favorable.
> If there is nowhere to go return brings good fortune.
> If there is somewhere to go, to be early brings good fortune.

Liberation is the aftermath of the previous hexagram: 39 - *Hampered*. It means release from bondage and hardship.

In the *Yijing* south-west indicates retreat and the community, thus it means that to get free from troubles you should retreat, move away from a situation that is bad for you and avoid being isolated.

A stressful and complicated situation can be unraveled by taking a step back and looking for a new approach.

Take care of not leaving behind loose ends after the situation starts to untangle and you can leave. If there is anything that requires your attention before turning back, you should attend to it promptly.

The Image

> Thunder and rain in action: The image of Liberation.
> Thus the noble forgives excesses and excuses offenses.

40 - Liberation

Thunder and rain clean the atmosphere, they represent liberation from stress and anxiety, since a storm clears the air.

To get proper release from a time of conflict and troubles, you should leave behind hatreds, misgivings and ill feelings, cultivating instead tolerance and being broad-minded.

A new cycle is starting, and you should face it without carrying worries and resentments from the past.

First Six

> No defect.

Relax and restore your energies.

Everything is going well, you will make no mistakes.

Career: You will progress smoothly.

Private life: You will have no worries because you are in touch with the time.

Health, Feelings and Social life: Good spiritual and physical balance.

Second Nine

> One catches three foxes in the hunt and gets a golden arrow. Determination brings good fortune.

The hunt is the will to purge the situation from undesirable elements, either internal or external: the three foxes.

The foxes symbolize greed, ignorance and fear. They are elements of corruption, which create difficulties and harm the progress.

The golden arrow was bestowed to people who did great things (the **hexagram 21.4** also mentions getting arrows, but they are metallic instead of golden), this means that after removing the bad factors (the foxes) you will get rewards. To persevere in the hunt and catch the foxes will bring good fortune.

Career: After you get rid of the people that are disrupting the situation you will prosper and may get a promotion.

Private life: Some bad influences are damaging your life. If you are able to eradicate them you will succeed and be happy.

Health, Feelings and Social life: Greed, ignorance and fear are things that can stop your spiritual development. Do not tolerate them.

Third Six

> One who bears a burden on his back but rides on a carriage attracts bandits.
> The determination is humiliating.

In ancient China, carriages were only used by high-ranking people, hence a baggage bearer had no place into them.

This line describes a low rank person, who sneaked into an elevated position, but he is not ready for his new responsibilities and it shows.

Since his appearance doesn't match reality he will receive no help but instead draw bandits and transgressors around him. If he persists in his charade he will be exposed for what he is and will be shamed.

The line also indicates a debasement of correct behavior, such as impersonating righteousness.

Career: You may be demoted and humiliated. Be aware of your limitations and do not try to do more than you can handle with ease.

Private life: If you insist in living above your means or pretending to be someone you are not, you will regret it. You may get robbed.

Health, Feelings and Social life: Your health will get compromised if you force your body beyond his capabilities. Stop pretending and recognize your limitations.

Fourth Nine

> Deliver yourself from your big toe.
> Then a trusty companion will come.

The big toe helps to walk, but here the big toe indicates dependence on an inferior and unreliable element.

It may be a habit, some people, or anything that you use as a prop for advancing, but it is surely damaging your prospects.

It is time to look elsewhere for support and discard such unworthy element. After you get rid of it, new possibilities will be opened to you and you will get help from good people.

Career: Emancipate yourself for bad relations; do not let evil people draw you into their circle. Your progress will be stopped until you left such people behind.

Private life: You are hampered by a parasitic relation with somebody who is not worth of being your friend. Get rid of him and you will get better friends.

Health, Feelings and Social life: Substance abuse, unhealthy dependences and vices will stop your spiritual progress and damage your health.

Fifth Six

Only the noble can have liberation.
Good fortune.
Inferior people trust him.

Only you can disengage yourself from links with inferior people and degrading habits.

If you are strong enough to liberate yourself you will be successful. Those inferior people whose links you severed will understand that you are in earnest and will not stop your parting.

Career: You will be promoted or advance in your business, leaving behind your current associates.

Private life: After you break your links with the people that are holding you down you will have good fortune.

Health, Feelings and Social life: Focus in you well-being and what is good for you and you will be free from weaknesses and bad habits from your past.

Top Six

The prince shoots at a hawk on a high wall and hits the target.
Nothing that is not favorable.

The hawk symbolizes an evil element in a high position and the last obstacle in your deliverance.

Shooting and hitting the hawk indicates that you should use the appropriate means to take down what is hampering your progress.

There will be no further problems.

Career: You have to do away with a powerful enemy by using the right methods to take him down.

Private life: The hawk on the wall symbolizes what is stopping you from deliverance, what keeps you restricted and in bondage. You will have to act with firmness to get rid of such obstacle, afterwards the outcome will be entirely favorable.

Health, Feelings and Social life: A new cycle will begin in your life as soon you surmount the obstacles that keep you blocked.

41

sǔn
Decrease

Associated meanings

Decrease, diminish, lessen, damage, loss, reduction, sacrifice, sublimation.

Judgment

Decrease with sincerity brings outstanding good fortune.
No defect.
Can be determined.
It is favorable to have somewhere to go.
What should be done?
Two bowls can be used for the offering.

All things increase and decrease periodically with the pass of time, but if you adjust your behavior to the needs of the current time you will be successful in the long run.

In times of shortage what matters most is your attitude. You cannot ignore reality and must be ready to accept some losses and give up some comfort. To be sincere means to accept your position; do not live in the past and make good use of the little things you still have.

Decrease also indicates that you should balance your resources. What exceeds should be restrained, and what is deficient increased.

The bowls were ritual vessels used to offer cooked grain to the spirits. They show the need to give up something and to do more with less, since the bowls were used for modest offerings.

41 - Decrease

The Image

> Down the mountain is the lake: The image of the Decrease.
> Thus the noble controls his anger and restrains his passions.

The lake waters evaporate and fertilize the mountain. In the same way you should apply self-control and keep in check your passions and anger. In return, the restricted energy can be used to improve your spiritual growth.

What is inferior is decreased to increase a superior cause. This is not the time for sensual gratifications and indulgence, but for restrain and servicing the needs of other people.

First Nine

> There is no defect if after finishing your work you go quickly,
> but think about how much you can sacrifice.

Helping other people after doing your tasks is fine and good. In this case the first line (a person who is in a low position), is helping the fourth line (somebody in a more elevated, directive position).

When you help your superiors you must draw the line at some point. Do not let others abuse you and neither be servile towards them.

Career: Putting your work before your own needs will bring praise from your superiors but also will diminish your private life.

Private life: Charitable work is commendable, but do not forget the needs of your family.

Health, Feelings and Social life: You have plenty of energy and goals. Take care of not overexerting yourself or your health will suffer.

Second Nine

> The determination is favorable.
> Going forward with violence brings misfortune.
> Without loss one may increase.

It is favorable to keep to your normal tasks, but to take on new risky or aggressive endeavors would be unfortunate.

Do not innovate, instead carry on with your current duties; with your work you can help others.

Career: Focus on your responsibilities, you will not be able to advance in the short term.

Private life: Keep with your routine chores and meet your obligations with others. Do not act aggressively.

Health, Feelings and Social life: Your health will be good if you keep your temper under control.

Third Six

> Three men walking along the road together are decreased,
> but one man walking gains a companion.

Increase conduces to decrease and decrease leads to increase, following the normal cycles.

If you are alone you will find company, but if you are part of group, it will be decreased.

This line speaks about keeping a proper balance in social relations. You should be perceptive enough to know where it is time to enter a group and when you should leave.

Career: You know well how to interact and work with other people. Be flexible and open-minded.

Private life: If you are alone you will find company, if you are single you may marry. A family or a group of friends may lose some member.

Health, Feelings and Social life: You will have losses and gains.

Fourth Six

> As a result of reducing his anxiety, he will have joy quickly.
> No defect.

The word translated as "anxiety" also means "defect, stress, affliction, haste, illness". It means that if you relax a bit and are more accessible, your troubles will decrease and you will be less stressed.

Career: If you moderate your ambitions, you will be more relaxed in your workplace and will enjoy more your duty.

Private life: You will have relief from heavy preoccupations and responsibilities.

Health, Feelings and Social life: You will feel better after diminishing your stress and bad habits.

Fifth Six

> Someone increases him by ten pairs of tortoise shells.
> Nobody can resist.
> Outstanding happiness.

41 - Decrease

Tortoise shells were both used as currency and for divination. Ten pairs of tortoise shells mean a great number of good omens and to receive an important amount of resources or money. They also indicate that fate is on your side, you will receive blessings from above.

Nothing can stand in the way of your success and happiness.

Career: You will receive a great increase in authority and income. Your prospects are brilliant.

Private life: You will enjoy a very lucky period. Expect great prosperity and happiness.

Health, Feelings and Social life: Enjoy your blessings.

Top Nine

> There is no Decrease but increase.
> No defect.
> The determination brings good fortune.
> It is favorable to have where to go.
> One gets servants but not a household.

The time for decrease is ending. What you do will benefit everybody without decreasing yourself. You will make no mistakes and having a worthy goal to follow will allow you to do still more.

To get servants but not a household means that you are working for the public good, unselfishly.

Career: You are an influential person doing an altruistic job; you will attract many helpers.

Private life: You don't have much of a private life, since you are focused in helping others instead raising a family. You will reach your goals and with the help of other people will achieve many good things.

Health, Feelings and Social life: Good health and excellent spiritual elevation.

42

yì
Increase

Associated meanings

Increase, augment, expansion, progress, benefit, profit, advantage, more and more.

Judgment

> Increase.
> It is favorable to have where to go.
> It is favorable to cross the great river.

In this time people in high position are dedicated to strengthen the people under them, cooperating freely and helping out more humble people.

There is a spirit of collaboration for the greater good because people see that the leadership objectives are beneficial for everyone, not only a few.

But this good time will not last for long, increase means a favorable opportunity that should be used before it vanishes.

To have where to go means that you should have a definite goal where to concentrate your efforts to reap the benefits of this time.

Since the meaning of Increase is cooperation, it is also related with providing services to others and working for the greater good.

In ancient China, crossing rivers, either at a ford or when the river was frozen, was not an easy task. It implicated dangers and hardships; hence crossing the great river means to carry out a difficult undertaking.

The Image

> Wind and thunder: The image of Increase.
> Thus the noble moves toward the good when he sees it;
> and corrects any excesses.

Wind and thunder symbolize complementary forces that cooperate between them to undertake something.

The noble always looks for positive things and improvements to be done, but also is ready to correct mistakes and transgressions.

To be ready to make continuous adjustments and improvements, avoiding excesses and overindulgence, is the way to success.

First Nine

> It is favorable to begin great endeavors.
> Outstanding good fortune.
> No defect.

You will receive great support and already have plenty of resources to enable you to carry out great endeavors with very good results.

Increase is a time for concentrating in your duty and servicing others, there is no margin for selfish attitudes.

Career: You will be promoted and given important responsibilities. If you have your own business you will have an extraordinary opportunity for developing it.

Private life: Your will progress greatly and have a very happy time sharing with others your prosperity.

Health, Feelings and Social life: If you are sick your health will greatly improve. In any case you will have a superabundance of energy.

Second Six

> Someone increases him by ten pairs of tortoise shells.
> Nobody can resist.
> Long-term determination brings good fortune.
> Used by the king in an offering to the Divine Ruler.
> Good fortune.

Tortoise shells were used both as currency and for divination. Ten pairs of tortoise shells mean a great number of good omens and to receive an important amount of resources or money. They also indicate that fate is on your side, you will receive blessings from above.

Nothing can stand in the way of your success and great happiness.

Long-term determination means that long-term planning and endurance is required.

To be used in an offering to God means that your reputation will be greatly increased and your deeds recognized by the higher authorities.

Career: You will receive an important promotion and will be honored; nothing will be able to stop your progress. It is important to have well defined, strategic goals.

Private life: You will have great prosperity and will be admired by other people.

Health, Feelings and Social life: Very good health and strength.

Third Six

Increased by unfortunate events.
If your service is sincere there is no defect.
Walk in the middle and report to the prince with a jade baton.

Although the situation is not good, you will make the most of it. Others may have losses but you will benefit from the adverse circumstances.

The important thing is to avoid using the misfortune of others for selfish aggrandizement, but instead having a service mindset.

If you behave with moderation your will receive recognition and support from your superiors.

Career: The situation is not normal, and extraordinary circumstances will help you to get support from people situated in an elevated position, bypassing your current bosses. If you are careful, discreet and unselfish, you will succeed and will get an important promotion.

Private life: You will experience sorrow and suffer some losses but at the end you will prosper, provided that you exercise good judgment.

Health, Feelings and Social life: Adversity may help you to grow spiritually.

Fourth Six

If you walk in the middle and report to the prince, he will follow.
It is favorable to be assigned to relocate the capital.

This line is the place of an officer who works as a consultant or mediator, providing guidance to the direction of his organization.

To walk in the middle means to have a balanced approach. As a mediator you have to understand how different people see the situation and avoid taking sides, but you your principal duty is to serve loyalty the prince –your superiors– giving him a non-partisan report of the current circumstances.

Your proposal will be well accepted and you will be trusted for carrying on important projects.

Career: You will have an important advisory position and will help with restructuring projects.

Private life: You may move to a new house or renovate your current home.

Health, Feelings and Social life: Be ready to adjust your views and accept new ideas.

Fifth Nine

> If you have a sincere and kind heart you do not need to ask.
> Outstanding good fortune.
> One has sincerity and is favored with spiritual power.

If you act moved by a sincere desire to help others you will have no doubts and will not need to ask the oracle about your plans.

People will trust you because they will sense your goodwill. Your influence will grow, that will be your spiritual power.

Your wishes will become true for the benefit of all people around you, since your will is oriented towards the common good.

Career: Your plans will come true and other persons will trust and follow you in your endeavors.

Private life: You will help others, who in turn will love and respect you.

Health, Feelings and Social life: Moral integrity and altruism will enrich your spiritual life.

Top Nine

> He increases no one.
> Perhaps somebody will attack him.
> Doesn't keep his heart constant.
> Misfortune.

Acting with greed will isolate you and make you hated.

By failing to help others and acting with injustice you may attract just retribution from the people that you are harming.

If you do not learn to share with others you will have many troubles.

Career: If you are too pushy and greedy you will lose all support and in the end you will fall down.

Private life: Avarice and an inconsiderate behavior will make you the object of other's people hate. You will have no help from anyone when you fall into disgrace.

Health, Feelings and Social life: Greed and egoism will isolate you and make you unhappy. You may be injured seriously.

43

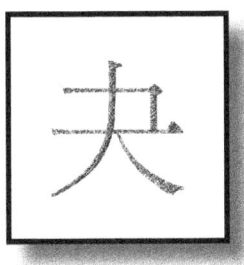

guài
Breakthrough /
Resoluteness / Parting

Associated meanings

Breakthrough, make a breach, split, cut off, pull off, flight, run away; resolute, decisive.

The ancient form of the character for this hexagram tag seems to show an archer's thumb ring or thimble, which was called *jué*. The meaning breakthrough may come from the bursting loose of the bow string.

Judgment

> Breakthrough.
> Proclaim the matter truthfully in the king's court.
> Danger.
> Report to your own city.
> It is not favorable to resort to weapons.
> It is favorable to have where to go.

Breakthrough means that the situation is more than ripe for change.

Tension has accumulated for a long time and the last remaining bad influences (symbolized by the sixth line) should be resolutely eradicated. It is not possible to reach compromises of any sort with evil forces; they should be eliminated by using soft power, and diplomacy, but not violence.

This is a decisive moment; you can't stand aside any longer. You have to make a stand and voice publicly your views.

To proclaim the issue in the king's court means that the crisis should be handled by common accord and publicly. In the same way, to report to your

43 - Breakthrough / Resoluteness / Parting

own city stresses out the importance of gathering support from your own sphere of influence before taking a public stand. Also it is important to have definite objectives.

From a psychological viewpoint, breakthrough indicates that vices and weaknesses should be not tolerated inside your own self.

The Image

> The lake rises above the heaven: The image of the Breakthrough.
> Thus the noble distributes benefits downward,
> while avoiding presumption of virtue.

The lake waters evaporate and generate clouds in heaven. Those clouds symbolize the tension that has accumulated, which can generate a dangerous outburst of rain.

To prevent such violent outbursts the noble doesn't hoard things for himself, but shares them with others.

Not presuming of virtue means to avoid boasting and not having selfish attitudes.

First Nine

> Powerful in the toes.
> He goes forward but cannot triumph, and makes a mistake.

To be powerful in the toes means that you are overeager to advance, but the conditions for a successful advance are not yet in place. You need more planning, also your position is not consolidated enough to allow you advancing successfully.

Acting now would be a mistake, if you are not able to stop yourself you will fail.

Make an effort to control your emotions and behaving more calmly.

Career: You will be blamed for your ill-timed actions.

Private life: If you cannot exercise self-control and are too bold or boastful you will fail and will be criticized.

Health, Feelings and Social life: Your feet may be injured or you may experience mobility issues.

Second Nine

> Cries of alarm at evening and night.
> If you are armed there is nothing to fear.

The situation is neither safe nor stable. Do not lower your guard and look out for signs of trouble.

To be armed means to be ready to face emergencies, contingency planning is critical for long-term success.

Career: By prepared beforehand for trouble. Do not let people slip under your guard.

Private life: You may take some losses, be ready for the unexpected and protect well your home and family.

Health, Feelings and Social life: Take precautions to protect your health because you are at risk.

Third Nine

> To be powerful in the cheeks brings misfortune.
> The noble is perfectly resolved.
> Walks alone in the rain, wet and grieved.
> No defect.

To be powerful in the cheeks indicates a pushy or overbearing temperament; such character traits will cause you trouble.

You will have to endure some level of conflict with other people and sacrifice some comforts to keep up your resolution, but you will make no mistake.

To minimize the unavoidable troubles, try to be tolerant of the limitations of the other people. They neither will understand nor support you but that is not reason for being harsh with them.

Career: You will not receive any help and will be criticized. Keep working for your goals and avoid unnecessary conflicts, be discreet.

Private life: You will find hardship in your way, but that is the price to pay to be consistent with your principles. People will desert and criticize you, but you can reduce your troubles by behaving peacefully.

Health, Feelings and Social life: Do not indulge in righteous anger. You will be isolated for a while; that is the price to pay for standing up for your principles.

Fourth Nine

> There is no flesh on his buttocks.
> Walks haltingly and leading a sheep.
> Regret disappears.
> Hearing complaints, not to be believed.

43 - Breakthrough / Resoluteness / Parting

You were stubborn and insisted in doing things your own way for a long time. You never listened to good advice.

Now you don't have strength enough to continue forward on your own and you will have to accept unquestioningly the terms of others.

In ancient China to lead a sheep being half dressed was a ceremony that indicated surrender, to ask mercy from a conqueror.

To resign independence and your own goals is a hard thing to do, but you have no other choices left to you.

Career: You may be criticized and demoted because justified complaints against you. It would be better to accept any position that is offered to you instead fighting to the end.

Private life: You better listen to good advice and recognize that you cannot do things your own way all the time.

Health, Feelings and Social life: You may have problems with your feet, legs or hearing.

Fifth Nine

A goat mountain breaks through and goes along the middle of the road.
No defect.

Finally a breakthrough is achieved; the weak line at the top of the hexagram symbolizes an open way ahead.

To go along the middle of the road indicates balance and commitment to solid principles. For that reason there will be no fault.

Career: You will be able to press forward and go ahead with your plans without making any mistakes.

Private life: Your wishes will be achieved; there are no more obstacles ahead.

Health, Feelings and Social life: If you had any mobility problems, they will be gone. Good health.

Top Six

There is no cry.
At the end there will be misfortune.
All seems good but there is unexpected trouble ahead.

The word "cry" means to cry for help or to make some signal. You will not have any warning of a coming danger and you will not receive any help, as a result you will suffer misfortune.

Being the only *yin* line in the hexagram, the sixth line symbolizes an inferior person who will be rejected by the other five *yang* lines and will suffer for it.

Career: Lack of support will create troubles for you.

Private life: You may have unexpected losses without any warning and you will not receive help from others.

Health, Feelings and Social life: You may have an accident. An older person may die.

44

gòu
Close Encounter / Meeting

Associated meanings

Couple, mate, meet, meeting of opposites, interlock, locking, coming to meet, brief encounter, temptation.

Judgment

> Close encounter.
> The woman is powerful.
> Do not take her as wife.

The structure of this hexagram is the inverse of the previous one, where the only *yin* line is at the top. Here the *yin* force is entering from the bottom, in 43 it is leaving.

Close encounter describes a time when opposite forces meet: the first *yin* line is entering the situation and meeting the other *yang* lines.

The first line symbolizes an inferior element, and because it is a *yin* line in low position, it is symbolized by a loose woman. The present danger is to become infatuated with this seemingly weak and attractive element, because she is more powerful and dangerous that she looks.

Not taking her as wife means that the inferior element may have a proper place in your life but only for a brief time and under some restrictions. But there is no chance of having a good and lasting relationship, since she would bring shame on your life and may even subjugate you.

44 - Close Encounter / Meeting

Although the inferior element is symbolized by a woman, in real life it may refer to persons of any sex or to any type of situation where some kind of temptation or foul play is happening.

From a psychological point of view, the first line symbolizes a primal force of the unconscious that, if not checked properly can take command of the whole self with destructive results.

The Image

> Under the sky is the wind: The image of Close Encounter.
> Thus the sovereign dispenses his orders to the four corners of the world.

The sovereign position is at the highest point of the social order, his subjects are below him. Like the wind, which connects the sky with the things below, stirring what it touches, the sovereign influences people by using his laws; he goes to the encounter of his subjects by mean of his laws.

In the same way that an encounter between opposites can be bad or good, laws affect the life of the people in different ways, depending on the goodness of the current government.

First Six

> Tie it to a metal brake.
> The determination brings good fortune.
> If it moves in any direction evil will appear.
> When one relies on a skinny pig it will falter.

It is better to apply restrain than to fall into danger.

Here the inferior element is compared to a skinny pig. If it is not controlled properly, in the end it will break havoc.

It cannot be trusted, it seems inoffensive and lean but it will grow more powerful and cause trouble if is not stopped now.

Career: Some inferior elements are infiltrating your organization. Keep such influences held in check while you can do that easily or they will cause trouble ahead.

Private life: You may meet an enticing person from outside your social sphere. Do not let such person encroach on you, keep your distance or you will be subjugated.

Health, Feelings and Social life: Keep in check your passions and primal urges, if you let them grow on you without limit, they will control you.

Second Nine

> There is a fish in the wrapping
> No defect.
> Not fitting for guests.

The second *yang* line is keeping the first yin *line* isolated. It means that you should prevent inferior influences from increasing, keeping them in place, to protect other people (the guests).

Career: You should handle any problematic influences by yourself. Keep them contained and do not let others take part on it. Be discreet and firm.

Private life: Some things should not be mixed. You may have a place in your life for some unconventional relation, but keep it apart from your family and friends for the good of everyone.

Health, Feelings and Social life: Something you may not be able to eliminate bad feelings or negative thoughts, but you should keep such feelings under control, not letting them spread.

Third Nine

> There is no flesh on his buttocks and he walks unsteadily.
> Danger.
> There will be no great defect.

You are sorely tempted but you will not be able do what you want because you lack enough strength.

In the end, the circumstances will prevent you from doing anything dangerous.

Career: You will not be able to advance, but that will save you from trouble. Your position is not secure, be careful.

Private life: You will have some troubles and may suffer some losses caused by bad decisions.

Health, Feelings and Social life: Your mind is disturbed by strong desire. Lack of stamina.

Fourth Nine

> There are no fish in the wrapping.
> This causes misfortune.

If you are too self-righteous and lack tolerance with the common folk you will lose their support when you more need it.

44 - Close Encounter / Meeting

Lack of cooperation and understanding between people from different walks of life will cause trouble.

Career: You may lose your position because you will receive no support from your subordinates.

Private life: You will be isolated because you are too hard and distant with people.

Health, Feelings and Social life: If you repress your feelings and are out of touch with them, your health will suffer.

Fifth Nine

> A melon wrapped in willow leaves.
> Hidden brilliance.
> It falls from Heaven.

The melon symbolizes something that needs a period of maturation, without being seen.

A melon, like a fish, is something that can be spoiled or can decompose easily. To wrap the melon indicates that it is not only preserved but also hidden.

The wrapped melon also symbolizes keeping good relations with your subordinates, protecting them.

Be prudent, cultivate your talents and your plans without ostentation, avoid pushing others.

If you are careful and discreet, when all things are in place you will achieve your objectives with ease, as if they fell from the sky into your hands.

Career: If you nurture carefully your plans and keep a low profile, you will achieve you aims with ease. You may get a new job or a promotion.

Private life: You will get your wishes fulfilled because you are a discreet person that knows how to handle things smoothly.

Health, Feelings and Social life: Women may become pregnant.

Top Nine

> Close encounter with his horns.
> Some regrets.
> No defect.

A close encounter with the horns means the interlocking of horns by two animals fighting one another. The top line is often associated with horns or the top of the head and also with extreme attitudes.

You do not suffer fools gladly and will stop inferior people who make advances on you with severity.

Although you are not doing anything bad, your attitude will generate friction with some people and in the long run you behavior will generate some troubles in your life.

Career: You will have some conflicts because you are too strict.

Private life: Your strong character will make you clash with some impertinent people. Your life would be easier if you were more tolerant.

Health, Feelings and Social life: Try to relax or you may suffer some stress.

45

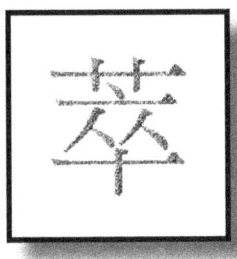
cuì
Gathering together

Associated meanings

Collect, assemble, gather together, massing, bunched, thick, dense, crowd, collection, group.

Judgment

> Gathering together.
> Success.
> The king approaches his temple.
> It is favorable to see the great man.
> Success.
> The determination is favorable.
> Offering great sacrifices brings good fortune.
> It is favorable to have where to go.

People gather together in families, organizations and states. The king is a leader that gathers people around him.

To join a mass of people, a sense of shared purpose and identity is required. The temple symbolizes such central point, which focuses the attention of the people in a single point and motivates them.

Seeing the great man may mean that you should ask for support from a wise person, but it also indicates that you should rise spiritually and intellectually to be able to gather other people around you. If you can do that you will have success.

45- Gathering together

Sacrifices are required from people in communities; all members should curb their own selfish desires up to a point, to contribute to the shared purpose that unifies the community.

To have determination and a definite goal is required to keep people working together for the greater good.

The Image

> The lake rises above earth: The image of Gathering together.
> Thus the noble gets his weapons in order,
> to be on guard against the unexpected.

The lake is a mass of water gathered together in one place.

Water can cause dangerous floods; in a group of people the danger comes from the conflicts that may arise between them.

To prevent unexpected dangers you should be alert and ready to make adjustments to avoid personal conflicts from escalating into nasty fights.

First Six

> One has confidence but not to the end, hence there will be confusion.
> Gathering together.
> One calls out, after one handclasp he will laugh.
> Do not worry.
> Going has no defect.

To be sincere, but not to the end, means that you are confused and insecure, fearing rejection. You still don't know to which group you belong or who you should follow.

To call out means to request admission to a group clearly. This will bring happiness.

Career: You are not sure if you should commit yourself to some business. Maybe you don't know well your potential boss or associates and that makes you feel insecure. The only way to know if it will work well is to try it out. You will never regret going forward.

Private life: If you are not sure about what to do or have some trouble, do not hesitate and ask for help. After you take the first step all will go well.

Health, Feelings and Social life: You may have some minor health issues. If you ask for help you will receive it, do not stay alone.

Second Six

> Drawn out.
> Good fortune.
> No defect.
> If he is sincere it is favorable to make a small offering.

A friend or some acquaintance may ask you to join some group, or some authority in an organization may summon you to take part with others in some activity.

May be you cannot offer much, but your sincerity and good will be more than enough to be admitted into the gathering and your participation will be propitious.

Career: With the help of a friend situated in a high position you will be offered a new job or promoted to a better position.

Private life: With help from your friends you will be drawn out from you current routine to face new possibilities.

Health, Feelings and Social life: Your feelings of isolation will be gone after you establish a good connection with a kindred spirit.

Third Six

> Gathering together between moans.
> Nothing is favorable.
> Going is without defect.
> Small humiliation.

Entering the group where you want to belong is difficult and you will have some trouble being accepted.

You should find some kind of sponsor to help you entering there. You will make no mistake if you go that way, although you will lose some face.

Career: You will need the right recommendation to get what you are looking for. At the beginning you may experience some trouble.

Private life: There will be some troubles in the family. You may depart from or arrive to a new place which is not up to your expectations.

Health, Feelings and Social life: An older relative may die.

Fourth Nine

> Great good fortune.
> No defect.

45- Gathering together

You have an important mission in the group, supporting and working closely with the group leader, helping him to gather followers.

Your generous efforts will conduce you to great success.

Career: You have many responsibilities as an administrator, but if you are cautious all will go well.

Private life: Because you care more for the common good than your own and you are earnest, you will have great success.

Health, Feelings and Social life: Excellent health.

Fifth Nine

> Gathering together has a good position.
> No defect.
> There is no trust.
> Having outstanding long term determination regret disappears.

This line symbolizes the leader who gathers people around a shared goal, but some of them may have joined the group only to get some rewards and do not really share the group's goals.

In time, by keeping committed to the group objectives, the leader will gain the trust of all people in the gathering. Until that moment the group will not work as a unified force.

Career: You will have to work hard to gain the trust and support of some individuals, before they are fully committed to their work.

Private life: Some of your relatives or friends do not trust and will not support you. But if you persevere in the right path, in the end all will go well.

Health, Feelings and Social life: Hesitation and conflicting desires makes hard for you to stay focused.

Top Six

> Sighing and moaning, copious tears.
> No defect.

You are sorry and frustrated because your contributions to the group are not recognized and you are left alone.

May be there is some conflict between you and the other people; try to understand what is preventing your from participating as a full member of the group.

If you are sincere, let them know that you want to join the group and that you are hurt. In the end, you will have a good chance of being admitted inside.

Career: If you cannot get the job or achieve the objective that you seek for you should concentrate in improving yourself in order to get there.

Private life: Alone and seeking comradeship you grieve. If you keep your determination up you will succeed.

Health, Feelings and Social life: Look inward and try to find peace inside yourself.

46

shēng
Ascending

Associated meanings

Climb, push upwards, ascend, rise, go up, arise.

The lower trigram for this hexagram is *xùn,* The Gentle, whose natural symbol is wood; the upper trigram is *kūn,* The Earth. This hexagram shows wood growing in the earth.

Judgment

> Ascending has outstanding success.
> It is useful to see the great man.
> Do not worry.
> Marching forth toward the south brings good fortune.

Ascending is a steady and continuous form of progress, not swift, but unstoppable.

To see the great man means not only to seek advice and help from those who can support and guide you but also to rise to the occasion, to meet the challenge of this propitious time.

This is a good moment to ascend in your organization or to make your business grow. Your progress will be steady and you will get support along the way.

You should not worry because you already have the necessary potentiality for success; it is only matter of developing yourself with determination. Departing toward the south means to undertake the necessary actions to reach your goals, the south is related with the community and the north with solitude.

46 - Ascending

The Image

> In the middle of the earth grows wood: The image of Ascending.
> Thus the noble, with yielding character,
> accumulates the small to achieve the great.

A tree seed growing below the earth is not seen, and its growth is unceasing but slow. It pushes upward until breaks ground and it adapts its way to the terrain. If it finds an obstacle, searches for a way around, but always pushing upward, towards the sun, which was traditionally placed in the south in ancient Chinese maps.

Ascending shows how by the sum of many imperceptible steps you can achieve great elevation, in the same way than a growing tree.

First Six

> Trusted and ascending.
> Great good fortune.

The first line symbolizes the root. It is the beginning of the ascension and it is very successful because people in high places will support it.

Career: You will get a promotion and recognition for your efforts.

Private life: You will get help to realize your dreams.

Health, Feelings and Social life: Good time to start moving your feet.

Second Nine

> If one is sincere it is favorable to present a small offering.
> No defect.

The second and third lines symbolize the tree trunk.

Even a small contribution will be favorable because it will show your sincerity and that you have the potential to still give more.

You will not make mistakes because what you do is the true expression of your potentialities.

Career: You will get promoted after you prove what you are capable of.

Private life: Although you still don't have many resources, your dedication will be noticed and you will receive help to advance forward.

Health, Feelings and Social life: If you had some health problem your health will improve.

Third Nine

>One ascends into an empty city.

To ascend into an empty city means to advance easily, without resistance and to take possession of a vacated territory.

This line doesn't tell if there will be fortune or misfortune, thus you may suspect that the situation is too good to be true, nevertheless such opportunity should not be discarded, but you should be careful.

In another interpretation level to ascend into an empty city may indicate to rise under a ruler who is going to fall or to follow a pipe dream.

Career: You will take over a vacant position with important responsibilities, but it may be less good than you expect.

Private life: You may move to a new home, but you will be alone for a time.

Health, Feelings and Social life: It will take some time to adapt to your new position in life. Be careful.

Fourth Six

>The King presents an offering on Mount Qi.
>Good fortune.
>No defect.

The fourth line is the place of the minister, who is privileged to take part in the ceremony when the king sacrifices to his ancestors.

The king represents a powerful person; to be along him in an important occasion means that you have been favored and honored by him.

In a practical level this means that you will fulfill your wishes and will ascend to a high position.

Career: You will be recognized and rewarded by your superiors. If you have a business, it will receive support from high spheres.

Private life: You will make important contacts and prosper materially and spiritually.

Health, Feelings and Social life: To be present during an offering in a sacred place symbolizes spiritual elevation and harmony.

Fifth Six

>The determination brings good fortune.
>One ascends on stairs.

46 - Ascending

To ascend with determination and on stairs indicates that you know clearly what you have to do. It also means to complete all stages carefully without skipping a single step. Do not look for shortcuts, take care of every detail.

You ascension will be achieved by entrusting responsibilities on others and by acting with softness and constancy.

Career: You will advance in your career and will reach an eminent position. By cautious and do not disregard the rules.

Private life: You will prosper smoothly if you are constant and careful.

Health, Feelings and Social life: Good spiritual and physical health.

Top Six

> Ascending in the dark.
> It is favorable an untiring determination.

The good times are coming to an end. You do not know what lies ahead. Do not stop ascending now, but be alert.

In this case, an untiring determination means to take all possible precautions to avoid danger.

Career: You are entering into uncharted waters. Do not take risks and be very careful.

Private life: Do not be greedy. Keep your mind focused in doing the right thing, because you may fall into danger if you are not vigilant.

Health, Feelings and Social life: Confusion and possible death.

47

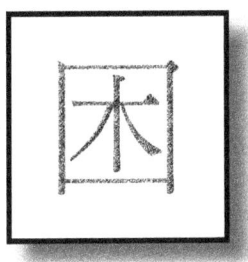

kùn
Oppression / Besieged / Impasse

Associated meanings

Oppression, obstruction; besieged, surrounded, beset; entangled, burdened, harassed; distress, exhaustion, anxiety, hardship, adversity.

The Chinese character constituents for this hexagram tag are: *mù*, "tree", and *wéi*, "enclosure, surround": a tree enclosed in a restricted space, where it cannot spread its branches nor grow.

Judgment

>Oppression.
>Success.
>The determination brings good fortune to the great man.
>No defect.
>Talk is not to be trusted.

You are caught by oppressive forces that are beyond your control and hinder you; neither advance nor withdraw is possible.

Good fortune means here to keep your willpower intact and never give up.

Words will make no effect, since you will not be trusted, instead they may make your situation worse.

Since you cannot neither change the current situation nor escape, the only way out is to endure the hard times until them improve.

If you keep up the faith in yourself you will prevail in the end.

47 - Oppression / Besieged / Impasse

The Image

> The lake has no water: The image of Oppression.
> Thus the noble will sacrifice his own life to achieve his objective.

The water sipping from the lake will make it dry and lifeless; this symbolizes lack of nourishment and support that may exhaust you.

The oppression is a test of your character. The external things that you may lose are not important in the long run, the critical thing is to not surrender to the pressure mounting around you; stand up and do not give up your goals.

First Six

> Buttocks oppressed by a tree stump.
> Enters a dark valley and is not seen for three years.

Oppression has sapped your willpower; to sit down uncomfortably on a tree stump means that your will is exhausted.

Entering a dark valley symbolizes a period of depression and defeatist attitudes. To overcome it, try to look ahead to a brighter future and do not isolate yourself. Three years indicate a long time.

In another interpretation level this may indicate a stint in jail or to be under some kind of restriction. The dark valley may depict a hole a in the ground; pits were used to hold prisoners in ancient China. The wooden stick indicates that punishment is used to overcome your will, as when the guards beat up a prisoner with a stick.

Career: Your fear and doubts are working against you. Your pessimism and confused attitude will limit your options.

Private life: You will be trapped in a vicious circle of anxiety and gloom until you put yourself together. You may be in mourning.

Health, Feelings and Social life: You may face a long period of depression and uncertainty.

Second Nine

> Oppressed between wine and food.
> Scarlet knee bands arrive from all sides.
> Offering a sacrifice is favorable.
> Marching forth will bring misfortune.
> No defect.

The wine and food indicate that you have a comfortable position, but your oppression is an internal state. You feel entangled with the boring circumstances of your life. Those who wore scarlet knee bands were men of rank and authority, to be approached by them means that you will be offered an opportunity to carry on some important endeavor.

To offer a sacrifice means to work for the sake of others, giving generously from your time and resources, but you have to wait for a clear sign before committing. Do not act rashly, only for your own benefit.

An alternative translation would be "oppressed by wine and food", meaning that you have been too self-indulgent and as a result you are entangled in sensual pleasures.

Career: You will be promoted or offered a job. It will open new opportunities for you, but you will have to work hard under the guidance of other people.

Private life: You will receive help from important people. Do not make any movement until you see a clear opening. Think what you can do for others instead of thinking "what do I want".

Health, Feelings and Social life: A self-indulgent period is coming to an end.

Third Six

Oppressed by stones.
Leans on thorny bushes and thistles.
Enters his house but does not see his wife.
Misfortune.

Being restless and irresolute, you will receive no support because you are looking for it in the wrong places. To be oppressed by stones and prickled by thorns indicates that you are expecting support from those that will not help you.

Calm down and reevaluate your priorities before it is too late.

In another interpretation level, to lean on thorns may indicate a period in prison, since prisons were surrounded by thorny bushes. You may not find any support or solace after you recover your freedom and return to your previous home.

Career: You may lose your job or go broke because you lost the way.

Private life: Trouble with your family and friends. Your partner may abandon you.

Health, Feelings and Social life: Delusional state. Health trouble.

Fourth Nine

> He comes very slowly, oppressed in a golden carriage.
> Humiliation, but it will be carried to conclusion.

To be in a golden carriage indicates a high social position and riches. You have good intentions and want to help a friend in need (symbolized by the first line) but you are afraid of criticism from powerful people and you delay doing the right thing.

At the end you will do what you should have done in the first place, but your lack of fortitude will shame you.

Career: You will have to overcome interferences coming from other people but also get over your own lack of resolve to get your work done. Do not let your boss bully you.

Private life: Doubts and insecurity will delay you. Do not worry about the opinion of other people, follow your own counsel.

Health, Feelings and Social life: Insecurity and dependence. You should strengthen your will.

Fifth Nine

> His nose and feet are severed.
> Oppressed by scarlet knee bands.
> The joy comes slowly.
> It is favorable to present offerings and libations.

You are oppressed from above and below. The cut nose indicates that your perception of detail is obliterated. The cut feet mean that your movement is restrained. Those who wore scarlet knee bands were men of high position; they may be bureaucrats or people with power over you.

Because you cannot overcome the superior powers that oppress you, the only way out is to accept your situation in life and learn to live in reduced circumstances.

Focus in your spiritual development and keep up your composure. With the pass of time things will slowly improve.

In another interpretation level, to be oppressed by scarlet knee bands may mean to be burdened by the responsibilities of your job.

Career: Both your bosses and your subordinates will cause you trouble, limiting severely your options. Do not fight; wait patiently for a good opportunity to do something useful.

Private life: You will have plenty of trouble with people and will face hindrances everywhere. You may have to make some sacrifices, but in time things will improve.

Health, Feelings and Social life: You may have some health issues, especially mobility trouble.

Top Six

Oppressed by climbing plants.
He is anxious and insecure.
He says to himself that movement will bring regret.
With repentance, marching forth brings good fortune.

Climbing plants symbolize restrictions that can be easily torn.

The oppression has ended, but you continue to fear it and don't dare to move.

The situation has changed for the better, be ready to cope with new challenges and to learn something new. You need to reevaluate your perspective and overcome your fears; that is the meaning of the word "repentance" in this context.

By moving forward you will leave all your troubles in the past.

Career: You can progress in your career only after overcoming your fears. The obstacles ahead you are not as big as you think; you have enough strength to broke through and prosper.

Private life: Fear to change will hold you in the same place forever. If you are brave enough to go forward you will be rewarded.

Health, Feelings and Social life: You feel secure inside your restricted world. But you will be missing many vital opportunities if you don't dare to break your confinement.

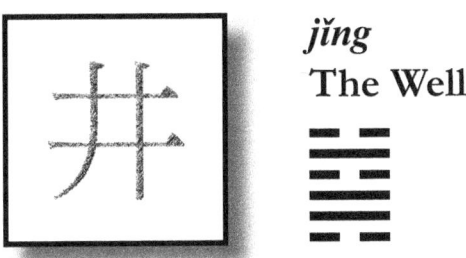

jǐng
The Well

In ancient times wells were placed in the center of a grid of nine fields. The center field, which had the well, was property of the feudal lord and the eight families living around it cultivated that field in common, in benefit of his lord and had shared use of the well.

Associated meanings

Water well, wellspring, life water, nourishment, foundation or source of life, inner source of truth, nucleus.

Judgment

> The Well.
> Changing the town, not changing the well.
> No loss, no gain.
> Going to take water from the well nearly dry.
> If the rope does not reach the water or the jar breaks, misfortune.

The well is the foundation of life, a non-changing nucleus that remains the same through life, your roots in life.

The well also represents the government of a city or the head of a family, if it fails to provide nourishment for the people, it should be corrected or replaced.

Changing the town but not changing the well indicates that although you may make big changes in your external life, your essence will remain the same through your whole life.

Reaching the water means to reach the truth, and to receive real nourishment from the sources of life, to get in contact with your inner sources.

When the rope is not long enough or the jar breaks the truth is not reached, because you don't know how or you are not are able to do it.

The Image

> Wood above the water: The image of the Well.
> Thus the noble encourages people at their work
> to cooperate among themselves.

A well is to the people around it, and to society in general, what a ruler is to the people. The value of the well depends on the water being actually raised, not empty promises.

In the same way, the principles of government must be actually carried out. If they are not working as intended, the people will not get nourishment and will stop cooperating between themselves.

To keep the social order healthy, cooperation between people and good communication between rulers and citizens is required.

The same principles apply to both countries, organizations, families and any other human groups.

First Six

> One does not drink from a muddy well
> There are no animals (birds) in an old well.

A muddy well symbolizes a misuse of resources. If you do not take care of your own development your life will be useless, both for yourself and for other people.

It also symbolizes a source that is not providing nourishment anymore or –in the external level– a man with authority who is corrupt and useless and because that has been left alone.

Career: If you don't help anyone, you will be ignored by the people. You will not get support from anybody.

Private life: You are alone; you will be at an impasse until you put your life in order and clean your own house.

Health, Feelings and Social life: You spiritual and physical health are stagnant because you have stopped caring about yourself.

Second Nine

> Shooting fishes in the well.
> The jar is broken and leaks.

A well is not the proper place to shoot fishes (they were shoot using arrows with attached strings). You are squandering away your talents in trivial pursuits.

The broken and leaking jar indicates that you are not using the correct method to get to the source of nourishment.

If you continue neglecting your potentialities you will not accomplish anything worthwhile and will stay in darkness.

You should set yourself higher goals.

Career: Your talents and resources are not being used well. May be you are in the wrong place or you are mismanaging the situation.

Private life: Until you polish more your natural talents you will not be of use to anybody.

Health, Feelings and Social life: Following hollow dreams will prevent you from improving your life.

Third Nine

> The well is cleaned but its water is not drunk.
> Our hearts grieve, because the water might be drawn out and used.
> If the king were clear-minded all would receive the blessings.

A well that is cleaned means plenty of potentialities and assets that have been restored, but sadly your person and abilities are still ignored by the authorities.

Do not disregard the opportunities for progress that you may find along the way. Use productively your resources, apply them to useful pursuits and do not isolate yourself.

Career: You superiors do not value you as they should. You may find more opportunities working in another place.

Private life: The people around you do not appreciate your true value. Your potential is wasted where you are.

Health, Feelings and Social life: Good spiritual and physical health. Isolation. You may not be fully aware about your capabilities.

48 - The Well

Fourth Six

> The well is lined.
> No defect.

The well is under restoration, that is a good thing and hence, doing so will mean no mistake.

It is time to put your life in order, reform what is wrong and develop your capacities.

You will not be able to do anything useful until your get your life organized.

Career: Do not start anything new but instead try to improve your current situation and correct any faults you may find.

Private life: Time for restoration of anything that is not up-to-date. You may build or renovate your house.

Health, Feelings and Social life: Your health will improve if you take proper care of it.

Fifth Nine

> The well has clear, cold spring water for drinking.

This line is the place of the ruler. You have the potential capacity to be a leader and to nurture the people. Both your work and words can benefit others, like pure drinkable water.

Still, there is not mention here about good fortune, since your capabilities have yet to be applied to the real world.

Career: You have at your disposal the talents and resources for achieving great results. Apply them well.

Private life: You can be of great help to the people around you.

Health, Feelings and Social life: You have excellent health and purity of purpose.

Top Six

> Taking water from the well.
> Not covering.
> It inspires confidence.
> Outstanding good fortune.

Notice that this is the only line where the well water is actually reached and used productively.

The well is accessible to everyone without hindrance.

In the same way, a leader of people inspires trust and is generous and tolerant with everyone.

Because there is a pure and nourishing source available for everyone and a spirit of cooperation prevails, outstanding good fortune is the outcome.

Career: You will reach a high position and will use your capacities to help people.

Private life: You will have plenty of good things and will share them with the people around you.

Health, Feelings and Social life: Your wisdom will guide others.

49

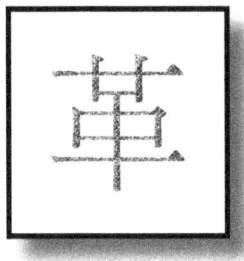

gé
Revolution /
Getting rid of

Associated meanings

Change, change of seasons; revolution, metamorphosis, overthrow; skin or hide, rawhide, leather, hide without the hair; flay, peel off, skinning, molting.

Judgment

> The Revolution is trusted after it has been accomplished.
> Outstanding good fortune.
> The determination is favorable.
> Repentance fades.

Revolution indicates a great personal change, a change in some external social structure or adjustment to new circumstances.

People will support the new order only after it is established and it will take time to win their trust. Hence, although radical change is needed, it should be done on a timely basis, or you will not have enough support and so the revolution will fail.

After the change is accomplished successfully, repentance will fade, since only then the revolution will be justified.

This is one of the few hexagrams that mention the "four cardinal virtues": *yuan*: outstanding (fundamentality, primal, originating, spring season, head, sublime, great, grand); *heng*: success (prevalence, growing, penetrating, treat, offering, sacrifice); *li*: determination (perseverance, constancy, correct and firm) and *heng*: favorable (advantageous, suitable, beneficial, lucky). One or more of the cardinal virtues appear in 50 different hexagrams, but only the

49 - Revolution / Getting rid of

hexagrams 1, 2 (with some modification), 3, 17, 19, 25 and 49 have the four virtues in its Judgment. Since the *Han* Dynasty onwards they have become keywords of Confucian thought, four qualities or virtues applicable both to Heaven and to the noble-minded person.

Any oracle encompassing the four cardinal virtues indicates that success is granted, but only if you don't stray from the good; for this reason determination in the right way is the key to success.

The Image

> Within the lake is fire: The image of the Revolution.
> Thus the noble regulates the calendar and makes clear the seasons.

The lower trigram is fire and above it is located the trigram of the lake. Fire and water are antagonistic, putting fire below water either makes the water boil or extinguishes the fire. Fire within the lake indicates conflict and change.

In the natural world the seasons bring ordered change to Earth. Each season starts a new renovation cycle, involving life and death. Notice that the character translated as "seasons" also means "time, epoch, opportune moment".

In the same way that proper timing is important to synchronize the crops with the seasons; when implementing important changes, finding the correct moment is of the utmost importance.

Most persons will resist change until it is firmly established, providing people with an ordered and timely transition will soothe them.

First Nine

> The Revolution is tied with a yellow cow hide.

The time for change has not arrived yet. Yellow indicates balance and moderation. To be tied in a yellow hide indicates that you should not advance, but wait for a propitious moment.

Career: This isn't the right time for introducing innovations. Keep to proved and traditional ways, do not start anything new.

Private life: Accept what you have. A cow is a docile animal, in the same way, be content with your situation and do not try to change it.

Health, Feelings and Social life: Your situation is stable, do not try anything new. You may have some mobility issues.

Second Six

> Revolution after the end of the day.
> It is favorable to attack.
> No defect.

Depending on the translation, the first line may read either the "end of the day" or "your own day".

In any case it means that the time will be ripe for change soon.

A full renovation is required and it will be auspicious. To attack means to advance boldly, you will make no mistakes moving forward now.

Career: You can change your position for the better and assume the control or management of your sphere of influence.

Private life: Renovate your life, changing it for good. Taking some risks now will be worthwhile.

Health, Feelings and Social life: Your health can be improved if you are ready to make big changes.

Third Nine

> Attacking brings misfortune.
> The determination is dangerous.
> Only after you have spoken about three times the revolution will be trusted.

If you act before you are ready, lacking the necessary support, you will fail.

To speak about three times means to check your plans and evaluate the perspectives carefully and to reach firm agreement with all involved people before acting. You have to be sure that you have enough support before making any bold movement forward. Make sure that you are trusted and that you can trust your followers as well.

Career: Acting without enough preparation will be dangerous. It will take time to make sure that your plan is feasible and to get the confidence and support of your collaborators.

Private life: When trying to make important changes in a family, it is important to talk with each family member and to make any necessary adjustments to your plan until you get the support of all them.

Health, Feelings and Social life: Untimely and rash change will affect your health for the worse. It is important to get as many informed opinions as possible before making any drastic change.

49 - Revolution / Getting rid of

Fourth Nine

> Repentance fades.
> There is confidence.
> Reforming the form of government brings good fortune.

A substantial transformation is possible now.

The Chinese character translated as "form of government" also means "heaven's will, fate, highest law". It means either to implement a radical change to modify the orientation of your life, or a profound change in the structure of an organization or human group.

People will feel that they can rely on the new order and they will support it, hence repentance will fade.

Career: You will get new responsibilities and support for implementing comprehensive and wide-ranging reforms.

Private life: Good time for renovating your life, starting new projects and trying alternative lifestyles.

Health, Feelings and Social life: The times are changing and you should keep pace with them. Changing and adapting old beliefs to the present will make you happier.

Fifth Nine

> The great man changes like a tiger.
> Even before asking the oracle he has confidence.

The great man indicates a highly principled person.

To change like a tiger means to innovate, adapt to new circumstances, to be ready to meet new challenges. The tiger symbolizes raw power; it is an emblem of bravery, ferocity and strength.

Having confidence before asking the oracle means that you are not only free of any doubts but also you are in tune with the times and you know perfectly what you should do to have success.

Your firm convictions and high ideals will help you to get the support of the people.

Career: You will progress brilliantly in your career or business because you have knowledge, skill and confidence.

Private life: You will be able to implement easily any changes you want because you are in the right and you know best what should be done.

Health, Feelings and Social life: Trust your intuition. Good health.

Top Six

> The noble changes as a leopard.
> The petty man changes its face.
> Attacking brings misfortune.
> The determination brings good fortune.

The revolution is already done. Now people should adapt to the new order.

The leopard symbolizes versatility, beauty and independence. To change like a leopard means to innovate, adapt to new circumstances with elegance. Also, to change like a leopard traditionally means to go from rags to riches.

Since attacking brings misfortune, change should be carried on without violence, with diplomacy. Also, since the main transformation has been already performed; to push ahead with more radical changes would be dangerous, only minor adjustments should be done now.

The change will bring good fortune only if performed deeply and with sincerity, like a leopard; passive acceptance or faking a change, like a petty man, will not do. Inferior people will only change their appearance, but not their hearts; they are not trustworthy.

Career: The rules of the game have changed. It is time to cooperate, learn to play by the new rules and prosper.

Private life: If you truly adapt to the new circumstances you will be happy and will prosper.

Health, Feelings and Social life: A new spiritual horizon appears before you. Learn to live by the new paradigm.

50

dǐng
The Cauldron / Sacrificial Vessel

Associated meanings

Cauldron; three-legged bronze cauldron with two ears; establish, renew, transform. Sacred bronze vessels were used during by the *Shang* and *Zhou* dynasties to offer sacrificial meals to the spirits in rituals.

Judgment

> The Cauldron.
> Outstanding good fortune.
> Success.

In ancient China, when a dynasty began, the first thing done was to cast a new cauldron with the fundamental laws inscribed on it, to symbolize the new epoch begun under the new king. Thus, when starting new life cycle (after Revolution, the previous hexagram) you should transform yourself to be able to face the new conditions and establish them firmly.

The Cauldron symbolizes purification, like it happened during sacrifice offerings; it also means initiation and transformation. The Cauldron also indicates something that tempers, transforms and harmonizes its contents.

In another interpretation level you are the sacrificial vessel, hence the Cauldron means the full realization of your potential, to develop your talents and gifts.

50 - The Cauldron / Sacrificial Vessel

The Image

>Fire over wood: The image of the Cauldron.
>Thus the noble corrects his position to consolidate his fate.

Fire over wood suggests the idea of cooking. The head of the family cooked his sacrifices to the spirits and served the food from the Cauldron into the bowls of the guests

Nourishing people with consecrated food indicates spiritual development, maturing and learning how to realize the innate potential: the fate.

The hexagram 48: **The Well** indicates the nourishment of the people in general, but the Cauldron means the spiritual nourishment of noble persons.

Wood keeps the fire running, in the same way the noble cultivates his fate with his acts, making sure he is on the correct path.

Fire over wood also indicates the importance of the correct placement of things. Thus, the noble rectifies the position of the people, to fully realize their potential.

First Six

>The Cauldron is lying upside down.
>It is favorable to remove debris.
>One takes a concubine to bear a child.
>No defect.

A Cauldron lying upside down means to produce a radical change of attitude when starting a new cycle in life. This transposition of values means that much of what previously was seen as good (the old content of the cauldron), it is no longer useful, and that what was previously disdained (the concubine) now has good development possibilities (the son).

In times of renovation, unorthodox methods should be used, what was low (the concubine, or handmaiden in other translations) will generate new opportunities and what was of high value is now worthless.

Career: You should get rid of what is no longer useful for your business and introduce new people and new methods to cope with a new reality. Long-term planning is required; the new strategy will take time to produce good results.

Private life: Your life has become stale, like a family that has produced no offspring. With help from humble people you will start a new life. You may take a nurse for raising your children.

Health, Feelings and Social life: If your health is bad it will improve. Non-conventional methods may help you.

Second Nine

> The Cauldron is full.
> My counterpart is anxious, but cannot get at me.
> Good fortune.

Your achievements may cause resentment in some people. The anxious counterpart (comrade or enemy in other translations) means somebody who wants to take from you the content of the Cauldron, without having any rights to it.

But they cannot get what belongs to you. Continue ahead with dedication and you will be fortunate.

Career: Some people will envy your achievements, but if you continue doing your work right they will not be able to damage you. You may not have support from them, but you will do just fine on your own.

Private life: You will prosper but may have disagreements and quarrels with some people.

Health, Feelings and Social life: Somebody in your family may get ill.

Third Nine

> The handles of the Cauldron are removed.
> Progress is impeded.
> The fat pheasant meat is not eaten.
> Rain falls all around, and regrets disappear.
> Finally there will be good fortune.

The missing handles mean that your talents are not appreciated and because that they are misused or are unproductive.

The meat not eaten indicates lost opportunities and wasted resources.

The rain symbolizes clearing up misunderstandings and overcoming conflicts.

At the end your true value will be recognized and you will be able to make good use of your talents and abilities.

Career: Your advance is blocked by some person above you, but with time you will clarify things out and will be successful.

Private life: Tensions and criticism will stop you from enjoying life and prospering. Finally all conflicts will be left in the past and you will be happy and prosperous.

Health, Feelings and Social life: You are stressed out and your own anxiety is hampering you. Try to relax, after you overcome your internal disturbances you will be happier.

50 - The Cauldron / Sacrificial Vessel

Fourth Nine

> The Cauldron legs are broken.
> The stew is spilled and stains the Prince's figure.
> Misfortune.

The broken legs mean lack of support that make your plans fail, lack of judgment, wrong start, overambitious plans that you are not qualified to handle.

The stained figure (or punishment by branding in other translations) means that as a result of your failure your reputation will be in tatters and you may be even punished.

Career: You will not be able to meet your responsibilities and will lose face. As a result you may be fired or demoted.

Private life: Serious blunder. Your lack of judgment will damage your reputation.

Health, Feelings and Social life: You may have trouble with your lower extremities.

Fifth Six

> The Cauldron has yellow handles and metal carrying-bars.
> The determination is favorable.

The carrying-bars pass through the handles (ears) of the Cauldron and allow its proper use.

This line is the place of the ruler, who is represented by the carrying-bars; his helpers are the cauldron handles. Yellow symbolizes balance and modesty.

An open-minded and wise ruler will attract good people to cooperate with him.

Career: You will be recognized, supported, and you will prosper.

Private life: A level headed and approachable attitude will allow you to achieve prosperity, helped by your friends.

Health, Feelings and Social life: Good health and wisdom.

Top Nine

> The Cauldron has carrying-bars of jade.
> Great good fortune.
> Nothing that is not favorable.

The jade carrying-bars are impervious to corrosion, they are hard, smooth, and have a soft luster; they symbolize an advisor who can handle with great strength and compliance the more delicate tasks. He is free of partiality and can do his work with the summit of perfection.

The sixth line of a hexagram frequently symbolizes a sage who is outside the situation and helps the ruler with his wisdom, as happens in this case.

Career: You will act as a consultant, offering your valued advice with great success.

Private life: Your firm but receptive demeanor will win you the trust from the people. You will be a very good influence in the life of the persons around you. Prosperity and happiness.

Health, Feelings and Social life: You are receptive to the highest spiritual influences.

51

zhèn
Shock

This is one of the eight hexagrams that are comprised by the same trigram repeated twice, in this case *zhèn*, The Arousing. Please see **The Eight Trigrams** (p. 369) for more information.

Associated meanings

Shock; clap of thunder; fear, awe inspiring, to terrify; stimulation, movement, quake, excitation, upheaval; to quicken; endow, succor.

Judgment

> Shock. Success.
> The arrival of Shock causes great fear.
> But afterwards there are laughing words.
> Shock terrifies for a hundred *li*.
> But he doesn't drop the libation in the sacrificial ladle.

An unexpected violent disruption in your life will shock you.

Uncertainty and awe inspiring changes will shake the structure of your life. Laughing words indicate the excitement mixed with fear that such times arouse.

Notice that shock may came in waves, in such case you will experience several periods of fear followed by distension moments when you will laugh.

To avoid dropping the sacrificial ladle means to keep your balance and to be ready to face the new times.

51 - Shock

These are interesting times, if you are able to adapt to the new circumstances you will grow as a person.

The Image

> The thunder repeated: the image of Shock.
> Thus the noble with apprehension and fear, puts his life in order and evaluates himself.

The duplicated trigram that forms this hexagram is exciting, arousing and shaking.

Thunder repeated means that your daily routine will be unsettled by unexpected events; they may be the result of completely unpredictable factor or they may happen because you chose to ignore some facts and hence you are no ready to handle its consequences.

These events may be unexpected situations, seemly fortuitous events, or a person that enters your life disrupting it.

At this moment you cannot ignore any longer what is happening. You have to grow and learn how to cope with the challenge.

To put your life in order means to be ready to adjust your attitude and your beliefs and to leave behind what is not useful anymore.

First Nine

> The arrival of Shock causes great fear.
> But afterwards there are laughing words.
> Good fortune.

The words in this line are similar to the text of the Judgment.

At first, shock will terrify you but after the first effect passes you will adapt and relax.

The new fearful things that have irrupted in your life will be indeed a blessing in disguise.

Career: What seems to be a disruptive experience or an undesired interference will help you to progress and learn more.

Private life: You will face unexpected and frightening events, but in the end all will turn right and you will rejoice.

Health, Feelings and Social life: Your composure will be jolted by some news, but Shock will help you to grow as a person.

Second Six

>Shock comes with risk.
>You lose one hundred thousand cowries and climb the nine hills
>Do not go in pursuit.
>In seven days you will get them.

You will be greatly disturbed and suffer some emotional or material losses, represented by the lost cowries (they were a form of coin).

If you accept your losses and instead striving to recover them, retreat until the danger is gone, all will end well.

In another level, to climb the hills indicates the need to grow and mature to be able to handle the new situation.

The seven days represent a necessary cycle, which cannot be skipped. After it ends you will get back what you lost before.

Besides this hexagram, the Chinese character for seven only appears in the **hexagram 24**, in the Judgment and in the second line of the **hexagram 63**. Here it indicates the return of money, in the hexagram 24 is related with a return and in the hexagram 63 with the return of the curtain of a carriage.

Career: You may be stripped of your influence or sidestepped for a while. You will have to resign some things and accept some losses. Be patient and avoid head on confrontations. In the end you will recover your strength and position.

Private life: Troubles and quarrels will disturb your life and you will have to resign some things and accept some losses. Avoid entering in conflict and fighting back with people. In the end you will recover your losses. If somebody leaves you, it will be only for a while.

Health, Feelings and Social life: Your health may take a sudden turn for the worse but it will improve with the pass of time. Emotional upheaval. Be patient.

Third Six

>Shock stimulates and terrifies one.
>If shock excites one to action, there will be no defect.

Shock is dangerous, but if it awakens you to the need to change and adapt to the new times, you will make no mistake.

You may get confused at first, but after you recover your balance you will find a way to handle the disturbing events.

If you take no action, ignoring the need for change, you will be ashamed.

51 - Shock

On other level, to take action also may mean to leave the place of danger, to run away.

Career: You need to adapt to the new circumstances, to change your perspective and focus on going on in a creative way. If you do not react soon you will be ashamed later.

Private life: Be flexible and ready to make adjustments, but be very cautious as well. Keeping still is not an option; to face the present challenging times you have to keep moving ahead.

Health, Feelings and Social life: Wake up. You need new ideas. Conservative thinking will not help you anymore.

Fourth Nine

> After Shock mud.

You are mired in doubt and confusion, because you lost your chance for escaping the turmoil.

Try to recover your balance and composure and to find new solutions for your troubles or your life will stagnate.

Career: Your career or business is petrified and stale. Ignorance and an unyielding attitude are dragging you down.

Private life: At this moment you are not able to change with the times. You see no viable options or any hope because you are very confused. You may be in detention for a while.

Health, Feelings and Social life: You may have mobility issues. Depression and confusion.

Fifth Six

> Shock comes and goes.
> Danger.
> But nothing is lost.
> There are things to do.

You are in the middle of great turmoil and danger, but if you stay focused in your objectives and keep balanced and rolling with the waves you will do well.

Career: Although the situation is unstable you will keep your position and will manage your duties successfully.

Private life: If you can keep your calm in the middle of unsettled conditions you will avoid danger and will be able to keep going ahead.

Health, Feelings and Social life: If you stick to your ideals you will keep your internal peace, no matter the external conditions.

Top Six

Shock causes fear and agitation.
One looks around in terror.
Marching forth brings misfortune.
The shock does not reach you but your neighbor.
No defect.
There is talk of marriage.

Shock has reached its highest point and unrest and confusion are extensive. Because people are afraid and unsettled they will be prone to act without thinking, making still worse their situation.

You have a chance to stay out of that collective psychosis. Do not follow the masses, but keep yourself calm and withdrawn.

The talk of marriage indicates plans or a chance to establish an alliance to overcome the current commotion.

Career: Defeatism and fear rule. You can keep yourself apart from trouble if you stay calm in spite of the chaos and do not let others hurry you. You may receive a job offer.

Private life: Be careful and prudent. This is no time to starting anything new or making changes. Learn from the mistakes of your neighbors. You may find a suitable partner.

Health, Feelings and Social life: Make an effort to control your emotions and behaving more calmly.

52

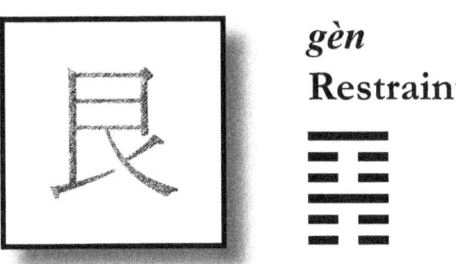

gèn
Restraint

This is one of the eight hexagrams that are comprised by the same trigram repeated twice, in this case *gèn*, Keeping Still. Please see **The Eight Trigrams** (p. 369) for more information.

Associated meanings

Keeping still, limit, check, hold steady, restrain, being quiet, non-action, stop; mind at peace, meditation.

Judgment

> Restraining his back. Doesn't feel his body.
> Goes to his courtyard and doesn't see his people. No defect.

Besides its literal sense, restraining the back means to keep both action and stillness in the proper place.

Not feeling his body and not seeing his people indicates to avoid following blindly impulsive instincts or the call of the group; to let things happen without reacting to them.

Restrain can be applied in two levels: inner restraint means to keep the mind in peace and outer restraint means to stay focused in what you are doing.

By mastering restrain you will be free of anxiety in two ways:

Your mind will not wander and worry about all the possible outcomes on your current situation.

52 - Restraint

You will not care about what other people think about you, because you will be focused in what you are doing not in how you look or what others may say about you.

The Image

>Joined mountains: The image of Restraint.
>Thus the noble doesn't let his thoughts wander beyond his position.

A range of mountains stays in place as an insurmountable barrier. It teaches us how to put a stop to our wandering thoughts.

Not allowing the thoughts to wander means to put a stop to vain speculations, to restrain the mind from idly rambling, to stay focused in the matters at hand, and to stay in the here and now.

It also means being realistic, to avoid chasing illusions.

First Six

>Restraining his toes.
>No defect.
>Long term steadiness is favorable.

You will be tempted to take action, but still this is not the right time to proceed forward.

If you keep your position steadily you will not make any mistakes.

Career: Stay where you are, neither seek advancement nor try to change your situation. Keep up with your responsibilities and you will be fine.

Private life: Be satisfied with things as they are. Be steady with your daily chores.

Health, Feelings and Social life: You may have some issues with your feet.

Second Six

>Restraining his calves doesn't help the one he follows.
>His heart is not happy.

The second line symbolizes a follower of the person indicated by the third line, the second line would like to help the third one, but it is unable to do so.

You are carried in the wake of a powerful will. The calves cannot move independently from the legs, they are dependent. In the same way you cannot stop the movement that has already started because a force more powerful than you is pushing ahead.

Career: You will not be able to make your own choices. You are limited by the decisions of your superiors, and they will not hear you.

Private life: You will find obstacles and your plans will not fructify because other people in your family will not leave you free to do your wishes.

Health, Feelings and Social life: You may have trouble with your legs.

Third Nine

> Restraining his hips.
> Tears his lumbar area.
> Danger.
> The heart is suffocated.

Here restraint is applied to the wrong point and with excess.

In the external world, this indicates an unyielding attitude and lack of adaptation to reality. If you do not know how to bend you will break.

Internally, it means an excessive repression of your feelings. This unwholesome attitude will generate too much stress and will suffocate your spirit.

Career: You should adapt to the situation and be more flexible. Otherwise you will wear yourself out. Do not overstrain yourself.

Private life: Excessive self-control and incessant striving will make you a bitter person.

Health, Feelings and Social life: If you do not learn to relax and take life more lightly you will make your own life insufferable.

Fourth Six

> Restrains his body.
> No defect.

To maintain still the body means to control the whole individuality in a balanced manner, without being influenced by external factors.

It also indicates that you know how to relax and rest properly.

Career: All is under control. Do not innovate. Keep things going as always and you will have no trouble.

Private life: If you stay quiet in your place you will avoid problems.

Health, Feelings and Social life: Rest properly and you will preserve your health.

Fifth Six

> Restrains his jaws.
> What he says is orderly.
> Repentance fades.

52 - Restraint

To restrain the jaws means to not indulge in idle chatter and to think before speaking.

Speaking orderly signifies to say the proper words and also to avoid saying things that will cause unrest between the people.

Career: Your discourse should be coherent with the policy of your company. Do not push your luck with continuous complaining.

Private life: If you are careful with what you say you will avoid disputes and future trouble.

Health, Feelings and Social life: Learn to control yourself. To restrain your jaws you have to master yourself, which is not an easy task.

Top Nine

>Earnest restrain.
>Good fortune.

Your deep inner composure allows you to contemplate with equanimity and an impartial perspective all things that happen to yourself and in the world in general.

Such attitude will bring good fortune to you and the people around you.

Career: Self-control and an unselfish demeanor will help you to have great success.

Private life: You are completely at ease in your life and your generosity will make you and your family happy.

Health, Feelings and Social life: You are at peace with yourself and with the world. High spiritual development.

53

jiàn
Gradual Development

Four hexagrams are related with marriage and the preliminary steps leading to it: **31-Influence**, depicts the initial attraction and courtship in a couple; **32-Duration**, indicates the institution of marriage; 53-Gradual Development, shows the steps and ceremonies leading to marriage and **54-The Marrying Maiden**, describes a young maiden entering an older man's house as a secondary wife.

Associated meanings

Gradual development, gradually, increasingly, advance by degrees, slow growth; moisten, dip down into, imbue; influence. Advance like the water, infiltrating gradually.

Judgment

> Gradual Development.
> The maiden's marriage brings good fortune.
> The determination is favorable.

In traditional Chinese society after a maiden was engaged, a number of ceremonies had to be performed before her marriage.

In the same way, Gradual Development requires proceeding on a step-by-step basis. Preliminary steps cannot be skipped if you want to lay solid bases for any project. In time your determination will allow reaching the concretion point, symbolized by the marriage of the maiden.

53 - Gradual Development

The Image

> On the mountain is a tree: The image of Gradual Development.
> Thus the noble dwells in virtue and so improves the manners of the people.

Gradual Development indicates a slow but impressive ascent, from the low riverbanks up to the highlands. In the same way that a growing tree, you should progress slowly and properly, establishing firm bases for your development.

The slow growing of a tree also indicates how a sage, gradually along his own development, influences other people improving their life and teaching them. In time, your ascent will put you as a prominent role model for the people around you, such as a grown tree on a high place, which can be seen from afar.

First Six

> The goose gradually moves toward the riverbank.
> The small child is in danger and will be spoken against.
> No defect.

The goose appears in all the lines of this hexagram, symbolizing the steps in Gradual Development, from the water to the sky.

The goose is an animal that can swim in water, walk on land of fly on the sky. The goose is safer on water or when flying than in land, where it is in danger from its predators. Here it approaches a dangerous limit, symbolized by the riverbank.

This is the beginning of Gradual Development, you are alone and entering a new territory, attractive, but full of unknown perils.

You will be criticized, because you are crossing a line and daring to try something new. You are inexperienced and people will not trust you, hence you will face some trouble.

If you follow your goals with determination you will learn new things and will do well, without making any mistakes.

Career: You will have to learn the basics of a new job or assignment. Be careful and ready to take some criticism.

Private life: There will be difficulties and some gossip against you, which is the price of innovating and starting something new.

Health, Feelings and Social life: Be open to new experiences and knowledge. Do not be afraid to follow your dreams.

Second Six

The goose gradually moves towards a big rock.
Eats and drinks joyfully.
Good fortune.

You have reached some security here and you can look to the future with hope. The big rock represents a stable and secure base, a place where your basic necessities are satisfied.

The Chinese character translated as "joyfully" also means feasting, which gives the idea of a social reunion.

Also the same character, which is repeated twice, is an onomatopoeia for the honking sound of geese. It has been said that geese call other of their same kind when they find food, to share it, hence this line suggest sharing happily the good things of life with other people.

Career: You will prosper and consolidate your position. You work will give you joy and also an opportunity to socialize.

Private life: You have found a safe haven. Now you can relax and enjoy your well earned money with your friends and family.

Health, Feelings and Social life: Good health and happiness. Nurture yourself properly.

Third Nine

The goose gradually moves to the highlands.
The man goes on an expedition but does not return;
the woman is pregnant but does not give birth.
Misfortune.
It is favorable to fend off bandits.

The highlands are not a proper place for a goose, because there is no food or shelter for it there. To go to the highlands or on an expedition (notice that the word "expedition" may be also translated as "go to war") means to start some bold and risky advance without proper preparation.

If you start a conflict or try to something dangerous beyond your real possibilities, you will fail. The not returning man indicates loses and lack of support; the woman not giving birth symbolizes a plan that doesn't fructify.

By trying to force advance where it is not possible to do so you will lose your way.

To fend off bandits means that instead following ahead with impossible goals you should protect what you have already got.

53 - Gradual Development

Career: If you act boldly before having enough support you will fail and put in danger your job or your business. Be conservative and focus in keeping your business running instead taking risks.

Private life: Trying to gets things done by force or by yourself alone will put your family in danger. You may be robbed if you are not careful.

Health, Feelings and Social life: Reckless behavior will endanger your life. Bad prospects for pregnancies.

Fourth Six

> The goose gradually moves towards a tree.
> It may find a flat branch.
> No defect.

A flat branch in a tree is not the best place for a goose, but in times of hardship and danger you should be flexible, and accept what you can get.

The important thing is to find shelter, it may not be the perfect place for you but if it puts your out of danger is a good option.

The flat branch also indicates temporary solutions.

Career: You may have to take some job that is below your expectations or doesn't fell right for you. If you are a businessperson you may have to make some compromises to keep your business going.

Private life: You can find support in unlikely places if you are ready to adapt to the needs of the moment. You may buy or expand your house.

Health, Feelings and Social life: Be open to new ideas.

Fifth Nine

> The goose gradually moves towards the top of the hill.
> The woman cannot conceive for three years.
> Finally, nothing can stop it.
> Good fortune.

Conceiving a child symbolizes accomplishing the desires of your heart, but there are some obstacles that will stop that from happening for a time.

The *yin* line in the second place symbolizes a woman, who is separated from the fifth *yang* line —which is on the hilltop— by the intermediate lines. Applied to human relations it means that deceitful people or misunderstandings will create barriers that will prevent you for a time from achieving what you wish.

Also, the top of the hill indicates a person in a high position, who may become isolated and suffer abuse and slander from invidious people.

In the end all obstacles will be overcame and you will have good fortune.

Career: Some people may envy your position and will slander you, creating some trouble and misunderstandings between you and other persons depending on you. This will delay your goals but will not stop them. Be careful to have the real facts before taking important decisions.

Private life: Malicious rumors will make some trouble for you and cause interference in your relations and plans. In time all issues will be cleared up and you will fulfill your wishes.

Health, Feelings and Social life: Pregnancy difficulties. Protracted labor. In the end all will go well.

Top Nine

> The goose gradually moves towards the highlands.
> Its feathers can be used to practice the rites.
> Good fortune.

The highlands are the culmination of Gradual Advance.

To use the feathers of the goose for the rites means that your advancement makes you an example and also an inspiration for others; in a more mundane level it may indicate a consummated marriage.

Career: You have reached the pinnacle of success. You may retire and serve as a valued consultant.

Private life: If you produce some kind of creative work you will have high success with it. Your wishes will become true.

Health, Feelings and Social life: Because your spiritual elevation, you are seen as a role model by the people around you, who will cooperate freely with you. Excellent health.

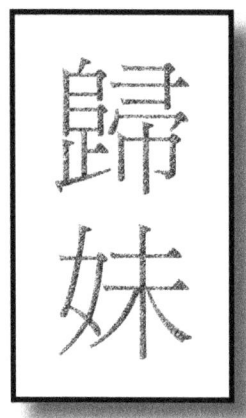

guī mèi
The Marrying Maiden

Four hexagrams are related with marriage and the preliminary steps leading to it: **31-Influence**, depicts the initial attraction and courtship in a couple; **32-Duration**, indicates the institution of marriage; **53-Gradual Development**, shows the steps and ceremonies leading to marriage and 54-The Marrying Maiden, describes a young maiden entering an older man's house as a secondary wife.

The two Chinese characters for this hexagram tag are: *guī*: "send in marriage" and *mèi*: "maiden, daughter, younger sister".

In ancient China a noble could have several wives and a ruler should have not less than three, all from the same family. The secondary wives were called younger sisters, since they usually were normally junior sisters, step-sisters or cousins of the primary bride.

The secondary wives were subservient to the principal wife, whose children had precedence over the other children.

Associated meanings

The marriage of the younger sister, the second wife, playing a subordinate role, concubine.

Judgment

> The Marrying Maiden.
> Marching forth brings misfortune.
> Nothing that is favorable.

54 - The Marrying Maiden

A girl entering a household as a secondary wife symbolizes becoming part of a human group in a subservient, informal or temporary position.

Taking an unassuming attitude and doing what is expected from you is the best choice when you are a subordinate.

Do not assume inappropriate prerogatives and do not undermine the people above you by influencing your common boss bypassing them.

The Image

> On the lake is the thunder: The image of the Marrying Maiden.
> Thus the noble persists to the end and knows the cause of the damage.

Thunder symbolizes the eldest son, who is leading the lake, the younger sister. This shows a young girl entering the house of an elder man in a low position, like a secondary wife or concubine.

Applied to current times, when entering in non-symmetric relationships, on the weaker side, you should be very careful to avoid damage, and behave with endurance.

Notice that neither good fortune nor blame is mentioned here. This kind of position is fraught with disadvantages, but as in most situations, with the proper attitude –patient and tactful in this case–, you can get the most of it.

This sentence also gives the idea of a transitory union that can't last forever because its initial flaws are the seeds of its final destruction.

First Nine

> She marries as a concubine.
> A lame man can walk.
> Marching forth brings good fortune.

The first line indicates a person with low social standing, as a concubine who has a humble position in a household. You are becoming part of some group, but you have little influence and you are very low in the pecking order.

Nevertheless, in spite of the disadvantages you can advance successfully, like a lame man who cannot walk fast but still advances on.

This is a good moment to start something new, if you are humble you will advance unimpeded, for that reason, marching forth brings good fortune.

Yi was the name of the penultimate *Shang* Emperor who gave a bride to the lord of *Zhou*. The **hexagram 11.5** has a similar oracle.

Career: If you stay in the background and support your boss loyally, you will progress.

Private life: You do not have much influence or power, but if you advance step by step, you will get ahead. Do not try to impose your views in your circle, in that way you will have a good welcome and may even receive some help.

Health, Feelings and Social life: Some mobility issues. Do not overexert yourself.

Second Nine

A one-eyed man can see.
The determination of a solitary man is favorable.

The one-eyed man that can see means to lose a partner and becoming solitary, to be in disadvantage or to suffer some loss or disappointment. Also it indicates having only a partial view of the situation.

To be determined as a solitary man indicates to go ahead on your own, without asking for help, in isolation.

In another interpretation level this line may indicate that if you do not have good prospects it is better to remain alone.

Career: You will receive no help from others, but you will manage yourself well.

Private life: In spite of your disadvantages you will be able to keep your position. This augury is good for somebody who is a recluse or is alone.

Health, Feelings and Social life: Vision troubles.

Third Six

The Marrying Maiden in servitude.
She returns and marries as a secondary wife.

To marry in servitude indicates a failing union or project; hence you will return back and accept a secondary role.

The sense of this line is that after your main ambition is thwarted you may go back and accept a compromise, taking the best possible alternative.

Career: You will be demoted, lose a job or fail in some project. Afterwards you will have to accept what you can get.

Private life: You will suffer some losses and your status will be affected. You may end some relation and then start a new one.

Health, Feelings and Social life: Lack of self-control will create troubles.

Fourth Nine

> The Marrying Maiden delays marriage, waiting for the right time.
> There will be a late marriage.

It is better to wait until you have a good opportunity instead compromising yourself with something that is below you.

In the end you will achieve your wishes.

Career: You will find some obstacles in your career but finally you will get what you were waiting for.

Private life: After postponing your wishes for a long time you will get what you yearn for. If you are seeking marriage you will have to wait until finding the right partner.

Health, Feelings and Social life: If you have health problems, they will improve after a long interval.

Fifth Six

> The emperor *Yi* gives his daughter in marriage.
> The sleeves of her dress were less gorgeous than her bridesmaid's.
> The moon is almost full.
> Good fortune.

The bridesmaids were secondary wives. In this case the more important thing —the daughter of the emperor— looked less attractive or was more humble than a less important factor —the bridesmaid—.

Appearance is not the main theme here, but modesty and a having a service vocation; that is what will allow you to complete a cycle —as the reference to the full moon indicates— and to be successful.

Career: You may be assigned to a new post; you will prosper in your new position if you are unassuming.

Private life: You will find happiness if you are attentive to the essentials and are not distracted by the appearances. A successful alliance will enrich your life.

Health, Feelings and Social life: Good health. Concentrate in simple things and avoid unrestrained fancy.

Top Six

> The woman has a basket, but it contains no fruit.
> The man stabs a sheep but it does not bleed.
> Nothing is favorable.

The Marrying Maiden - 54

The empty basket indicates falsity and meanness, the sheep that doesn't bleed is an insincere sacrifice, since the animal was already dead.

Also, the empty basket symbolizes an infertile womb and the non-bleeding sheep a man with no seed.

Lack of real commitment and hypocritical attitudes will poison any good chances in a marriage or union of any type.

Career: Your efforts will be wasted because they lack substance and are only for show. You will have little income and will not achieve anything good.

Private life: A union based on false premises will be fruitless and in the end will fail. Insincere and feeble efforts will not avail you.

Health, Feelings and Social life: Hypocrisy will poison your spiritual development. Your health may take a turn for the worse; old persons may die.

55

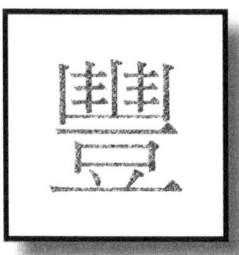
fēng
Fullness / Abundance

Associated meanings

Abundance, fullness; luxurious, bountiful, fruitful, prolific, ripe, full; prosperity, affluence; reaching the zenith. Some scholars think it describes a solar eclipse, which serves as an analogy for the eclipse of the influence or capable men.

Judgment

> Fullness has success.
> The king is coming.
> Do not be sad.
> Suitable at midday.

Both the king and the reference to the sun at midday denote personal growth and elevation.

You will reach a high point in your life, but since the sun starts descending as soon it reaches its zenith, it will be a transient moment of glory as well. That is the reason for the warning: do not be sad.

Also the sun gives warmth and light to all things; it shares its energy with all human beings. Do not try to hoard the fullness of this moment, it is not possible and such behavior goes against the requirements of this time. On the contrary, be ready to help and sustain others, share your blessings with an open heart.

55 - Fullness /Abundance

The Image

> Thunder and lightning culminate altogether: The image of Fullness.
> Thus the noble decides legal cases and applies punishments.

Thunder and lightning symbolize power exercised from a superior and enlightened position.

In several lines of Fullness, lack of clarity and suspicions make difficult the interaction between people.

Legal cases and punishments are the main tools to restore the public trust and to avoid lowly persons from interfering and darkening the light of justice.

First Nine

> Meets the master that is his match.
> Even if they are together for a ten-day week there will be no mistake.
> Going forward attains rewards.

You will meet somebody that shares your values and views –the fourth line– but is placed in a position higher than yours; this person will help you to realize your goals.

The ten-day week describes a period without harm that is granted between both parties. It will be a temporary meeting but you will complete a full cycle in that time.

The ten days together will allow you to accomplish a shared project with help from your master.

If you try to prolong the allowed time together, to reach still more benefits, you will attract calamity over yourself.

In ancient China the ten days weeks in use was based only on numeric considerations, without any astronomic relation.

Career: You will be promoted with the help of friends in high places. Use your new position constructively and do not abuse the confidence that you are granted.

Private life: A powerful friend will help you to advance, and you will work together along with him for a shared cause.

Health, Feelings and Social life: Good health.

Second Six

> The curtain has such fullness that the Big Dipper could be seen at noon.
> Going forwards attains distrust and hatred.
> Manifest sincerity will have good fortune.

The text of this line has several possible translations, but the general meaning is that your advance will be checked because you are distrusted. The curtains are prejudices and envy that will keep your merits unnoticed by your superiors.

Direct action will not work well, but if you demonstrate your sincerity by doing worthy deeds, finally you will be successful and will gain the trust of your superiors.

The Big Dipper is a cluster of seven stars in the constellation *Ursa Major*, four forming the bowl and three the handle of a dipper-shaped configuration, also called Plow or Plough.

Career: Your advice will not be heeded and your merits will be dismissed, but in the long run you will succeed.

Private life: Your plans will be hindered by some people, but if you are patient and sincere you will prevail at the end.

Health, Feelings and Social life: In time your health will improve.

Third Nine

> The covering has such fullness that the dimmest starts could be seen at noon.
> Breaks his right arm.
> No defect.

Unfavorable conditions will block any intent on your part to overcome them. The broken arm means that your influence and power will be diminished after an unsuccessful intent for advancing.

The dimmest starts symbolize petty people who will prosper meanwhile you are obstructed.

Nevertheless, you will make no mistake.

Career: You will be handicapped by the incompetent people who run the show. Capable men will be isolated and inoperative.

Private life: Your plans will not prosper, you will face trouble and your efforts will not be recognized.

Health, Feelings and Social life: You may have trouble with your arms.

Fourth Nine

> The curtain has such fullness that the Big Dipper could be seen at noon.
> He meets his master in secret.
> Good fortune.

55 - Fullness /Abundance

The darkness can be overcame with the help of a powerful ally, the fifth line, who is the ruler.

You will complement well the qualities of your master and by joining your efforts in a concerted way you will advance successfully.

To meet in secret stresses out the need for extreme care and caution.

Career: A superior will help you to be promoted.

Private life: You will start to overcome the darkness and the obstacles in your life with the help of a friend.

Health, Feelings and Social life: If you have any illness, your health will start to improve.

Fifth Six

> Brilliance is coming.
> You will have blessings and fame.
> Good fortune.

You will get over the pressing darkness with the help of capable helpers and the application of your inner abilities.

Your merits will be recognized and honored and with the cooperation of your supporters you will achieve great accomplishments.

Career: You will receive rewards for a well done team work and as a result you will progress.

Private life: The darkness and isolation of the previous times are gone. You will get support from your friends and family and happiness and prosperity will return.

Health, Feelings and Social life: You will be blessed with stamina and spiritual clarity. Flourishing health.

Top Six

> A large canopy hides his house.
> He peeks from his door, silent and with no one at his side.
> For three years he sees nothing.
> Misfortune.

Instead of facing the troubles of daily life you prefer to abode in the past, being afraid of the external world.

You are becoming isolated because you are not ready to share your blessings but look at others with arrogance and contempt.

Your rigid attitude will keep you apart from other people for a full period of seclusion.

Career: If you are not ready to face reality you will be discarded.

Private life: You family life will suffer because of your arrogance and egoism. In the end you will lose your family and friends and may lose your property as well.

Health, Feelings and Social life: Paranoid suspicions may paralyze your life.

56

lǔ
Sojourner / Wanderer

Associated meanings

Sojourner, guest, to lodge, wanderer, traveler, stranger, outsider, exile, expatriate, stay away from home, transition, temporary situation, wandering troops.

Judgment

> The Sojourner.
> Success in small things.
> The determination of the Sojourner brings good fortune.

You are residing in a strange land. Because you don't have support from your family or a wide network of friends, your perspectives are restricted, thus only small things can be done.

The determination of the Sojourner indicates adaptation to the limits of your current situation and to act accordingly to your possibilities.

As a Sojourner you are looking for a place to call home and perhaps employment as well. Until you secure a good place for settling, you should be satisfied with small comforts and avoid asking too much from people. You are a stranger and you will be respected only if you behave with dignity and modesty.

In another interpretation level this hexagram indicates a transitional phase, a temporary situation that will pass in time.

The Image

> Above the mountain is fire: The image of the Sojourner.
> Thus the noble applies punishments with clarity
> and doesn't prolong litigations.

Conflicts may have unpredictable and dangerous results, like a fire on a mountain summit that is swayed by the winds, they can easily grow beyond your control.

Fire will only last while it has something to burn, in the same way punishments should only be applied for a short while and when there is no other chance.

You may have to defend yourself, but you do not have the resources to sustain protracted conflicts.

First Six

> The Sojourner is too fussy.
> He will bring calamity upon himself.

The character translated as "fussy" also means "trivial, petty, annoying, touchy, contemptible". The general idea is that the Sojourner has an exaggerated opinion of his own importance and he is an annoyance to other people, a troublemaker.

Notice that being this the first line, it depicts a person of scarce resources and low social position. Such a petty person will fall in disgrace because his inappropriate behavior.

Career: You may lose your work because you are not up to your responsibilities.

Private life: If you are intolerant and narrow-minded you will cause trouble for yourself.

Health, Feelings and Social life: For your own sake, you should review your priorities and focus in what is important.

Second Six

> The Sojourner comes to a resting place.
> Keeps his belongings safely and gets a young and loyal servant.

You will find a good place to stop for a while.

The character translated here as "belongings" also means "money, means of livelihood and property"; besides its literal meaning, it symbolizes your resources, knowledge, and ability. To keep your belongings safe also means that you are coping well with your journey, that you behave with self-possession and modesty.

To get a young servant indicates that you will receive support, which will be good within its limits, since a young servant wouldn't be highly qualified.

Career: You will secure a position that provides a base for further advancement. Also you may get an assistant.

Private life: After a transition period you are learning how to cope with your new environment. You are adapting well, since you have got both a place to stay and a loyal helper.

Health, Feelings and Social life: You will feel secure and supported.

Third Nine

The Sojourner burns his resting place.
He loses his young servant.
The determination is dangerous.

To burn the resting place indicates a violent and overbearing behavior that will undermine your own security.

If you treat other people with arrogance and insensitivity you will lose their cooperation.

If you follow such wrong path, you will be alienated from other people, and will find only trouble in your future.

Career: If don't moderate your extreme behavior you will lose your position and any support that you previously had.

Private life: Do not act without caring for the feelings or opinions of others or you will lose their support. Do not be stubborn; stop before it is too late. You may lose your property or some member of your family.

Health, Feelings and Social life: You are too stressed out, your health will suffer.

Fourth Nine

The Sojourner stays at one place and obtains property and an ax. My heart is not happy.

You have found a temporary resting place and some security.

Still uneasy, you don't feel safe. The ax also may indicate hard work to get settled or the need for security measures.

Your aspirations are not yet fulfilled; you know that your current lodgings are not the proper place for you.

The general sense is that you will find temporary solutions that are acceptable but not very good.

Career: To get a property and an ax means to get recognition and a position good enough. But you are not comfortable in your new job and feel the need to secure it.

Private life: You are just passing through a place. Although you have found temporary accommodations it is a hard life.

Health, Feelings and Social life: Anxiety and solitude.

Fifth Six

He shoots a pheasant.
Although the first arrow fails finally he is praised and given employment.

To shoot a pheasant means to seek employment by way of showing your abilities.

You may have some troubles demonstrating your value, but in the end you will get what you look for, after you prove what you are capable of.

In another interpretation level you will have to offer something of value before getting accepted.

"The shooting at a target was used in antiquity, for the election of feudatories and officials. The precision in shooting was supposed to represent the uprightness of the heart, and vice-versa." (*Wieger*).

Career: You will get a promotion or a new job from your superiors after they recognize your merits.

Private life: You will prosper and get public recognition.

Health, Feelings and Social life: Feeling good.

Top Nine

The bird burns its nest.
The Sojourner laughs at first but afterward cries out and weeps.
He loses his cow in *Yi*.
Misfortune.

The nest indicates an elevated position, at the top of the hexagram. To laugh first and weep afterwards means that if you are being arrogant and careless you will lose your position, a thing that happens many times in the top line, when people cross the line of proper behavior.

The reference to the lost cow in *Yi* is related to an historical-mythical Chinese figure, associated to birdlike characters, which took his herds to pasture in *Yi* and was murdered there.

To lose the cow means to lose the livelihood and to be unable to adapt to the exigencies of the time.

The character for bird, *niao*, who appears in this line, only is used four times in the *Yijing* and always indicates that extreme attitudes will cause misfortune.

Career: Your lack of adaptability and your arrogance will destroy your base of power.

Private life: You will suffer losses caused by negligence and overconfidence. A fire may damage your property.

Health, Feelings and Social life: Your feelings will sway from joy to distress. You may contract a disease of the eye.

57

xùn

Gentle Influence / Penetration / The Wind

This is one of the eight hexagrams that are comprised by the same trigram repeated twice, in this case *xùn*, The Gentle. Please see **The Eight Trigrams** (p. 369) for more information.

Associated meanings

Humble, yield, compliant, obedient, mild, bland, insinuating, bowing down, food offering, bending to enter.

Judgment

> Gentle Influence.
> Success in small things.
> It is favorable to have a place to go.
> It is favorable to see the great man.

Success in small things indicates certain attitude, compliant and humble, but persistent and determined. This means that you will achieve your ends little by little, but in a sure way.

To have a place where to go means that you should have perseverance and clear objectives; otherwise your gentle influence would dissipate soon without having any lasting effects.

To see the great man not only indicates to seek advice and help from a qualified source, but also to rise mentally and spiritually to be up to the situation.

57 - Gentle Influence / Penetration / The Wind

The Image

> Winds that follow each other: The image of Gentle Influence.
> Thus the noble proclaims his commands and acts to carry out his tasks.

Confucius said: "The relation between superiors and inferiors is like that between the wind and the grass: the grass is bound to bend when the wind blows across it". This quotation indicates clearly the meaning of the image.

Wind influences the grass without being visible. In the same way, you should influence unceasingly the people that you are leading, inspiring and supporting them to perform their tasks.

The words "proclaims his commands" mean that you should be always behind your projects supporting them but also indicates the need to concentrate your mind in your objectives, avoiding unnecessary distractions.

First Six

> Advancing and retreating.
> The determination is favorable for a warrior.

To advance and then retreat indicates a state of indecision and hesitation and hence lack of stability.

What is required is the determination of a warrior: assume your duty firmly, be single-minded and valiant.

Career: The situation is not stable; you will have ups and downs. Keep focused in your main goal and strive purposefully to reach it.

Private life: Profit and loss. If you act more firmly you will get better results.

Health, Feelings and Social life: Your will is weak and you feel insecure. Your health may have ups and downs.

Second Nine

> Penetration under the bed.
> Using invokers and sorcerers in large number brings good fortune.
> No defect.

The invokers and sorcerers indicate the way to catch hidden factors or influences. Invokers can be also translated as "chronicles", which suggests unseen influences from the past.

The message is that you will need special methods and specialists to clarify the situation and uncover hidden forces. Also, this kind of work should be done with subtleness and finesse; a frontal assault would be useless.

You will make no mistake uncovering what is hidden beneath the surface, because such disclosure will benefit you.

Career: There may be some people around you with hidden agendas or some negative influences unknown to you. Seek help from qualified people, to help you clarify the situation.

Private life: Something is not what it seems in your family or circle of friends. May be somebody has a hidden grudge against you or some secret design that may harm you. It will be good for you to bring to the light such hidden machinations.

Health, Feelings and Social life: To penetrate under the bed means to cast light over hidden factors in you unconscious mind, to unveil feelings or prejudices that are repressed. You will need professional help to do that.

Third Nine

Repeated penetration.
Humiliation.

If you can't accomplish your will and try to force you way blindly, you will be shamed.

In another interpretation level it also may indicate that you cannot reach a decision, and will ruminate without end about some matter. Such indecision will not allow you to do anything good and in the end will humiliate you.

Career: You will be disgraced by your lack of decision or your intransigent attitude.

Private life: If you don't strengthen your will and soften your methods you will be shamed.

Health, Feelings and Social life: Lack of internal balance may damage your spiritual and physical health.

Fourth Six

Repentance fades.
Captures three types of prey in hunting.

Traditionally, animals caught in real hunts were divided in three categories: a) for sacrifices; b) for guests and c) provisions for the sovereign's kitchen. A hunt that yielded enough for all purposes was considered very successful.

Applied to current situations it means to achieve very good results at all levels and to get all that you need.

Troubles will disappear.

57 - Gentle Influence / Penetration / The Wind

Career: You will very extremely successful and will achieve your goals.

Private life: You will find what you are looking for and will have a prosperous time.

Health, Feelings and Social life: If you are ill, you will get a proper diagnosis and treatment and your health will improve.

Fifth Nine

> The determination is fortunate.
> Repentance fades.
> Nothing that is not favorable.
> There is no beginning, but an end.
> Before the seventh day, three days; after the seventh day, three days.
> Good fortune.

You should change your approach after you realize that your first intents were wrong. If you act with determination and flexibility you will avoid trouble.

The mention to the seventh day and the three days is related to the ancient ten-day week. It means that if you make adjustments by the middle of the week, by the end of it you will see good results –do not take the number of days literally–. It also means that any changes in your methods should be done gradually and that your new approach will take some time to produce visible results.

In ancient China, the ten days weeks in use was based only on numerical considerations, without any astronomic relation. The ten days were associated with the Ten Heavenly Stems *(tian gan)*, that are a Chinese system of cyclic numbers from the *Shang* dynasty.

Career: You will have to apply some corrections and adjustments to your plans. If you are firm in your new modus operandi you will succeed.

Private life: Now is the proper time to rectify errors from the past. If you do so, you will avoid being humiliated and will have good fortune.

Health, Feelings and Social life: This is a decisive moment. A time to put to right what is wrong. If you do what is right now, you will gain good emotional balance.

Top Nine

> Penetration under the bed.
> He loses his belongings and an ax.
> The determination is ominous.

Penetration under the bed means to be obsessed with elucidating every detail of some issue before taking action.

If you waste all your energy and time in vain speculation you will have nothing left to face the real problems in your life.

In another interpretation level it means that if you follow some issue too far, you will generate more trouble than good results.

If you persist in your obsession you will lose your means of defense and attack, and will squander your resources.

Career: If you are too suspicious and insecure you will achieve nothing good and may even lose your work or business.

Private life: You will suffer some losses. Stop procrastinating and ruminating endlessly or you will experience real trouble.

Health, Feelings and Social life: Paranoid compulsion. You may suffer an illness.

58

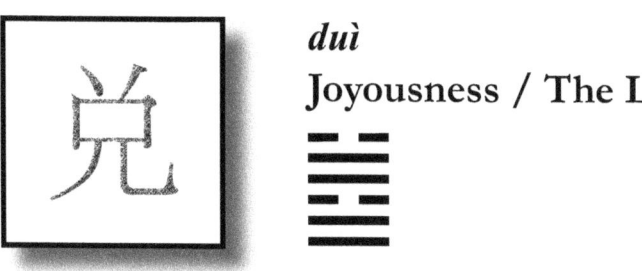

duì
Joyousness / The Lake

This is one of the eight hexagrams that are comprised by the same trigram repeated twice, in this case *duì*, The Joyous. Please see **The Eight Trigrams** (p. 369) for more information.

Associated meanings

Joyousness, happiness, satisfaction; cheerful talk, openness, interaction, exchange, communication, mouth; barter.

"Good words that dispel grief and rejoice the hearer; hence the two meanings, to speak, to rejoice." (*Wieger*).

Judgment

> Joyousness.
> Success.
> Determination is favorable.

A joyous attitude is easily communicable to others and will help to foster good communications and friendly relations between people.

Joy should flow from within and not depend on external circumstances. If you run after joy you will not find true joy. The essence of joy is an open and cheerful nature, not a mindless search of external pleasures.

Determination is required to avoid joy from becoming immoderate and weakening.

The Image

> Two lakes together: The image of Joyousness.
> Thus the noble joins his friends for discussion and training.

58 - Joyousness / The Lake

As two lakes linked together mingle their waters and avoid stagnation, free communication with other people will enrich your ideas and give proper perspective to your thoughts, keeping your notions up-to-date and vital.

Open communication with friends will not only give you knowledge, will keep you happy as well.

First Nine

> Harmonious joy.
> Good fortune.

The word translated as "harmonious" also means "balance, rhythm, respond to, agreement", indicating that you are in tune with the current situation and with the people around you.

You are free to do your will because you have inner calm and good balance.

Career: You will prosper and receive help because you are in very good terms with your associates.

Private life: Domestic harmony will prevail. Do not make demands on people but be gentle with all them.

Health, Feelings and Social life: Very good health and happiness.

Second Nine

> Sincere joy.
> Good fortune.
> Regrets go away.

Do not let others complicate your life with dubious pleasures. Follow what you think is best, disregarding what others say.

In that way you will avoid trouble and will enjoy good fortune.

Career: Have faith in your own plans; do not be enticed to take unproved shortcuts.

Private life: You may be tempted to stray from your path, or to do something improper to satisfy other people. Never give up on your principles.

Health, Feelings and Social life: Hesitation and doubts when facing unbecoming desires.

Third Six

> Coming joy.
> Misfortune.

Excessive indulgence of your own appetites and desires will cost you dearly and will destroy your hopes.

Career: Seeking advancement through obsequious behavior will cause you misfortune. Keep focused in your duty.

Private life: You will lose yourself and weaken your will if you only live for external pleasures, amusements and money.

Health, Feelings and Social life: Do not trade your inner stability and peace for vain dreams.

Fourth Nine

> Haggling joy.
> Still not at peace.

After limiting your anxiety there will be happiness.

You are restless and undecided, trying to balance external pressures with your own desires.

Choose wisely; select what will give you true and lasting value and not only temporary pleasure.

Once you find the correct path you will be happy.

Career: You may have to decide between the right path and an easy way. Do not let fawning people sway you from your duty.

Private life: Do not be unduly concerned with your pleasures. Relax and take things easy; you will do well.

Health, Feelings and Social life: Indecision and stress, but it will pass. Temporary illness.

Fifth Nine

> Trusting degrading influences is dangerous.

To trust degrading influences means to trust unworthy people or to be involved in a dubious situation.

It also indicates overconfidence in your capacity and strength disregarding possible dangers.

Career: Do not put your trust in the wrong people or in shady schemes.

Private life: You will commit a judgment error if you trust nefarious people.

Health, Feelings and Social life: Evil influences in action. Substance abuse.

58 - Joyousness / The Lake

Top Six

> Alluring joyousness.

Vain and fun loving people will only care about their pleasures and follies, dragging others with them in their wake.

Career: If you are a public relations or sales person you may prosper materially. This is not a good moment for hard work.

Private life: You will lead others in the search of pleasure with clever words. You will have no profit or loss.

Health, Feelings and Social life: Intense social life. For you life is a game of mirrors.

59

huàn
Dispersion / Dissolution / The Flood

Associated meanings

Dispersion, dissolution, scattering; dispel misunderstandings, fantasies and fears; overcoming dissension; gush, splash; slack, relaxed.

Judgment

> Dispersion.
> Success.
> The king approaches his temple.
> It is favorable to cross the great river.
> The determination is favorable.

This hexagram has a double meaning:

To disperse the obstacles or misunderstandings that prevent an union.

Avoiding to be dispersed or separated by obstacles, illusions and prejudices.

People are keep apart by prejudices and petty intolerance, but the time of Dispersion is like a flood that will carry away such obstructions and melt the ice in the hearts of the people.

The king is a leader that gathers people around him. To join a mass of people, a sense of shared purpose and identify is required. The temple symbolizes such central point, which focuses the attention of the people in a single goal and brings people together.

In ancient China, crossing rivers, either at a ford or when the river was frozen, was not an easy task. It implicated dangers and hardships; hence crossing the great river means to carry out a difficult undertaking.

59 - Dispersion / Dissolution / The Flood

The Image

> Wind moving over the water: The image of Dispersion.
> Thus the ancient kings made offerings to the Supreme Lord
> and erected temples.

The wind blowing over the water melts the solid ice and pushes the water around. In the same way barriers between people should be overcame.

The ancient kings symbolize a pattern or model of good governance, which we should strive to follow.

To make offerings means to get over egoism, grudges and prejudices, to make a contribution for the sake of the community. The temple symbolizes a shared project or idea that summons peoples around.

First Six

> Uses the strength of a horse for rescue.
> Good fortune.

You are located at the beginning of Dispersion and you should try to prevent dissension. To help with the strength of a horse means to go quickly and energetically to fix the problems.

Good fortune means that you can avoid further troubles by taking early care.

Career: You will have quick advancement with help from your superiors.

Private life: Strong progress and loyalty between friends.

Health, Feelings and Social life: Spirited energy and good health.

Second Nine

> Dispersion.
> Run to your support.
> Repentance fades.

You are in danger of becoming isolated and alienated from others, swept by the flood of the circumstances.

You should adjust your attitude to prevent trouble, get in touch with other people and help them instead ruminating and bearing ill will towards them.

Running to your support also means to use your energy in constructive ways, doing what is your real vocation.

Career: Be ready to seize an opportunity instead grumbling against others.

Private life: You will attain your wishes if you overcome your misanthropy.

Health, Feelings and Social life: Ill humor and hatred will disperse if you focus your thoughts in some inspiring goal.

Third Six

> Disperses himself.
> No repentance.

You will need all your energy concentrated in the undertaking that you are carrying out, do not waste time or energy regarding your own personal trivial interests.

Putting all your efforts towards the common good will benefit not only other people but yourself, in the long run.

Career: Working in the service business will be beneficial.

Private life: You will dedicate your time to altruistic purposes with good success.

Health, Feelings and Social life: Expansive feelings of kinship, care and concern towards other people will make you a stronger and better person.

Fourth Six

> Disperses his group.
> Outstanding good fortune.
> Dispersion is accumulation.
> Common people do not consider that point.

To disperse his group means to leave behind self-centered partisanship, and narrow factions, to be open-minded and ready to benefit others beyond your close friends. Also it indicates to overcome prejudices, outdated rules and customs.

By dispersing the benefits outside your own group of associates you will work for the common good and achieve far greater results in the end, which is the meaning of the phrase: dispersion is accumulation.

This can be only done by an enlightened person, who can see beyond what common people realize.

Career: Try to see the big picture, consider all options and don't be narrow-minded.

Private life: If you are able to prevail against parochial attitudes you will prosper and enrich your family.

Health, Feelings and Social life: You will have a chance to rise spiritually and expand the scope of your mind, but that will only happen if you are open to new ideas.

59 - Dispersion / Dissolution / The Flood

Fifth Nine

> Dispersing sweat, proclaiming aloud.
> Disperses the king dwellings.
> No defect.

"Dispersing sweat" can also be translated as "imperial edict". In the same way that sweating can break a fever, the king's edicts will break –disperse or dissolve– conflicts and grudges between his subjects.

Notice that the fifth line is the place of the ruler and symbolizes somebody with authority. To disperse the king dwellings means to share what you have with others, to give first and ask later, to take the first step in helping others.

Career: You will have to rally people around your project to get the support that you need. But to get help from qualified people you will have to offer them more than kind words.

Private life: Some kind of adjustment or change should be made in your family, perhaps redistributing some property.

Health, Feelings and Social life: If you are ill, your health will improve. If you relax your mood will be better.

Top Nine

> Disperses his blood.
> Going away, keeping at a distance, departing.
> No defect.

Blood symbolizes danger and hatred. To disperse the blood means that the risk of spilling blood (bitter conflicts) should be avoided by whatever means necessary.

Anything that can cause serious trouble should be put away. Risks should not be taken and caution should prevail.

You should be ready to give up, depart or discard some of your projects if that is necessary to avoid danger.

Career: Perhaps you will be reassigned to a new workplace or may have to start your business anew in another location.

Private life: A bad agreement is better than a good lawsuit. Be ready to accept a compromise in order to settle disputes or lawsuits.

Health, Feelings and Social life: You are excessively stressed. Laid back and relax, learn to give up and do not try to control everything or always having the last word.

60

 *jié*
Limitation

Associated meanings

Regulate, moderate, constraint, contain, restrict, articulate; moral integrity, self-control.

"The primary application of *jié* was to denote the joints of the bamboo; it is used also for the joints of the human frame; and for the solar and other terms of the year. Whatever makes regular division may be denominated a *jié*; there enter into it the ideas of regulating and restraining; and the subject of this hexagram is the regulation of government". (*Legge*)

Judgment

> Limitation.
> Success.
> A severe limitation cannot be applied with persistence.

Limitation means to put each thing in its right place at the proper time and to restrain all things to their proper spheres.

Restrictions should be applied to put order in your live, like when limiting how much you eat or controlling your temper. In other cases, temporary limitations are required to adapt to some circumstance, like when limiting expenditures in times of hardship.

Severe limitation refers to excessive control that can cause counterproductive results instead of being beneficial.

60 - Limitation

The Image

> Above the lake is water: The image of Limitation.
> Thus the noble establishes the number and measure
> and deliberates about morality and conduct.

The lake puts boundaries to the water inside it, defining its shape and depth.

In the same way, through self-imposed limitations, we shape our life and channel our energy in the chosen path.

To establish number and measure means to regulate properly our work along time. It also indicates to discard some things and to keep others, establishing proper priorities.

To deliberate about morality and conduct means to adjust our behavior to the present situation, to actualize the norms to the current necessities.

First Nine

> Not going out of the door to the courtyard.
> No defect.

Here, not stepping into the courtyard means to remain in a safe and familiar place.

Stay well inside your limits, wait for an opportunity, and do not make a false start.

Career: Do not try to force changes or to expand your responsibilities. Stick to proven methods.

Private life: Maintain your daily routine without changes. Do not travel.

Health, Feelings and Social life: You will have no trouble if you remain quiet and resting. Be discreet.

Second Nine

> Not going out of the gate of the courtyard
> Misfortune.

If you do not act quickly you will lose a good opportunity.

The gate separates the courtyard from the outside world, crossing it means to venture in the world.

Open yourself to new possibilities, travel, be ready to meet new people and to take some risks.

Do not let doubts and fears stop you from acting.

Career: You should be open to learn new things and innovate to face new opportunities.

Private life: Change will do you good. Staying at home following the same old routines will make you lose a good opportunity.

Health, Feelings and Social life: If you do not express what you are feeling you will be sorry. You need some physical exercise.

Third Six

Disregarding the limits leads to sorrow.
No defect.

Lack of self-control and moderation may put you in some embarrassing situations when relating to other people.

Each sphere of society has its own rules and if you ignore them you will create unnecessary conflicts.

In another interpretation level, self-indulgence may make you to violate your own rules and you will harm yourself.

Career: If you overstep your sphere of influence or try to take shortcuts bypassing the rules you will shame yourself.

Private life: Keep your word and avoid extravagances or you will be sorry.

Health, Feelings and Social life: Be moderate and avoid abusing food and drink. Do not stress yourself too much.

Fourth Six

Contented limitation.
Success.

A realist attitude, accepting willingly the restraints imposed on your life will be successful.

Once you have learned to control your behavior in order to get the most of your life, self-control will come to you naturally and easily.

This also means being capable of following the leading of your bosses.

Career: Your loyal and dedicated work will be rewarded.

Private life: By adapting yourself to the current situation and accepting your limits without struggling against reality, you will progress.

Health, Feelings and Social life: Bear your physical or emotional restrictions with patience; in time, you will prevail against the odds.

Fifth Nine

> Pleasant limitation.
> Good fortune.
> Going forward has praise.

A well-balanced person applies restrictions to himself before requesting them to other people.

By setting the correct example he incites others to follow his good example. Going smoothly he will be able to achieve his goal and will gain the public esteem.

Career: Always set an example for others by accepting yourself in the first place the regulations that you will apply to them afterwards. If you are fair minded and realistic, you will earn the support of your subordinates and will be praised by your superiors.

Private life: Discipline combined with benevolence will help you to prosper and have a very happy family life.

Health, Feelings and Social life: Good health and excellent relations with the people around you.

Top Six

> Bitter limitation.
> The determination is ominous.
> Repentance fades.

Exaggerated limitations will cause undesirable consequences, for that reason to continue this way will bring misfortune.

Treating others in a hard way will generate resentment and resistance; being too harsh on yourself may make you bitter.

Such bitter limitation can be useful only for a while and just in extreme cases.

Career: If you are overbearing and harsh with your subordinates you will brew up trouble.

Private life: Stern discipline can be sustained only for a while. If you overdo it you will cause trouble.

Health, Feelings and Social life: If you ask too much of yourself your health will be harmed and you will lose your emotional balance.

61

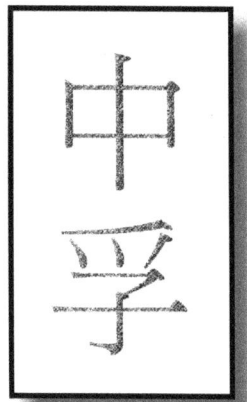

zhōng fú
Inner Truth

Associated meanings

Inner sincerity; reliability, to inspire confidence in others, inner confidence.

Judgment

> Inner truth.
> Pigs and fishes.
> Good fortune.
> It is favorable to cross the great river.
> The determination is favorable.

This hexagram shows how inner reliability and confidence will be advantageous and will allow you to earn the trust of other people.

Pigs and fishes were presented to the Lord of Heaven by the common people, but these humble contributions, presented with inner sincerity were worthy of blessings. No matter how small is your contribution, if it is presented with sincerity it will be appreciated. Also, if you inner truth can even influence pigs and fishes, it is great indeed.

In ancient China, crossing rivers, either at a ford or when the river was frozen, was not an easy task. It implicated dangers and hardships; hence crossing the great river means to carry out a difficult undertaking.

If you are true to yourself and proceed with confidence you will be successful.

61 - Inner Truth

The Image

Above the lake is the wind: The image of Inner Truth.
Thus the noble discusses criminal cases and delays executions.

The two empty lines in the middle of this hexagram symbolize the heart and mind free from all preoccupations, without any consciousness of self, indicating inner truth.

A truthful person in a position of authority tries to understand deeply the conduct of people and is not hasty to condemn them, taking all necessary care to understand all the facts before taking action.

First Nine

It is auspicious to be prepared.
If there is something else, it is unsettling.

Take preventive steps, don't leave anything to chance.

Rely in your own resources; do not depend on the support of others.

If you are focused and do not vacillate all will go well.

Career: You will prosper if you are self-reliant and are well prepared. Stick to proven methods.

Private life: You have all that you need for enjoying a happy life. Be wary of strangers.

Health, Feelings and Social life: Be on your guard; stand by your ethical principles.

Second Nine

A crane calling from the shadows.
His young replies.
I have a good cup.
I will share it with you.

If you cultivate sincerity, all those who share the same temperament will answer your call.

You will prosper and receive help from others.

The crane is an emblem of longevity, wisdom and nobility. Also notice that the meaning of *fú*, the second character in the hexagram tag (*zhōng fú*) means "to brood over eggs", "to hatch".

Career: You will be promoted and supported by your superiors.

Private life: Share the good things of life with your friends. A child may be born in your family.

Health, Feelings and Social life: Good health and happiness.

Third Six

> Gets a mate.
> Sometimes beats the drum, sometimes stops.
> Sometimes weeps, sometimes sings.

Other translations for "mate" would be "comrade, antagonist or enemy".

If you depend on relations with other people for your happiness or self-confidence, your emotional stability will be erratic, according to the changes in the mood and esteem of the others toward you.

Try to be more independent.

Career: You will have ups and downs in your work, depending on the whims of other people.

Private life: Good moments will alternate with trouble. You will have gains and losses.

Health, Feelings and Social life: It would be good for you to learn to be more independent, to correct your life's imbalances.

Fourth Six

> The moon is almost full.
> One of the team's horses goes away.
> No defect.

The moon almost full indicates that a cycle is ending and changes are coming.

The horse going away means that somebody is going his own way. It may also indicate the end of a relation, society or project.

A lost horse also is an image of distress and loss of strength.

This is the proper time to choose a new path, leaving something behind and following higher goals.

Do not vacillate in accepting advice from wiser people, but in the end, trust your own opinion.

Career: You may be reassigned or promoted and start a new project.

Private life: You may part with old friends or relations in search of something new, or some friend may leave you behind.

Health, Feelings and Social life: You will make no mistake following your insights to advance spiritually.

61 - Inner Truth

Fifth Nine

> He has truth that links them together.
> No defect.

This line is the place of the ruler. The truth that links them together is the confidence and sincerity of the leader that binds all his followers together under his leadership

This is the proper time to establish relationships and to attach associates.

Career: You will have the confidence of the people around you and you will be successful.

Private life: Your sincerity and reliability will gain the trust and loyalty of your family and friends. No problems.

Health, Feelings and Social life: Good health. You are completely honest with yourself and with the people around you.

Top Nine

> The cry of the pheasant rises up into heaven.
> The determination is ominous.

When reputation is higher than capability, promises can't be carried out. Sooner or later reality will take charge of the situation and misfortune will arrive.

Do not promise more than you can achieve, you will not accomplish anything good with only words.

The cry of the pheasant can be taken as a bad omen. Compare with the second nine where the crane and his young answering it are a sign of sincerity and comradeship.

Career: Be realist and conservative. Do not try to improve reality with lies or misrepresentations, stick to the facts.

Private life: Arrogance and unrealistic expectations will cause your downfall. Stop before going too far.

Health, Feelings and Social life: Pride and hollow illusions will mislead you.

62

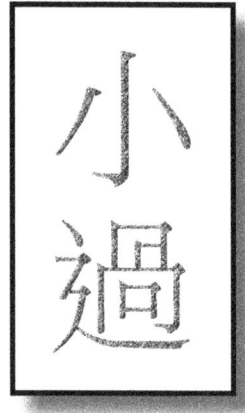

xiǎo guò
Excess of the Small

Associated meanings

Preponderance of the small, keeping a low profile, small gains, scrupulous and humble work, small gets by.

Judgment

> The Excess of the Small.
> Success.
> The determination is favorable.
> Proper for small matters, not suitable for great matters.
> The flying bird leaves the message:
> It is not right to ascend, it is fit to go below.
> Great good fortune.

The Excess of the Small indicates lack of strength and resources for doing big things. Because the only two yang lines in this hexagram are placed in the center —the inner part of the hexagram— there is not enough strength to cope with the outer world.

The flying bird symbolizes the risk of carrying something too far, as a bird that flies too high and is shot down. The symbol of the bird (niao) only appears —besides this hexagram, where it is repeated three times— at the top line of the **hexagram 56**, where it indicates misfortune following hubris. In all cases it is a warning against the danger of ambition and reckless behavior. This is not the proper time to be bold.

62 - Excess of the Small

Good fortune is the result of being focused on your daily routines with care and modesty, giving proper attention to detail.

The Image

> On top of the mountain is the thunder: The image of the Excess of the Small.
> Thus the noble in his behavior is exceedingly reverent,
> in mourning is exceedingly sorrow,
> and in his expenditures is exceedingly frugal.

This is a time to accept and respect the social norms to the utmost grade, a time for humbleness, prudence and conscientious work.

Be willing to accept your present limitations; do not try to force the situation or to stand out, instead flow with the current.

First Six

> The flying bird will have misfortune.

Being the first line, it describes what will happen to a beginner when he tries to carry out something that is beyond his capacity or knowledge.

Do not take any chances or you will suffer trouble. Stay where you are, if you try to move to a higher position, you will fail.

Career: Focus in your normal duties, if you try to advance or you attract attention over yourself you will have trouble.

Private life: If you keep contented with your current position you will avoid trouble. Do not try to innovate; be modest.

Health, Feelings and Social life: Your dreams are not realistic; do not follow your fancy, but exercise restraint.

Second Six

> Passing by his ancestor, meeting his ancestress.
> Not reaching his ruler, meeting his minister.
> No defect.

To go towards the ancestress means to follow the hierarchies. To meet the ancestress instead of the ancestor or to meet the minister instead of the prince means that you should take exceptional care when approaching authority, not demanding too much. This also indicates to follow the line of minor resistance and to make the most with limited resources.

Career: Use your contacts wisely to support your plans. They don't need to be high level to be useful.

Private life: You may be helped unexpectedly by somebody with authority in your family, may be an old woman.

Health, Feelings and Social life: Be adaptable and realistic, you may find friends in unexpected places.

Third Nine

If he is not exceedingly careful, somebody may follow and strike him. Misfortune.

If you do not take good precautions you will be harmed by an unexpected aggression. The Chinese character translated as "strike" also means "kill, injure, violent assault, maltreat".

The attack will come without warning, like a stab on the back, and it may come from somebody that you trust.

An alternative translation would be "Not passing, somebody…", meaning that if you go too far you will put yourself in danger.

Career: Somebody may try to trick or deceive you. Trust no one.

Private life: Do not be overconfident. Take all necessary precautions to avoid being harmed.

Health, Feelings and Social life: Be extra careful with your health and be prudent in your dealings with people.

Fourth Nine

No defect.
Not passing, meeting.
Moving on is dangerous.
One must be alert.
Do not be unyielding.

This is a warning to be quiet and restrained. Do what you need to do and no more. Be humble, do not make others to lose face.

To be alert means to wait and see. This is not a good time for making any changes or to introduce new plans.

Career: Follow your duty and do not take the initiative. Keep a low profile and wait patiently.

Private life: Be on your guard. Respond as needed to the circumstances but do not try to force the situation. It is not advisable to travel.

Health, Feelings and Social life: Be discreet and quiet.

Fifth Six

> Heavy clouds but no rain from our western frontier.
> The prince catches the one in the cave.

Clouds without rain indicate that you have reached some results, but still you cannot achieve your final objective.

Search for something new that can help you; it may be hard to find, as if hidden in a cave. Perhaps some person can help you or you need some thing or knowledge to succeed.

Notice that the text neither prognosticates success nor error.

Career: The way ahead is blocked. You will need help from capable people to keep going ahead.

Private life: You have reached an impasse. Look for new ideas or new people to help you.

Health, Feelings and Social life: Stress and confusion. Try to clarify your mind and understand what you really feel.

Top Six

> Passes without finding him.
> The flying bird is netted.
> Misfortune.
> This means disaster.

If you don't know where to stop and try to fly too high you will become entangled in trouble.

Some translations say "the flying bird leaves" instead of "the flying bird is netted". The modern meaning for the character lí is "to leave, part from", but originally the phonetic element of this character showed a bird being caught in a net and some of its original meanings were "fall into, fasten, attach".

Career: Be satisfied with reasonable gains or you will meet with disaster.

Private life: Excessive arrogance and overconfidence will cause your downfall.

Health, Feelings and Social life: If you ask too much of your body your health will be harmed.

63

jì jì
Already Across

Associated meanings

After completion, after the climax, after crossing the river, already fording, already completed, mission accomplished.

Judgment

> Already Across.
> Success.
> The determination is favorable for small things.
> At first good fortune, at the end chaos.

In ancient China, crossing rivers, either at a ford or when the river was frozen, was not an easy task. It implicated dangers and hardships; hence having crossing the river means to have accomplished a difficult undertaking.

Success is achieved. Now you should handle the transition to a new stage. If you neglect to take precautions things may go downhill easily.

Do not take things or people for granted. Small things that are often overlooked can cause serious problems later on, take scrupulous attention to detail to stabilize the situation.

The Image

> Water over fire: The image of Already Across.
> Thus the noble meditates on misfortune in advance to prevent it.

63 - Already Across

Fire and water interacting usefully are used to cook or to produce vapor, but if the fire is too strong, the water will boil outside the cauldron, and if it is too weak the water will stop boiling.

As a boiling cauldron must be tended with care to obtain proper results, all factors in the current situation should be kept working seamlessly and in their proper places to prevent trouble.

Do not wait until trouble gets out of hand; prevent small problems from getting worse by stopping them as soon they start.

First Nine

> Drag his wheels and wets his tail.
> No defect.

To drag the wheels means to contain the advance, to avoid rushing blindly forward. Take your time and advance with care.

The next hexagram –which is the specular image of this one–, depicts a fox crossing a stream in its Judgment. The tail mentioned in this line is a reference to the tail of that same fox, which is implied here in the text. The wet tail symbolizes minor inconveniences, but the main idea here is that by applying restraint you can avoid falling into danger and minimize your loses.

Career: Plan carefully your moves. Do not take unnecessary risks and do not make hasty decisions.

Private life: Advance with caution and care and you will avoid trouble. Do not let others push you around. Take all the time that your need to decide what you will do.

Health, Feelings and Social life: Be conservative, this is not a good moment for innovation, instead preserve what you already have.

Second Six

> The woman loses the curtain of her carriage.
> Do not chase it; you will get it in seven days.

You will suffer a temporary setback that will stop you for a while. To lose the curtain means to get your plans exposed at the wrong moment, to be in danger, to lose strength.

Control your anxiety and be discreet, do not attract attention over yourself.

Instead of trying to press forward, bide you time and wait until the situation improves and you can advance without endangering yourself.

Besides this hexagram, the Chinese character for seven only appears in the **hexagram 24**, in the Judgment and in the second line of the **hexagram 51**. Here it indicates the return of the curtain of a carriage, in the hexagram 24 is related with a return and in the hexagram 63 with the return of money.

Career: You may lose the support from your superiors due to compromising circumstances; do not try to force it back. If you perform your duties flawlessly you will be reinstated to your previous status after a cycle is completed.

Private life: You will lose face and will struggle with a complicated situation for a while. If you endure the troubles with modesty and discretion, it all will pass.

Health, Feelings and Social life: Rest until your strength returns. Do not expose yourself, be discreet and prudent.

Third Nine

> The eminent ancestor attacks the Land of the Devil,
> after three years conquests it.
> Petty men must not be used.

The three years conquest campaign indicates a hard and dangerous enterprise. Three years symbolizes one long period of bitter conflicts. The triumph can be achieved, but not without paying a high cost.

The Land of the Devil indicates what is outside the laws, a factor of danger and corruption that must be subjugated by force.

To consolidate your gains you should use only reliable methods and people, otherwise you will endanger your achievements.

Career: If you are in the military you will face combat. In other cases you will suffer protracted difficulties when starting a new business.

Private life: You can achieve your ambitious goals, but it will take a long time and plenty of resources to do it. Be wary of lawsuits and legal proceedings.

Health, Feelings and Social life: Make an effort to control your weakness and behave more rationally. It will not be easy and will require strict self-discipline.

Fourth Six

> He has frayed silk and caulking rags.
> Be cautious until the end of the day.

63 - Already Across

The frayed silk and the rags are for stopping leaks in a boat that is crossing the river; they mean taking preventive measures when doing something dangerous.

You may find unexpected trouble along the way, be alert and take precautions beforehand.

Career: The best plans can have hidden flaws. Act in advance to deal with possible difficulties. Exercise extreme caution.

Private life: If you are careful and take every possible precaution you will avoid trouble.

Health, Feelings and Social life: You are at risk. Circumspection is advised.

Fifth Nine

> The eastern neighbor sacrifices an ox,
> but this falls short of the neighbor in
> the west with his small offering,
> whose sincerity receives blessings.

Sincerity will be rewarded, humble contributions presented with real feeling will fare better than pretentious exhibitions.

You don't need to do big things to cause a good impression, be sincere and modest.

Career: If you are too ambitious you will fail, but if you are straightforward and realistic you will succeed.

Private life: Do not behave in a conspicuous ways. Keep things simple and unpretentious and you will have good fortune.

Health, Feelings and Social life: Sincerity and modesty will be advantageous. Do not show off.

Top Six

> He immerses his head.
> Danger.

You have gone too far and too deep and now you will pay the price for your carelessness.

If you wait too long to turn back or to take corrective action, you will fall into danger. You may have a serious setback at the end of the crossing.

Career: If you try to take on more that you can handle you will put yourself in danger of losing all that you had achieved until now.

Private life: You are too deeply involved with someone or something, beyond what you can deal with. Danger of drowning.

Health, Feelings and Social life: Notice that the phrase "immerses his head" also means to overindulge in wine and sensual pleasures. It indicates danger of choking and a complete loss of self-control.

64

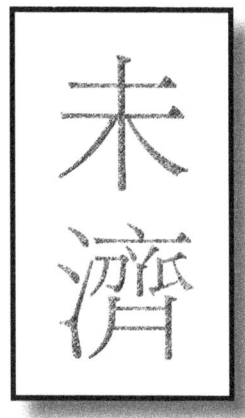

wèi jì
Before Crossing

Associated meanings

Before completion, before the climax, before crossing the river.

Judgment

> Before Crossing.
> Success.
> If the little fox tail gets wet when finishes fording the river
> nothing is favorable.

In ancient China, crossing rivers, either at a ford or when the river was frozen, was not an easy task. It implicated dangers and hardships. Before crossing the river, careful preparations must be made and proper precautions should be taken.

In this case the crossing of the river symbolizes a difficult transition between chaos and order.

The warning about getting the tail in the water points to the difficulties of the endeavor. You should have a surplus of strength and prudence to face such a task. If you can't carry the endeavor out to the end, everything done before will be in vain.

The Image

> Fire over water: The image of Before Crossing.
> The noble is careful discriminating things, so that each one is left in place.

Fire over water can't be used to cook food or anything useful because both forces are misplaced.

To discriminate things placing them in its correct positions means to recognize the potential of each thing and to order and structure them in function of your objective.

In that way order can be obtained from chaos.

First Six

> He wets his tail.
> Humiliation.

The character that wets his tail is the little fox mentioned in the Judgment. The wet tail is the result of rash action, without planning and with ignorance.

Humiliation will serve you to know your own limits, and to turn back, avoiding further danger.

Career: If you act based on the wrong assumptions, you will fail. You may be demoted or set back in your plans.

Private life: Your lack of experience and heedless actions will shame you.

Health, Feelings and Social life: You will be sorrow for your mistakes. Depression.

Second Nine

> Dragging his wheels.
> The determination is fortunate.

To drag the wheels means to contain the advance, to avoid rushing blindly forward and to advance with care.

Determination means to keep dedicated to your goals, to not skip any step and to keep full control.

Career: You have some obstacles to surmount, slow down and take proper care of every detail. With prudence you will advance slowly but safely.

Private life: Do not be tempted to do anything rush or dangerous. Stick to proven methods and you will be safe.

Health, Feelings and Social life: Do not let others hurry you; take your time to decide which course you will take.

Third Six

> Before Crossing.
> Attack brings misfortune.
> It is favorable to ford the great river.

Aggressive or unyielding advance will conduce to failure.

Be sure of getting support from good people and avoid being intransigent.

In this way you will be able to handle difficult endeavors, as symbolized by fording the river.

Career: You will need help and a good dose of diplomacy to achieve success.

Private life: Avoid facing trouble head on, but instead try to reach a compromise.

Health, Feelings and Social life: If you are ill, handle your illness with caution and avoid harsh treatments that may cause more harm than good.

Fourth Nine

> The determination is fortunate.
> Repentance fades.
> Shock to conquer the Land of the Devil.
> Three years of rewards from the great kingdom.

The carefully planned advance will be successful, thus repentance will fade.

Shock means fast and strong advancement (lit.: "as a thunderbolt") that inspires fear in the foes that are going to be conquered. It also means that you will face a hard and difficult struggle to achieve your objectives.

The Land of the Devil indicates what is outside the laws, a factor of danger and corruption that must be subjugated by force.

The three years of rewards indicate that you will get plenty of gains for a long time. Notice the difference with the third line in the previous hexagram, where it takes three years to conquer the Land of the Devil but there is no mention about any rewards.

Career: If you are in the military you will start a campaign. In other cases you will face a some conflicts and struggles in order to expand your business, but in the end you will succeed.

Private life: You will gain great profits after facing a difficult endeavor with plenty of disputes.

Health, Feelings and Social life: The Land of the Devil also indicates the internal fears and passions that should be conquered with discipline to achieve self-control over yourself.

64 - Before Crossing

Fifth Six

>The determination is fortunate.
>There is no repentance.
>The glory of the noble is true.
>Good fortune.

The struggle was won by using harsh methods, but to administer your new domains it is better to use more diplomatic ways.

The light of the noble indicates sincerity, civility and enlightenment. The fifth line is the ruler of the hexagram, who empowers capable people on the basis of objective merit.

Abiding in the middle of the trigram of the light (the upper trigram), nothing is concealed from the perception of the ruler.

Career: You may be promoted and your merits will be widely recognized.

Private life: Happiness and prosperity.

Health, Feelings and Social life: Good health and clarity of mind.

Top Nine

>They drink wine in confidence.
>No defect.
>But confidence will be lost if your head gets wet.

The new time is on the threshold, but the situation is still unfulfilled. To celebrate the end of the old stage and to get ready to receive a new time is not a bad idea. However, to wet the head indicates an unbalanced attitude and to lose control on the final step.

This line is a warning against getting dizzy when success is at hand.

Career: Celebrating your triumph is not incorrect but if you are extravagant you will damage your reputation.

Private life: If you cannot self-control yourself you will lose face and the people around you will stop trusting you.

Health, Feelings and Social life: To get the head wet also means to overindulge in wine and sensual pleasures. In any case it indicates a complete loss of self-control.

Get the Natal Hexagram

Step 1: Get the upper trigram, corresponding to the year of birth

We form the Natal Hexagram by combining two trigrams. First we will get the upper trigram, taking it from the following tables, according to the year of birth of the person. There are two tables, which show the trigrams for odd and even centuries.

Odd Centuries (like the 21st century)

Year	Upper Trigram	Year	Upper Trigram
0	☰	1	☷
2	☷	3	☳
4	☳	5	☴
6	☶	7	☰
8	☰	9	☷
10	☲	11	☴
12	☵	13	☴

Get the Natal Hexagram - Odd Centuries

Year	Upper Trigram	Year	Upper Trigram
14	☱	15	☳
16	☰	17	☷
18	☲	19	☴
20	☵	21	☶
22	☱	23	☳
24	☰	25	☷
26	☲	27	☴
28	☵	29	☶
30	☱	31	☳
32	☰	33	☷
34	☲	35	☴
36	☵	37	☶
38	☱	39	☳
40	☰	41	☷
42	☲	43	☴
44	☵	45	☶

Odd Centuries - Get the Natal Hexagram

Year	Upper Trigram	Year	Upper Trigram
46	☲	47	☶
48	☰	49	☳
50	☱	51	☵
52	☴	53	☲
54	☲	55	☷
56	☰	57	☳
58	☱	59	☵
60	☴	61	☲
62	☲	63	☶
64	☰	65	☳
66	☱	67	☵
68	☴	69	☲
70	☲	71	☷
72	☰	73	☳
74	☱	75	☵
76	☴	77	☲

Get the Natal Hexagram - Odd Centuries

Year	Upper Trigram	Year	Upper Trigram
78	☷	79	☰
80	☰	81	☷
82	☱	83	☴
84	☳	85	☲
86	☲	87	☶
88	☰	89	☷
90	☱	91	☴
92	☳	93	☲
94	☲	95	☶
96	☰	97	☷
98	☱	99	☵

Even Centuries (like the 20th century)

Year	Upper Trigram	Year	Upper Trigram
0	☷	1	☱
2	☴	3	☶
4	☰	5	☳
6	☵	7	☲
8	☷	9	☱
10	☴	11	☶
12	☰	13	☳
14	☵	15	☲
16	☷	17	☱
18	☴	19	☶
20	☰	21	☳
22	☵	23	☲
24	☷	25	☱
26	☴	27	☶
28	☰	29	☳
30	☵	31	☲
32	☷	33	☱

Get the Natal Hexagram - Even Centuries

Year	Upper Trigram	Year	Upper Trigram
34	☵	35	☶
36	☰	37	☷
38	☱	39	☲
40	☴	41	☳
42	☵	43	☶
44	☰	45	☷
46	☱	47	☲
48	☴	49	☳
50	☵	51	☶
52	☰	53	☷
54	☱	55	☲
56	☴	57	☳
58	☵	59	☶
60	☰	61	☷
62	☱	63	☲
64	☴	65	☳

Even Centuries - Get the Natal Hexagram

Year	Upper Trigram	Year	Upper Trigram
66		67	
68		69	
70		71	
72		73	
74		75	
76		77	
78		79	
80		81	
82		83	
84		85	
86		87	
88		89	
90		91	
92		93	
94		95	
96		97	
98		99	

Step 2: Get the lower trigram, corresponding to the month and day of birth

Now we will get the lower trigram, taking it from the following table, which shows the trigrams for the periods of the year.

Trigrams for each period of the year

Period	Trigram
01/01-02/15	☰
02/16-04/01	☷
04/02-05/17	☳
05/18-07/02	☵
07/03-08/16	☶
08/17-09/30	☱
10/01-11/15	☲
11/16-12/31	☴

Step 3: Get the changing lines

Now we will get the changing lines, taking them from the following table, which shows the different changing lines for the hours of odd and even days.

Changing lines for the different times of odd days

Hour	Changing Lines
00:00 to 00:44	6
00:45 to 01:29	1, 6
01:30 to 02:14	2, 6
02:15 to 03:59	1, 2, 6
03:00 to 03:44	3, 6
03:45 to 04:29	1, 3, 6
04:30 to 05:14	2, 3, 6
05:15 to 06:59	1, 2, 3, 6
06:00 to 06:44	4, 6
06:45 to 07:29	1, 4, 6
07:30 to 08:14	2, 4, 6
08:15 to 09:59	1, 2, 4, 6
09:00 to 09:44	3, 4, 6
09:45 to 10:29	1, 3, 4, 6
10:30 to 11:14	2, 3, 4, 6
11:15 to 12:59	1, 2, 3, 4, 6
12:00 to 12:44	5, 6
12:45 to 13:29	1, 5, 6
13:30 to 14:14	2, 5, 6
14:15 to 15:59	1, 2, 5, 6
15:00 to 15:44	3, 5, 6
15:45 to 16:29	1, 3, 5, 6

Get the Natal Hexagram - Changing Lines for Odd Days

Hour	Changing Lines
16:30 to 17:14	2, 3, 5, 6
17:15 to 18:59	1, 2, 3, 5, 6
18:00 to 18:44	4, 5, 6
18:45 to 19:29	1, 4, 5, 6
19:30 to 20:14	2, 4, 5, 6
20:15 to 21:59	1, 2, 4, 5, 6
21:00 to 21:44	3, 4, 5, 6
21:45 to 22:29	1, 3, 4, 5, 6
22:30 to 23:14	2, 3, 4, 5, 6
23:15 to 23:59	All Lines

Changing lines for the different times of even days

Hour	Changing Lines
00:00 to 00:44	None
00:45 to 01:29	1
01:30 to 02:14	2
02:15 to 03:59	1, 2
03:00 to 03:44	3
03:45 to 04:29	1, 3
04:30 to 05:14	2, 3
05:15 to 06:59	1, 2, 3
06:00 to 06:44	4
06:45 to 07:29	1, 4
07:30 to 08:14	2, 4
08:15 to 09:59	1, 2, 4
09:00 to 09:44	3, 4
09:45 to 10:29	1, 3, 4
10:30 to 11:14	2, 3, 4
11:15 to 12:59	1, 2, 3, 4
12:00 to 12:44	5
12:45 to 13:29	1, 5
13:30 to 14:14	2, 5
14:15 to 15:59	1, 2, 5
15:00 to 15:44	3, 5
15:45 to 16:29	1, 3, 5
16:30 to 17:14	2, 3, 5
17:15 to 18:59	1, 2, 3, 5

Get the Natal Hexagram - Changing Lines for Even Days

Hour	Changing Lines
18:00 to 18:44	4, 5
18:45 to 19:29	1, 4, 5
19:30 to 20:14	2, 4, 5
20:15 to 21:59	1, 2, 4, 5
21:00 to 21:44	3, 4, 5
21:45 to 22:29	1, 3, 4, 5
22:30 to 23:14	2, 3, 4, 5
23:15 to 23:59	1, 2, 3, 4, 5

Fourth and last step: Get the Natal Hexagram

Refer to the **Chart of the Trigrams and Hexagrams** (p. 379), for the number of the hexagram(s) obtained from the lower and upper trigrams.

If you do not know the time of birth, you will get only one hexagram, without changing lines.

Example for DOB: 1986-08-25. Time: 03.10 hs:

In this example, the hexagram on the left in the figure above (55) is the Natal Hexagram. Since this hexagram has two changing lines, you will also need to draw to second hexagram (21, shown at the right side), but replacing the changing lines with their opposite ones. If the changing line is *yang* replace it with to *yin* line and vice versa. In the above example the changing lines in the third and sixth positions are replaced by their opposites.

Changing lines are drawn differently from non-changing lines by adding an X or to circle in the middle. Remember that lines are always counted from the bottom up.

Returning to the previous example, where the hexagrams are 55 and 21, we must read the Judgment, the Image and the third and sixth lines of hexagram 55, but only the Judgment and the Image of hexagram 21.

Generally speaking, hexagram 55 is the starting point of the situation (in this case to person's life) that will lead to hexagram 21, which describes the final situation. Note that both hexagrams can be linked in other ways.

See **Understanding hexagram readings** to learn how to interpret the oracle readings.

You can also see other example about the Natal Hexagram in **How to get to Natal Hexagram** (p. 19).

The Eight Trigrams

Each hexagram is composed of two trigrams (*gua*), which are groups of three consecutive lines, one of them corresponds to the three lower lines and the other to the three upper lines. There are only eight trigrams (in Chinese *bagua*,i means eight) because there are only eight ways to combine broken and whole lines into groups of three.

The names of the eight trigrams refer to the natural elements: *Qian* (Sky), *Kun* (Earth), *Zhen* (Thunder), *Kan* (Water), *Gen* (Mountain), *Xun* (Wind or Wood), *Li*, (Fire) and *Dui* (Lake). The eight trigrams form four pairs, which show opposite polarities.

In each hexagram, the text called *The Image* explains the appropriate behavior for that time, based on the trigrams that form the hexagram.

In many hexagrams the lower trigram (lines 1, 2 and 3) is related to the interior, that is, the subjective part of a situation or internal side of an organization or family; instead, the upper trigram (lines 4, 5 and 6) is related to the objective external reality or characters that face the outside world in a company or family.

The movements of the trigrams help explain the meaning of many hexagrams. For example, if the lower trigram descends and the upper trigram rises (as in hexagram **12, The Standstill**), there will be a disconnection between the two trigrams; if the opposite is true, that is, the lower trigram ascends and the upper one descends, there will be a more dynamic relationship, as in hexagrams **11, Harmony**, and **49, Revolution**.

Many other factors help to define the relation between the trigrams of the hexagramas, in several cases the relation is explained in the text or the commentaries of the hexagram, in other cases, to capture its interaction remains in the hands of the reader.

The Eight Trigrams

Most of the meanings exposed below come from Wing 8 (the *Ten Wings* are the *YiJing* comments from the Confucian school), *Shuogua*.

THE CREATIVE / THE HEAVEN

≡

Heaven symbolizes strength and is the beginning of all things.

Related Trigram:	
	The mother.

Action: Rules.

Movement: Rising.

Pronunciation: qián.

Natural symbol: Heaven.

Member of the family: The father.

Body part: The head.

Animals: A good horse, an old horse, a thin horse, a wild horse, a piebald horse.

Season: Autumn.

Color: Deep red.

Cardinal points: North-West.

Deficiency: Arrogancy.

Other associations: A circle; a ruler, a prince; strength, hardness; strong movement, tireless work; jade; metal; cold; ice; the fruits from trees. God strives in *qián*. It means that *yang* and *yin* interact, stimulating each other.

THE RECEPTIVE / THE EARTH

Earth symbolizes gentleness and nourishes all beings.

Related Trigram:	
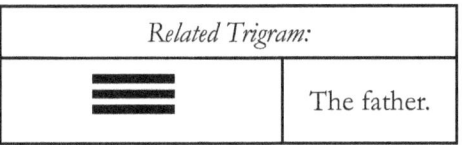	The father.

Action: Serves, nourishes.

Movement: Descendent.

Pronunciation: kūn.

Natural symbol: Earth, black soil.

Member of the family: The mother.

Body part: The belly.

Animals: Cow and calf; a heifer; a young mare.

Season: Summer.

Color: Yellow.

Cardinal points: South-West.

Deficiency: Extreme passivity.

Other associations: Cloth, a kettle, parsimony, a turning lathe, a large wagon, variegated things, a multitude, quantity, a handle and support; frugality, thrift, passionate delivery, devotion, protection, selflessness, generosity, gentleness, ductility, the number 10. God is served in *kūn*.

THE AROUSING / THE THUNDER

The Thunder symbolizes movement and speed.

Related Trigram:	
	The eldest daughter, Wind, because Thunder and Wind do not hinder one another, but they excite each other.

Action: Arouses, shakes, stirs, put the things in movement.

Movement: Ascending, shakes all things.

Pronunciation: zhèn.

Natural symbol: The thunder, wood.

Member of the family: The eldest son.

Body part: The feet, because they serve for movement.

Animals: The dragon; horses that neigh well, have white hind legs, are sprightly, or have a white star on the forehead.

Season and time: Spring, dawn.

Color: Dark yellow; violet blue and yellow; dark and pale.

Cardinal points: East.

Deficiency: Overbearing.

Other associations: Development; a great highway; vehement decisions; green bamboo shoots; reeds and rushes; in respect to cultivated plants it is those that grows back to life from its disappearance (like legumes); what in the end becomes the strongest and most luxuriant. God comes forth in zhèn.

THE GENTLE / THE WIND

The Wind symbolizes penetration.

	Related Trigram:
☴	The eldest son, Thunder, because Wind and Thunder do not hinder one another, but they excite each other.

Action: Scatters (the seeds of) the things.

Movement: Incessant, subtly influences all things.

Pronunciation: xùn.

Natural symbol: The wind, wood.

Member of the family: The eldest daughter.

Body part: The thighs; deficiency of hair; broad forehead; much white in the eye; crooked eyes.

Animal: The cock, fowl.

Season: Spring.

Color: White.

Cardinal points: South-East.

Deficiency: Hesitation.

Other associations: Firewood; a plumb line; a carpenter's square; long; lofty; advancing and receding; unresolved; strong scents; the close pursuit of gain, those who get nearly threefold in profit; work, business; a fair; a ten days cycle; at the end point of its development it becomes *Zhen* (The Thunder). God sets all things in order in *xùn*.

THE ABYSMAL / THE WATER

The Water is the symbol of what is precipitous and perilous.

	Related Trigram:
☲	The middle daughter, Fire, because Water and Fire do not fail to complement each other.

Action: Moistens.

Movement: Descending, falling into the abyss, the falling water flows inexorably seeking the lowest level.

Pronunciation: kan.

Natural symbol: Water, clouds, river, Moon.

Member of the family: The middle son.

Body part: The ears.

Animals: Pig; fox; horses with beautiful backs, with high spirit, with a drooping head, with thin hooves, who shamble along.

Season: Winter.

Color: Red.

Cardinal points: North.

Deficiency: Anxiety.

Other associations: Channels and ditches; lying hidden or concealed; bending and straightening; a bow, a wheel; anxiety, distress of mind; pain in the ears; blood; chariots that have many risks and damages; penetration; a thief; trees strong and sound-hearted. God toils in *kan*.

THE CLINGING / THE FIRE

The Fire is the symbol of what is bright and what is catching.

	Related Trigram:
☵	The middle son, Water, because Fire and Water do not fail to complement each other.

Action: Warms and dries.

Movement: Ascending, like the fire that flames up.

Pronunciation: lí.

Natural symbol: The Sun, fire, lightning.

Member of the family: The middle daughter.

Body part: The eyes.

Animals: Pheasant, cow, turtle, crab, clam, snail.

Season: Summer.

Cardinal points: South.

Deficiency: Violent anger.

Other associations: Armor and helmet; spear and sword; men with large bellies; it is the trigram of dryness; trees that are hollow and rotten above; clarity, discernment, clear perception. God causes creatures to perceive one another in *lí*.

KEEPING STILL / THE MOUNTAIN

The Mountain is the symbol of stoppage or arrest.

	Related Trigram:
☴	The youngest daughter, with whom it combines its force.

Action: Stops things, keep things in its place.

Movement: Stationary.

Pronunciation: gèn.

Natural symbol: The mountain.

Member of the family: The youngest son.

Body parts: The hands, the fingers, the annular finger, the nose.

Animals: Dog, rodents, panther, birds with a strong beak.

Season: Winter.

Cardinal points: South-East.

Deficiency: Avarice.

Other associations: Side roads; small rocks; doorways; tree and vine fruits; gatekeeper, porter, eunuch, palace guard; strong and gnarled trees; firm rules, rest; end and beginning. God brings things to perfection in *gèn*.

THE JOYOUS / THE LAKE

☱

The Lake is the symbol of pleasure and satisfaction.

	Related Trigram:
	The youngest son, with whom it combines its force.

Action: Brings joy.

Movement: Descending, like the water of a lake.

Pronunciation: duì.

Natural symbols: Lake, marsh, wetlands, pond, shallow water, calm and deep. The mirror of the lake.

Member of the family: The youngest daughter.

Body parts: Mouth and tongue, because that t is related not only to the pleasures of the table but also to the speech, words, orders, laughter and kisses

Animals: Sheep. The broken line at the top of this trigram shows the sheep horns. Sheep and goat have the same name and associations in China.

Season and time: Middle of autumn (harvest time); the evening.

Cardinal points: East.

Deficiency: Melancholy.

Other associations: A sorceress; decadence and discarding of things (in the harvest); rot and breakage; removal of the fruits that hang from the branches; fall to the ground and burst (like the fruits of the harvest); break, break; metal; defense, weapons; metal; kill; hard and salty land; a concubine. The structure of the trigram indicates hardness, tenacity and inner obstinacy, but outside (the upper *yin* line) is flexible and docile. God gives the creatures pleasure in *duì*. But the excess of pleasure has its dangers, that is why the double meaning pleasure/destruction is the axis of meaning of this trigram.

Chart of Trigrams and Hexagrams

Upper ▶ / Lower ▼	Quian	Zhen	Kan	Gen	Kun	Xun	Li	Dui
Quian	1	34	5	26	11	9	14	43
Zhen	25	51	3	27	24	42	21	17
Kan	6	40	29	4	7	59	64	47
Gen	33	62	39	52	15	53	56	31
Kun	12	16	8	23	2	20	35	45
Xun	44	32	48	18	46	57	50	28
Li	13	55	63	22	36	37	30	49
Dui	10	54	60	41	19	61	38	58

Each hexagram is composed by two trigrams, one comprises the lower three lines of the hexagram and the other corresponds to the three upper lines.

The above table shows all possible combinations of the eight trigrams, in that way you can find easily the number for any hexagram drawing.

www.ingramcontent.com/pod-product-compliance
Lightning Source LLC
Chambersburg PA
CBHW031312160426
43196CB00007B/505